"Bradshaw parachutes you directl_ of his playworlds with no map and you're going . . . the action move: ___ulldozer through a doomed grove of trees—it won't stop because you're sad, or offended, or don't believe that what you are seeing is actually happening before your eyes . . . By the end of the play, you can't help but admit that, yes, human beings are capable of all that, all of it, within a very short span of time."

—Lisa D'Amour, Playwright / Author of *Airline Highway*

"Bradshaw dismantles the standard stage narrative of blackness—suffering, anger, intuitive 'wisdom'—and exposes instead the combination of ego and self-loathing that has marked generations . . . A true satirist, Bradshaw is evangelical in his passion for demonstrating that race and sexuality are artificial constructs that lead to very real things, such as subjugation—and he does so with a kind of desperate humor. He shows us that human cruelty is learned. And learned. And then we try to pass it off as 'natural.'"

—Hilton Als, *New Yorker*

"These plays invade dangerous, treacherous territories . . . In a Bradshaw play, no one in the audience gets to sit back in safety and crow over the sins of others. In matters of vanity and perversity, our lust for psychic and social power—in addition to our secret angers: class, race and gender—are equal-opportunity employers."

—Margo Jefferson, *Bomb*

"Mr. Bradshaw is fast becoming the American theater's most distinctively provocative playwright."

—Ben Brantley, *New York Times*

"Clearly attacking the homophobia in the African-American community while exclaiming that deep-seated prejudices remain unconsciously latent in all of us, Bradshaw has created an entertainment—and make no mistake, this is an entertaining work—that views theater as a forum for goading audiences out of complacency, refusing to provide the pat but satisfying ending where everyone learns to be nice to each other."

—Steven Oxman, *Variety*

"Thomas Bradshaw continues to needle our notions of morality, making us laugh like madmen at things our internet browsers would flag as porn."

—Helen Shaw, *Time Out New York*

"Thomas Bradshaw writes plays that can get under your skin in very uncomfortable ways. To be sure, his work can be suave and entertaining, but as anyone who has seen his previous work would attest, this is a playwright who charts controversial pathways . . . with sometimes explosive results."

—Gerard Raymond, *Slant*

INTIMACY

and Other Plays

—

INTIMACY

and Other Plays

THOMAS BRADSHAW

THEATRE COMMUNICATIONS GROUP
NEW YORK
2015

Intimacy and Other Plays is published by Theatre Communications Group, Inc., 520 8th Avenue, 24th Floor, New York, NY 10018-4156

The publication of *Intimacy and Other Plays* by Thomas Bradshaw, through TCG's Book Program, is made possible in part by the New York State Council on the Arts with the support of Governor Andrew Cuomo and the New York State Legislature.

TCG books are exclusively distributed to the book trade by Consortium Book Sales and Distribution.

LIBRARY OF CONGRESS CATALOGING-IN-PUBLICATION DATA
Bradshaw, Thomas.
[Plays. Selections]
Intimacy and other plays / Thomas Bradshaw.
pages cm
ISBN 978-1-55936-469-0 (paperback)
ISBN 978-1-55936-783-7 (ebook)
I. Title.
PS3602.R34286A6   2015
812'.6—dc23   2015003177

Book design and composition by Lisa Govan
Cover art and design by Mark Melnick

First Edition, September 2015

For Roxane, Drake and Calder

CONTENTS

PLAYWRIGHT'S NOTE

All characters should be played with the utmost honesty and sincerity. The irony in the plays should be underplayed rather than overplayed at all times. The characters in these plays feel that all their actions are completely necessary and unavoidable. The plays should be directed in a straightforward and realistic manner.

—TB

FULFILLMENT

PRODUCTION HISTORY

Fulfillment was commissioned by the MTC/Ars Nova Writers Room in 2013. It was first produced by the Flea Theater (Niegel Smith, Artistic Director; Carol Ostrow, Producing Director) in New York City on September 21, 2015, in a co–world premiere with Chicago's American Theater Company, with support from the Venturous Theater Fund. It was directed by Ethan McSweeny; set and lighting design was by Brian Sidney Bembridge, costume design was by Andrea Lauer, sound design was by Mikhail Fiksel and Miles Polaski; the production stage manager was Ben Andersen. The cast was:

MICHAEL	Gbenga Akinnagbe
SARAH	Susannah Flood
SIMON	Christian Conn
TED/LEONARD	Jeff Biehl
MARK	Peter McCabe
BOB/REAL-ESTATE AGENT/WAITRESS	Denny Dillon
DELROY	Otoja Abit

This production of *Fulfillment* then opened at the American Theater Company (Bonnie Metzgar, Interim Artistic Director) in Chicago on November 9, 2015. The design and production personnel remained the same. The cast was:

MICHAEL	Stephen Conrad Moore
SARAH	Erin Barlow
SIMON	Jason Bradley
TED/LEONARD	Jeff Trainor
MARK	Scott Olson
BOB/REAL-ESTATE AGENT/WAITRESS	Erika Napoletano
DELROY	Justin Cornwell

CHARACTERS

MICHAEL, African-American, forty

SARAH, Michael's girlfriend, white, thirty-two

SIMON, Michael's best friend, white, forty

TED, Michael's upstairs neighbor, white, late thirties

MARK, Michael's boss, white, fifties

BOB, a very butch lesbian, president of Michael's condo
association

DELROY, a basketball star, African-American, twenties

LEONARD, a meditation instructor

REAL-ESTATE AGENT

WAITRESS

SETTING

New York City. The present.

SCENE 1

Michael is touring an apartment with a Real-Estate Agent.

AGENT: This building has a gym, indoor swimming pool, sauna, doorman, and concierge service just like you requested.

MICHAEL: I like the vibe of this place. It's got that chic hotel feel, just like I wanted.

AGENT: All the appliances are stainless steel, and the cabinets have been custom-made from Tanzanian Anigre wood. The counters are gray slate and the backsplash is green glass from Italy.

(They walk into the bathroom.)

The bathroom is wall-to-wall Rosa Aurora marble and there's a deep soaking tub.

MICHAEL: How big is this place?

AGENT: Seven hundred and fifty-two square feet.

MICHAEL: And how much is it?

AGENT: One point five.

MICHAEL: This place seems awfully small for that amount of money.

AGENT: You're the one who wants to live in a Newly Renovated Unit in Soho. We can find a cheaper one-bedroom if you're willing to sacrifice on the amenities and lose the doorman. One point five is actually a good price. Last month I sold a similar unit for one point six.

MICHAEL: I love these big windows.

AGENT: You couldn't ask for a better view.

MICHAEL: Do you think that we can get it for one point three? One point five is a bit steep.

AGENT: Honestly, I bet this unit will have multiple offers. If you really want it you're gonna have to bid more than asking.

SCENE 2

Michael is eating sushi with Simon.

SIMON: You sure that you want to drop that kind of money for a shoebox in Soho?

MICHAEL: It's a great investment.

SIMON: If it were my money I'd buy a place in Jersey. For a million five you could buy an estate.

MICHAEL: I work eighty hours a week. I'd never see the inside of my house. Besides, you live in the village. Why are you trying to banish me to another state?

SIMON: We inherited our place. Otherwise, there's no way we would have been able to afford to live there.

MICHAEL: Well, I want to walk. That way I'll get twenty minutes of exercise going to and from work. God knows that I don't have time to go to the gym.

SIMON: Suit yourself.

(Pause.)

How're things going with that girl? You know, um—

MICHAEL: The girl from my firm?

SIMON: Yeah.

MICHAEL: Sarah.

SIMON: Yeah.

MICHAEL: So, uh, a few days ago we took some clients out to dinner, and we both got a little drunk, and started, you know, to feel each other up under the table.

SIMON: That's a good first step.

MICHAEL: Then she invited me back to her place.

SIMON: No way!

MICHAEL: She's wild, dude. Really wild.

SIMON: Wild how?

MICHAEL: Well, uh, she really likes to be spanked.

SIMON: Is that so weird?

MICHAEL: Has your wife ever asked you to spank her?

SIMON: No.

MICHAEL: I rest my case. But here's what's really weird about it. When we got off the elevator on her floor she took me into the stairwell and made me spank her there.

SIMON: That's crazy, man!

MICHAEL: I think she orgasmed just from getting spanked. Her face got flush and her whole body started to shake.

SIMON: Holy shit! It's like that movie *Secretary*!

MICHAEL: Yeah, totally, man. So, then she pulls down my pants—

SIMON: In the stairwell?

MICHAEL: Uh-huh. And then she tells me to fuck her face.

SIMON: Jesus!

MICHAEL: And I said, what do you mean? And she said: "You heard me. I want you to fuck my face the same way you'd fuck my pussy."

SIMON: This story is making me hard.

MICHAEL: Yeah, me, too. I can't wait to get my hands on her again.

SIMON: So, did you fuck her face?

MICHAEL: Of course, but I didn't last too long.

SIMON: Did she swallow?

MICHAEL: No. She made me cum all over her dress.

SIMON: You sure you're not making this up?

MICHAEL: I swear to God this happened. Then she straightened herself up and said good night.

SIMON: She didn't invite you into her apartment?

MICHAEL: Nope.

SIMON: What's it like at work?

MICHAEL: It's weird. I can't get my mind off her. She's been acting like it didn't even happen. I've been going to the bathroom and masturbating like four times a day because every time I get a whiff of her hair . . . or see that tight little ass . . . or her nerdy glasses . . . those small tits . . .

SIMON: Small tits? You like small tits?

MICHAEL: Yeah. I love them. You ever seen me with a big-titted girl?

SIMON: I guess not.

MICHAEL: Think about it . . . Jessica, Martha, Corinne—

SIMON: I guess I never really thought about it.

MICHAEL: I've never felt this way about someone before. I think I love her.

(Pause.)

I gotta go to the bathroom.

(Michael exits to the bathroom. Simon continues to eat his sushi.)

SCENE 3

Michael is talking on the phone.

MICHAEL: That's great to hear. So, uh, I need to borrow some money.

   I know I have a good job, but there's an error on my credit report.

   Do you know how long it takes to get an error on your credit report corrected!? There are multiple bids on this place and I'll lose it if—

It says my credit score is 625, even though I've never paid a bill late in my life.

Well, they're asking me to bring twenty-five percent instead of twenty to the table.

An additional eighty thousand.

Calm down, calm down, you can take it out of your retirement account can't you?

Look, you know I'm good for it. I'll pay you back in two years tops.

I promise that you won't be bankrupt in your retirement.

Thanks, Mom.

(He hangs up the phone.)

SCENE 4

Sarah is in her office. She's beautiful. Very nerdy. Very conservative-looking. She types at her computer. Michael walks up and stands next to her. She ignores him. He clears his throat.

MICHAEL: Do you have a moment?
SARAH: Uh, I'm really busy. What do you need?

(Awkward pause.)

MICHAEL: I just wanted to tell you that I, um, I'm in contract to buy an apartment.
SARAH *(Not really paying attention. Still typing on her computer)*: Good for you.
MICHAEL: It's in Soho.
SARAH: Uh-huh.
MICHAEL: It's my fortieth birthday present to myself.

(She stops what she's doing and looks at him.)

SARAH: You're forty?

MICHAEL: Yup.

SARAH: Wow. You don't look a day over thirty.

MICHAEL: Thanks.

SARAH: How are you still an associate?

MICHAEL: I'm a senior associate.

SARAH: Junior, senior—it doesn't really matter. You're still an associate.

MICHAEL: I uh. Yeah. I don't know. How old are you?

SARAH: Thirty-two. If I don't make partner by the time I'm thirty-five I'll quit.

MICHAEL: Really?

SARAH: Yeah. You should go ask Mark why you didn't get promoted.

MICHAEL: Most ninth year associates got passed over for promotion. I bet this'll be my year.

SARAH: Where's your ambition?

MICHAEL: I just bought an apartment for one point six.

SARAH: Yeah, but you should be living in a five-million-dollar apartment.

(Michael looks weirded-out and confused.)

You know why I think you haven't been promoted?

MICHAEL: Why?

SARAH: Racism.

MICHAEL: That has nothing to do with it, Sarah.

SARAH: Do you see any black partners?

MICHAEL: No, but I don't see any black anybody. There's no control group.

SARAH: Just think about it. No women partners, no black partners. I'm telling you this because we're two of the only people from under-represented groups working here. We need to stick together.

(Sarah goes back to her typing. Michael stands there awkwardly for a moment, then he starts to walk away.)

Why aren't you married?

MICHAEL: I wanted to play the field I guess.

SARAH: Please. You haven't even been out on the field as far as I can tell.

MICHAEL: What's that supposed to mean?

SARAH: How many women have you slept with?

(Pause.)

MICHAEL: So many that I've lost count.

SARAH: Please.

MICHAEL: How many men have you slept with?

SARAH: You don't want to know. It would only make you jealous.

MICHAEL: Why would I get jealous?

(Sarah gives Michael a knowing look.)

SARAH: I belong to this group. This quasi-religious group. We chant and stuff. I think you'd like it.

MICHAEL: Would I?

SARAH: Yeah, I think you would. Want to come with me on Saturday morning?

SCENE 5

Leonard stands before a group of practitioners dressed in yoga outfits. Sarah and Michael sit on the floor with their legs crossed.

LEONARD: Here at Leonard's Chanting Meditation Studio your mind will become one with the earth—with the spirit of the universe. Is your mind constantly wracked with worry and anxiety? Do you obsess over that thing you said to your boss? Do you feel anxious about what your friends are saying behind your back? Are you worried that everyone thinks your personality sucks? Do you gorge yourself with food and pornography to make yourself feel better about the world?

Look no further. Leonard's Chanting Meditation is the best way to calm the mind. When we chant NA-MU-AMI-TA-BUL we become one with the Tao and are at peace.

(He points at Sarah.)

When you, Sarah, start to chant, you'll stop reprimanding yourself for getting that stupid haircut.

(Sarah nods approvingly.
Leonard points at Michael.)

When you, Michael, start to chant, you'll finally grow some balls, and stop letting Sarah yank you around like a little puppy dog!

(Michael looks at Leonard in amazement—How did he know that? Sarah doesn't seem to have registered the insult at all.)

And remember, no masturbation. It is essential that we preserve our chi.
    Repeat after me.
    NA-MU AMI-TA-BUL.
ALL: NA-MU AMI-TA-BUL.

(Sarah, Michael and the rest of the class repeat this. They start to chant.)

SCENE 6

Michael is sitting at his desk alone. He looks around to make sure no one is there, then he takes a quart of Bombay Sapphire out of his desk and guzzles it. He sits for a moment thinking. He then walks over to his boss Mark's office.

MICHAEL: Hey, Mark, can I talk to you for a moment?

MARK: Sure, Michael. What's up?

MICHAEL: Well. You've treated me well over the last few years but—

MARK: I have. Thank you.

MICHAEL: You're welcome.

MARK: I appreciate it when an employee recognizes how generous the firm has been to them. It's unusual and your gratitude will be remembered when the time comes.

MICHAEL: When the time comes? What are you talking about?

MARK: When it comes time to calculate your merit increase for the year.

MICHAEL: Do you regard me as a valuable employee?

MARK: Of course. That's why you got the raise you did last year.

MICHAEL *(Incredulous)*: You gave me a two-percent raise!

MARK: Two percent of uh-um, uh, what do you make?

MICHAEL: Two ninety.

MARK: Two percent of two ninety is almost six thousand dollars! And with your bonus—

MICHAEL: The bonus is pennies compared to what the partners make! Steven started at the firm the same time I did and he's a partner now! He made eight hundred thousand dollars last year!

MARK: Is that what this is about?

MICHAEL: Yes. For nine years I've put in eighty-hour work weeks. I've paid my dues. Why haven't I been made a partner?

MARK: You'll be promoted to partner when the time is right. Each has to wait his turn. Or not. Some never make partner.

MICHAEL: Every time you get a black client you trot me out like a show horse!

MARK: I'm not sure how to respond to that. Do you not want to work on cases where the client happens to be black? That sounds racist, Michael.

MICHAEL: You know what I'm saying!

MARK: No, I don't!

MICHAEL: I deserve to be made partner! Don't you think the image of the firm would improve if there was some diversity within the partnership?

MARK *(Looks around)*: We seem to be doing just fine.

MICHAEL: Fuck you!

MARK: What did you just say to me?

MICHAEL: You heard me. FUCK YOU.

MARK: You're skating on very thin ice.

MICHAEL: You're not going to fire your token blacky.

MARK: All right. You want to know why you haven't been made partner?

MICHAEL: Yes! Yes! I would like to know.

MARK: You have a drinking problem, Michael.

(Michael goes silent.)

You didn't think we knew, did you?

MICHAEL *(Softly)*: I don't have a drinking problem.

MARK: I can smell alcohol on your breath right now. The least you could do is keep some mouthwash in your desk.

(Michael looks lost.)

I'm sorry. I shouldn't have made the mouthwash comment.

(Silence.)

I want you to go to rehab. The firm will pay for it.

MICHAEL: I don't need to go to rehab.

MARK: Yes, you do.

MICHAEL: I can't be away from work that long. Please, please, don't send me away.

MARK: I'm sorry, Michael. I don't see any other option.

(Long pause.)

MICHAEL: How about AA? I could go to AA.

(Pause.)

MARK: I guess you could try AA. But if I catch you drinking again we're gonna send you away for thirty days.

MICHAEL: Please promise not to tell anyone about this.

(Mark nods his head.)

MARK: After you clean yourself up we can talk about you becoming a partner.

MICHAEL: Thank you.

SCENE 7

Michael is sitting alone in his apartment with a bottle of gin in his hand. He takes a few swigs. We watch him send a text. The lights change to indicate the passage of time. Michael takes a couple more swigs. There is a knock on the door. He opens the door still holding the bottle in his hand. Sarah is standing there. Michael is lucid. Sinister. Filled with desire. He intensely looks her in the eye.

SARAH: Nice place.

(He moves out of the way to let her in. She enters. He closes the door behind her.)

I'm glad you texted me.

(Michael puts the bottle down.)

I was just sitting at home—

(He grabs her firmly by the throat. She is surprised. Excited. A little scared. He starts to walk her across the room looking her directly in the eye.)

MICHAEL: I love you.

(He walks her some more. Their eyes are locked.)

I love you.

(He backs her into a wall. He takes his hand off her throat and puts his hand on her buttocks and pulls her against him.)

I need you, Sarah.
SARAH: I need you, too.

(They kiss. It is gentle. Intense. Deep.)

MICHAEL: Finger yourself.
SARAH: Leonard says that we are not supposed to masturbate.
MICHAEL: Do it for me. Do it for your daddy.

(She is unsure for a moment, then slides her hand into her skirt and starts to finger herself while standing against the wall. Their eyes are still locked. He starts to rub his penis through his pants.)

Good. Good. That's my good little girl.

(She closes her eyes and gasps then opens her eyes again.)

I'm not going to fuck you tonight. You don't deserve that yet.

(He turns her around so that her butt is facing him. She stops fingering herself. She turns around to see what he's about to do.)

I didn't tell you to stop fingering yourself.

*(She starts fingering herself again.
    He pulls down his pants and strokes his penis.)*

You want me to jerk off on your skirt don't you?

(She doesn't answer. She just keeps fingering herself.)

Don't you?!
SARAH: Yes. But spank me a little first.
MICHAEL: No, you don't deserve that either.
SARAH: Please?

(Michael stops jerking off. He looks at her bottom and gives her a hard swat.)

Oh, yes.

(Pause.
He swats her again. The lights start to fade.)

Yes. Again.

(Another swat.)

Again.

(Another swat.
Darkness.
Another swat.)

Faster!

SCENE 8

It is morning. Michael and Sarah lay in bed sleeping. Sun streams into the room onto the bed. It looks comforting. Comfortable. Beautiful. Michael lifts his head up and looks at Sarah. Suddenly we see a look of horror come over his face as he feels around where he's lying in bed. Then he grabs his stomach, jumps out of bed, and runs to the bathroom. We hear vomiting sounds. Sarah stirs. She sits up in bed. Michael exits the bathroom looking like shit.

SARAH: You okay?

MICHAEL: Yeah.

SARAH: Sounded like you were vomiting.

MICHAEL: No. no. I was uh. I'm okay.

(Suddenly Sarah notices that the bed is wet. She starts feeling around. She's perplexed.)

SARAH: The bed is wet.

MICHAEL *(Mock surprise)*: It is?

(He goes over and feels.)

Weird.

SARAH: Did you spill something in bed last night?

MICHAEL *(Glad that she's found a logical explanation for this)*: Yes. Yeah. You know what? I got up in the middle of the night and brought some water back to bed. Must have spilled it.

(Sarah puts her nose to the bed and smells. She makes a disgusted face.)

SARAH: Michael, this is urine.

(She looks at him concerned and climbs out of bed.)

MICHAEL *(Trying to laugh it off)*: I guess one of us must have pissed in the bed.

(He chuckles. She doesn't think this is funny. She is deeply concerned and looking at him in a piercing, motherly way.

Michael grabs the bottle of gin on the floor. It is empty. He leaves the room and comes back with a full bottle of gin and two glasses.)

Want a drink?

(Silence. She looks at him with horror. He pours two glasses of gin. He then starts to lift a glass to his mouth when she gently grabs his arm and stops him. She takes the glasses and the bottle of gin into the bathroom and pours them out. He follows her into the bathroom.)

What are you doing?!

SARAH: You've obviously got a very serious problem, Michael. You've got to stop!

MICHAEL: How would you know?

SARAH: You just pissed in the bed!

MICHAEL: I had a little too much, that's all.

SARAH: If you want to lie to me I'm going to leave. Otherwise, I'll help you.

MICHAEL: You'll help me?

SARAH: Yes.

(Pause. Michael is overwhelmed. He tears up.)

It's okay. It's okay.

(She pulls him close to her.
  He cries.)

It's okay.

(She strokes his head.)

MICHAEL: Mark said that I haven't made partner because of my drinking.

SARAH: That's bullshit. You're one of the hardest-working people at that firm. Mark's the last person who should be pointing fingers about someone having an alcohol problem. Last year he was so wasted that he had to be carried out of the Christmas party.

(Michael chuckles faintly.)

MICHAEL: He wanted me to go away to rehab for thirty days, but
I convinced him to let me go to AA instead.
SARAH: AA is the only thing that works. Rehab forces someone
to stop drinking for thirty days, but it often doesn't have
any lasting effect. AA is the only way to get sober for good.
MICHAEL: How do you know all this?
SARAH: My dad is an alcoholic. And my brother he—he—

(She chokes up.)

MICHAEL: What happened?
SARAH: He died in a drinking-and-driving accident.
MICHAEL: I'm sorry.
SARAH: It happened a long time ago. When I was a teenager.
But . . .

(She takes his hand and looks him in the eye.)

I'll go with you.
MICHAEL: To AA?
SARAH: Yeah. I'll stop drinking, too.
MICHAEL: Just for me?
SARAH: Why not?

SCENE 9

*Michael walks into the lobby of his new apartment building. Ted is
checking his mail. He notices Michael.*

TED: Hi.
MICHAEL: Hi.
TED: Do you live here?
MICHAEL: I just purchased a place. I'm here to take some mea-
surements.

(Ted extends his hand to shake Michael's.)

TED: I'm Ted.

(They shake hands.)

MICHAEL: Michael.

TED: Do you smell that?

MICHAEL: Smell what?

TED: It smells like uh, methane.

MICHAEL: Maybe there's a gas leak.

TED: No, that's a different kind of smell. This smells like, uh, uh, did you fart?

MICHAEL: No.

TED: Are you sure?

MICHAEL: Yes, I'm sure. Maybe you farted and didn't realize it.

TED: I have a very strong sphincter. I don't fart in the lobbies of buildings, or in elevators for that matter. That would be rude!

MICHAEL: Okay, well, I should be getting upstairs. It was nice to meet you.

TED: It was nice to meet you, too.

SCENE 10

A week later. Sarah and Michael are packing boxes in Michael's apartment.

SARAH: How does it feel?

MICHAEL: How does what feel?

SARAH: Being sober?

MICHAEL: It's amazing not to wake up with a hangover every day.

SARAH: You're sober, and moving into your new apartment. It's a fresh start.

MICHAEL: Well, I wouldn't be doing this without you.

(They kiss then go back to packing.)

You know, I like AA, but I don't get the God thing. It's really kind of bothering me.

SARAH: Stop thinking of God as some all-knowing, all-controlling being in the sky. God is freedom.

MICHAEL: What do you mean? I'm not free to drink anymore.

SARAH: This is what I'm talking about. God is what's going to allow you to become a different person. Right now you think that drinking is freedom when it's actually the opposite for you. Drinking had enslaved you. You weren't free not to drink. Now you are. Your higher power took away your desire to drink whether you like it or not.

MICHAEL: Really? You really think that?

SARAH: AA says that "no human power could have relieved our alcoholism." Walking into an AA meeting is an act of submission to God.

MICHAEL: You really know a lot about this.

SARAH: My dad has been in the program for eighteen years.

MICHAEL: I've been getting up in the middle of the night and eating a whole pint of ice cream.

SARAH: The body converts alcohol into sugar. Eating ice cream is a way of coping with the withdrawal.

MICHAEL: Huh.

SARAH: Of course, I don't want you to become obese. So you should probably try to chant when you get the urge to eat ice cream in the middle of the night.

MICHAEL: What am I supposed to do while I chant?

SARAH: You're supposed to envision the thing that you want.

MICHAEL: So, I should chant while envisioning a Bentley?

SARAH: Yeah, sure. If that's the thing that you desire most.

(Michael laughs.)

It really works. You'll see if you actually give it a chance.

MICHAEL: Okay. Let's chant right now.

(Michael and Sarah sit on the floor crossed-legged.
They repeat: NA-MU AMI-TA-BUL as the lights fade
to black.)

SCENE 11

Simon and Michael are unpacking boxes and moving furniture around in Michael's new apartment.

MICHAEL: Do you like where the couch is?

SIMON: Actually, I don't.

MICHAEL: You don't?

SIMON: No. It cuts off the flow of the room. We should move it against that wall, then the space will seem a lot bigger.

MICHAEL: Okay.

(They move the couch against the wall.)

Yeah, you're right. That really opened the place up.

SIMON: I told you.

MICHAEL: How did you know to do that?

SIMON: My wife is an interior decorator you idiot.

MICHAEL: Of course. How is she?

SIMON: Terrible. We just had another miscarriage, man.

MICHAEL: I'm sorry to hear that.

SIMON: Yeah.

MICHAEL: How many is that?

SIMON: This is the third.

MICHAEL: Have you guys seen a doctor?

SIMON: Of course we've seen a doctor.

MICHAEL: My mother had a bunch of miscarriages before and after she had me.

SIMON: Crazy.

MICHAEL: Yeah. And when she was five months pregnant with me she started to bleed and have contractions. They put her on bed rest for the rest of the pregnancy.

SIMON: You're a miracle baby.

MICHAEL: I guess. How far along was she?

SIMON: Eleven weeks.

MICHAEL: I know a couple who announced at twelve weeks, and lost the baby at thirteen.

SIMON: That's terrible.

MICHAEL: It's going to be okay. They have so many treatments for geriatric pregnancies these days. How old is she again?

SIMON: She's only thirty-eight.

MICHAEL: How's she holding up?

(Simon starts to speak, then he tears up. He starts to speak again, then stops. Then he wipes a tear from his eye.)

SIMON: Can we talk about something else?

MICHAEL: You're the one who brought it up.

(Simon snaps.)

SIMON: I know that I'm the one who fucking brought it up, but now I want to un-bring it up okay?

MICHAEL: Yeah, sure, man, sorry.

(They unpack things in silence for a little while.
A marble drops on the floor in the apartment above them and bounces.
Simon and Michael both look at the ceiling. Simon immediately goes back to what he's doing, but Michael continues to stare.)

What was that?

SIMON: It's just your neighbors.

MICHAEL: That was pretty loud.

SIMON: That was nothing, man. This place seems very quiet to me.

MICHAEL: It better be for one point six.

SIMON: So, you had sex with that girl yet?

MICHAEL: We're supposed to have sex for the first time tomorrow night.

SIMON: I can't believe you haven't had sex with her.

MICHAEL: Oh, believe me, we've been doing plenty, but no actual vaginal penetration.

SIMON: What does that mean? "No actual vaginal penetration." You been fucking her in the ass?

(Michael laughs.)

MICHAEL: I wish. We want the first time we have sex to be mean-
   ingful, so we've planned a special night.
SIMON: Special night, huh? What are you turning into a faggot?
MICHAEL: I really like her, Simon. I think that she might be the
   one.
SIMON: Just kidding around, man. I can't wait to meet her.

SCENE 12

*Sarah is lying on top of Michael's bed in elegant lingerie. The room
is lit by candles. Michael enters wearing a silk robe. He stands watching her for a moment. Their eyes are locked. He loosens the belt of the
robe and lets it slide onto the floor. He is completely naked. He climbs
on top of her and they kiss. Deep. Passionate. Romantic. She takes
his penis and glides it into her. She moans. He is motionless inside her.
He's absorbing the moment. He holds her tightly.*

MICHAEL: Oh, Sarah, you feel so good.

   *(They kiss deeply. He slowly glides his penis out and then glides
   it back in. She gasps. He stays deep inside her. The ecstasy he
   feels is palpable.)*

Oh, Sarah. Sarah. I love you.

   *(He kisses her forehead, her eyes, and her cheek, before he
   kisses her on the lips again. He begins to thrust into her deep
   and quick. She moans and gasps.
      She has an orgasm. Her whole body shakes.)*

God. God.

   *(A child loudly runs across the floor in the apartment above
   them. Michael is distracted a little but maintains his focus on
   trying to orgasm now that Sarah has climaxed.*

The child runs across the floor again. Michael tries to concentrate harder.

Now the child is completely out of control—jumping up and down on the floor, then running across the floor, tripping, then falling, getting up, running some more.

Michael loses his erection. He stops and looks at the ceiling.)

What the fuck is that?

SARAH: It's your neighbors.

MICHAEL: Yeah, but, but—

SARAH: It's the sound of a child playing.

MICHAEL: Jesus that's loud.

(It's suddenly silent. The child has stopped running.)

SARAH: It's no big deal, Michael. You'll get used to it. Now, relax.

(She feels for his penis and notices how soft it is.)

Let me help you with that.

(She starts to give him a blowjob. He relaxes. When he's hard she climbs on top and rides him. They're really getting into it when the child starts running and going crazy upstairs even worse than before. Sarah doesn't even notice. She has her eyes closed and is intensely trying to achieve orgasm again. Michael has his head lifted up, his eyes open, and he is moving his head in whichever direction the child runs. He's gone soft again. Sarah stops riding him. She's frustrated.)

Just ignore it!

MICHAEL: Hold on.

(He physically lifts her off him and tosses her onto the bed. He then jumps out of bed, runs into the kitchen, then comes back with a broom and starts banging it on the ceiling.)

SARAH: Michael! What the fuck are you doing?

(The running stops. Silence. Then an adult male stomps twice very loudly on the floor above. Michael's whole apartment shakes. Michael then hits the ceiling twice with the broom. The man upstairs immediately stomps twice. Michael hits the ceiling two more times, and the man stomps back two more times.)

Stop it, Michael! That isn't going to make things better.

(Sarah and Michael lock eyes. Then Michael yells to the neighbors above through their ceiling:)

MICHAEL: What the fuck is wrong with you?!
TED: Hey, man, we're just living up here. Normal living. So my question is: WHAT THE FUCK IS WRONG WITH YOU?!
MICHAEL: The sound of that child running is unbearable!
SARAH: Michael, stop it!
TED: The sound of your loud sex is what's unbearable!
MICHAEL: I've never heard a child run that much! Is your kid retarded or something?!
TED: Did you just call my kid a retard?!
MICHAEL: Yeah, your kid is a retard just like her fat fuck father! You sound as if you weigh four hundred pounds!
TED: That's it! I'm coming down there!
MICHAEL: No, I'm going up there!

(Michael bolts out of his apartment. The next thing we know he's banging loudly on his neighbor's door.)

Come out here, you coward!

(The neighbor swings the door open.)

TED: I'm not a coward. I was just putting on my shoes!

(They stand looking into each other's eyes for a moment. Then Michael peers into Ted's apartment.)

MICHAEL: I don't see any carpeting in your apartment.

TED: So what?

MICHAEL: The condo rules state that at least eighty percent of your floors have to be covered with carpet and padding that's half an inch thick.

TED: Do you have carpet in your apartment?

MICHAEL: No, but I just moved in. I plan to get rugs as soon as—

TED: When you get carpeting in your apartment then we can talk.

(Ted tries to shut the door in Michael's face but Michael sticks his foot in the door and keeps it open.)

MICHAEL: Don't shut the door in my face!

TED: Now you're trespassing! You've got your foot in my apartment! I'm calling the police if you don't leave right now.

MICHAEL: Let me talk to your daughter.

TED: How do you know I have a girl?

MICHAEL: I need to talk to her!

(Michael tries to force his way into the apartment and they struggle. Ted eventually is able to push Michael back into the hallway and slams the door behind him.)

SCENE 13

Later that night. Sarah is rubbing Tiger Balm on Michael's shoulder. Michael is calmer now but still tense. Ted has put on combat boots to retaliate against Michael. We hear Ted stomping back and forth throughout this scene. Sarah is being empathetic.

SARAH: You can't ever do that again.

MICHAEL: Why?

SARAH: Because he could sue you for harassment.

MICHAEL: For knocking on his door?!

SARAH: Yes! Just for knocking on his door. But you didn't just do that. You tried to force your way into his apartment. And why were you asking to speak to his daughter?!

MICHAEL: I just wanted to ask her to stop running in the house. Clearly her parents aren't going to make her stop running, so I thought that I would have a polite conversation with her.

SARAH: You're going to have to get used to this, Michael. *(Gestures toward the stomping going on above)*

MICHAEL: How the fuck am I supposed to get used to *THAT*?

SARAH: Through prayer and meditation.

MICHAEL *(Genuinely perplexed)*: What?

(She grabs the Big Book of Alcoholics Anonymous and flips through it looking for a specific page. She finds it.)

SARAH: The eleventh step of AA states: "Sought through prayer and meditation to improve our conscious contact with God, *as we understood Him*, praying only for knowledge of His will for us and the power to carry that out."

MICHAEL: Okay. What do you want me to do with that?

SARAH: Look, I know you've just started this program, and probably aren't ready to start working the steps, but I think that the eleventh step might be the solution to your problem.

MICHAEL: How is prayer and meditation going to help me with my asshole neighbors? I paid one point six for this place. That should give me the right to have peace in my home.

SARAH: Well, it doesn't. You'll never have peace if you look for it in external things.

MICHAEL: What does that mean?

SARAH: A new house is not going to make you happy, a new car isn't going to make you happy, neither is a new bathroom or a new kitchen, neither is sex or a relationship. Peace of mind comes from within. We can't control our external environment. We have no control over the things that people do. The only thing we have control over is how we respond to the obstacles that are placed before us in this life.

(Her words are clearly having an effect on Michael.)

You didn't have to react the way you did tonight. You didn't help the situation, you only made it worse.

(Michael nods his head.)

You've been an alcoholic half your life. It's only natural that you have no idea how to deal with people. You stopped maturing emotionally the second you started to drink alcoholically. How old were you when you started drinking?

MICHAEL: Sixteen.

SARAH: You have the emotional maturity of a sixteen year old.

(Pause.)

Think of praying as talking to God, and meditation as listening to God. If you talk to God and listen for his answers you'll never be led astray.

MICHAEL: I'm not an atheist, but I haven't thought that much about God.

SARAH: But you have. That's what you were looking for in the bottle. Something to comfort you. Something that you could rely on. Something to help bear the burden of living in this world.

(Michael nods. They kiss.)

Let's say a prayer from the Big Book.

(She flips through the pages until she finds the right one. She gets on her knees and clasps her hands with the book on the floor in front of her so she can read.)

C'mon Michael, get down on your knees.

(He gets on his knees and clasps his hands.)

Repeat after me.
"God, I offer myself to Thee—"
MICHAEL: "God, I offer myself to Thee—"
SARAH: "To build with me, and to do with me as Thou wilt."
MICHAEL: "To build with me, and to do with me as Thou wilt."
SARAH: "Relieve me of the bondage of self, that I may better do Thy will."
MICHAEL: "Relieve me of the bondage of self, that I may better do Thy will."
SARAH: "Take away my difficulties, that victory over them may bear witness—"
MICHAEL: "Take away my difficulties, that victory over them may bear witness—"
SARAH: "To those I would help of Thy Power, Thy Love, and Thy Way of Life."
MICHAEL: "To those I would help of Thy Power, Thy Love, and Thy Way of Life."
SARAH: "May I do Thy will always!"
MICHAEL: "May I do Thy will always!"

(They look into each other's eyes as they kneel side by side. Michael puts his hand on Sarah's back and firmly pushes her to the ground so that she's on all fours. He silently moves himself behind her, pulls up her nightie, and unceremoniously enters her. Her eyes go wide because of the lack of preparation and the animalistic nature of what he's just done. Michael roughly and steadily pumps into her until they reach a simultaneous orgasm. They stay in that position, motionless for a few moments.)

I love you, Sarah.
SARAH: I love you, too.

SCENE 14

*Michael knocks on Ted's door. He is holding a fruit basket. Ted
opens the door.*

TED: What do you want?

MICHAEL: Well, I'm, I, uh—

TED: What is it?

MICHAEL: I, uh, just wanted to apologize for last night. My
behavior was unacceptable and uncivilized. I'm sorry.

TED: I appreciate that. I'm sorry, too.

MICHAEL: I brought you this fruit basket. I thought about buying you chocolate, but then I thought that you might not
want to give chocolate to your kid, 'cause sugar makes kids
literally bounce off the walls, so I, uh, bought something
with unprocessed sugar so your kid won't act so crazy
when she eats it.

(Ted is confused and a little insulted by what Michael just said.)

TED: Uh, thanks.

(Michael hands Ted the basket. Awkward pause.)

So, I guess I'll see you around the building.

(Ted starts to close the door.)

MICHAEL: Oh, there's one more thing.

TED: What is it?

MICHAEL: We were wondering whether you could try to keep it
down in the mornings.

TED: What are you talking about?

MICHAEL: Your kid woke us up at five-thirty this morning with
all the running, banging, and dropping stuff.

TED: I'm not going to stop my kid from playing in her own home.

MICHAEL: I understand and accept that. But my girlfriend and I usually like to sleep until seven-fifteen on weekdays, and around ten on the weekends, so, I'm not asking you stop your child from playing, but I would really appreciate my sleep not being disturbed.

TED: I'll see what I can do.

(Ted slams the door in Michael's face.)

SCENE 15

A few days later. Michael is sitting in Mark's office. Michael looks like shit. He has dark circles under his eyes.

MARK: You're two days late with the Obtuku file. Do you need someone to help you get it done?

MICHAEL: I'm almost finished, Mark. It's just been a rough week.

MARK: You know, you seemed to be doing really well for a little while. I felt as if I was seeing a whole new Michael. The type of Michael that I'd want to make a partner at this firm. Where did that Michael go?

(Pause.)

Did you have a relapse? You can be honest with me.

MICHAEL: I didn't relapse. Look, I just bought this new apartment.

MARK: So?

MICHAEL: I can hear everything that my neighbors do, and they have this little kid who gets up at five A.M. each morning and wakes me up.

MARK: You should get soundproofing.

MICHAEL: I hadn't thought of that!

MARK: It's something to look into. You spent one point six to buy this place, it's probably worth the extra thirty or forty so that you can enjoy it. But make them get carpet first. You don't want to drop that kind of money if you don't have to.

MICHAEL: Thanks for the advice.

(Pause.)

MARK: We're hoping to sign a new client, and we think that you're the best man to seal the deal.

MICHAEL: Tell me a little about him.

MARK: Well, he's a celebrity.

MICHAEL: What kind of a celebrity?

MARK: A basketball star.

MICHAEL: Jesus, Mark.

MARK: What?!

MICHAEL: Nothing. Keep going.

MARK: I thought it would be a good idea for you to go out to dinner with him, one on one, and really establish a relationship, you know, like, uh, like—

MICHAEL: Like bros.

MARK: Yes! Exactly! Like bros.

MICHAEL: A partner is always the lead attorney for a celebrity client. Why are you making me the lead attorney on this?

MARK: I know you think it's because you're black. But it's not. That has nothing to do with it. I'm doing this because now you're officially being groomed to be a partner. You need to get your feet wet. As long as you stay sober, start getting some sleep, and finish working on the Obtuku file, I don't see any reason why you won't be made partner by the end of this year.

MICHAEL: Really?! This year?

MARK: Yup.

MICHAEL: Thank you, Mark. Thank you!

(He goes over and gives Mark an awkward hug.)

I'm sorry about all that stuff I said to you a few weeks ago.

MARK: Water under the bridge.

(Michael gives Mark a kiss on the forehead.)

Okay. Okay. It's time for you to get out of my office. I'm a little afraid that you're going to try and fuck me in the ass.

MICHAEL: Okay. Okay. I'm leaving. And I assure you that I wasn't going to try and fuck you in the ass.

(Michael exits.)

SCENE 16

Simon, Sarah and Michael are eating dinner at Michael's apartment. Ted is stomping around upstairs. Michael and Sarah are ignoring it and acting like everything is perfectly fine.

SARAH *(To Simon)*: Do you think that Michael is rude to the waitstaff at restaurants?

(Simon starts laughing.)

MICHAEL: What kind of question is that?

SIMON: Only when he's really hungry!

MICHAEL: That's not true!

SARAH: Yes, it is, Michael! The worst is when a waiter is taking too long to get something, so Michael goes and gets it himself!

(Simon laughs.)

SIMON: I hate it when he does that!

SARAH: It's the worst!

MICHAEL: I don't understand why the two of you are all right with being tyrannized by the waitstaff at restaurants. If I ask for water or ketchup I expect them to bring it immediately, and not take fifteen minutes.

SARAH: Yeah, but don't you think it's rude to go behind the counter, where customers aren't allowed, to grab the ketchup.

MICHAEL: This is not a matter of rudeness. It's a matter of necessity. I need my ketchup immediately or the food is going to get cold!

SARAH: Well, I wish you wouldn't do that.

MICHAEL: You couldn't have brought this up in private?

SARAH: You act like this behavior is so normal, that I started to think that I was the crazy one. I wanted to see if Simon agreed with me before I made an issue out of it.

MICHAEL: That's ridiculous.

SIMON: And while we're on the subject: Why do you have to send your food back like three times. Last time we were out together you made the waitress cry. It wasn't her fault that your food wasn't as hot as you would have liked it.

MICHAEL: She kept letting my food sit in the pickup area for like five minutes before she would pick it up and bring it over.

SARAH: Waitresses are really busy. They have a lot to do. You could try having some sympathy for people that are in a lower class than you are.

MICHAEL: Most of the waiters and waitresses in New York have college degrees.

SIMON: That's not true.

MICHAEL: Yes, it is! Lots of them are actors and writers who are trying to make ends meet. They're of the same social class as we are.

SARAH: Except that they need to wait tables. When we go out to restaurants you turn into a monster. You act like a coked-up rich guy from an eighties movie!

SIMON: And if you don't mind me saying so, it makes you seem like an Uncle Tom.

MICHAEL: What?!

SARAH: It is a bit Uncle Tomish.

MICHAEL: Have either of you even read *Uncle Tom's Cabin*!? He's the hero of the novel.

SIMON: I don't care about the historical figure of Uncle Tom. I'm interested in how the modern day terminology relates to you.

MICHAEL: The two of you are racists!

SARAH: I'm not saying that I think that you're an Uncle Tom.
I'm just talking about how an objective viewer might per-
ceive you.

SIMON: I feel the same way. *I* am not calling you an Uncle Tom.

MICHAEL: I waited tables for four years at a fine-dining estab-
lishment. Every one of us who worked there had pride in
our jobs. We were determined to make sure that the diners
had the best experience possible. I anticipated the custom-
er's every need. I noticed when their water glass was almost
empty and would make sure their plates were cleared the
second that they were finished eating. Now, most waiters
are too busy chatting with each other, texting and checking
their e-mail.

SARAH: You're lumping every waiter—

MICHAEL: Let me finish. Everyone thinks they should be famous
nowadays. No one is happy with the lot they've been dealt.
Every bagger in the grocery store, the baristas at Starbucks,
people who work in hotels, and garbagemen. They all think
that they should be on *American Idol* or *America's Top Model*,
or whatever reality drivel they're showing on television these
days. People no longer take pride in the work that they do
because they don't think the work that they do is important.
The only important work as far as they're concerned is the
work of becoming famous and how many people follow you
on Twitter and how many Facebook friends you have. But
the work that they do *is* important, and maybe they would
have some pride in what they did if they realized that.

(Simon is now looking at the ceiling.)

SIMON: What the hell is that?

MICHAEL: It's my neighbor Ted.

SIMON: Does he really have to walk like that? He sounds like an
elephant.

MICHAEL: Sarah thinks that I'm being ridiculous for having a
problem with the noise. She says that it's a normal part of
apartment living.

SIMON: That's not normal, man.

SARAH: Michael will get used to it.

MICHAEL: I've been praying and meditating to try to deal with it.

SIMON: How's that going?

MICHAEL: It's kind of working.

(The child starts running all over the place.)

SIMON: I'll tell you one thing: there's no way I could fucking deal with that. I'd move if I were you.

MICHAEL *(To Sarah)*: Maybe I should go to the board and make them get carpeting.

SARAH: I'm telling you, it's not going to do any good.

MICHAEL: We can't just let ourselves be terrorized because of some vague idea about being a good neighbor.

SARAH: I don't feel terrorized. That's all in your head.

MICHAEL: Well, I just had an epiphany from my Higher Power.

SARAH: What was this epiphany?

(Michael looks up at the ceiling and screams as loud as he can:)

MICHAEL: THAT THESE PEOPLE NEED TO GET FUCK-ING WALL-TO-WALL CARPETING. FUCK YOU, TED!

(The running and stomping stops. A moment passes.)

TED *(Through the floor)*: NO! FUCK YOU!

(Blackout.)

SCENE 17

Ted is on the phone.

TED: Hi, Bob, how's it going?
        Good. Good. Glad to hear that. How's your wife?

Oh, well, I'm glad she's recovered from the knee surgery. Why would you ask me that? Of course I have carpets and pads.

(Ted looks around his bare floors.)

Yup. They cover at *least* eighty percent of my floor if not more.

An inspection? Why?

He said that? He actually said that he saw into my apartment and that I didn't have carpeting??!!

Well, let me tell you about that guy. He's crazy! He came up here one night and tried to force his way into my apartment and demanded to speak to my daughter.

Yeah, it is disturbing. I don't want to spread rumors, but I think that he might be a pedophile.

Yeah. I mean, why else would he try to break into my apartment to see *my daughter?*

Glad that you're going to look into that.

Oh, you still want to do the inspection?

Yeah, okay, this week is actually really bad for me. I'm, uh, I, um, I'm going out of town. But the end of next week should be fine.

Great. See you then.

SCENE 18

Sarah walks into Michael's office and stands there watching him silently for a moment. He notices her but continues working.

SARAH: Can I borrow your stapler? Mine seems to be broken.

(He hands her the stapler without looking at her. He continues to work. She just stands there.)

I can't believe you're giving me the silent treatment. I thought only women did that.

(Silence.)

Are you on your period? 'Cause I have some tampons in case you need one to put in your vagina.

(Michael shakes his head to indicate that he's not going to engage her petty antics.)

C'mon, just tell me what's wrong? I seriously have no idea. Last night you said you were tired and went straight to bed, and this morning you refused to talk and just read your paper. You're acting really immature.

MICHAEL: Okay, you want to know what's wrong?

SARAH: YES!

MICHAEL: You flirted with Simon all through dinner last night.

SARAH *(Incredulous)*: What?

MICHAEL: You two were just laughing and smiling at each other, and pretty much leaving me out of every conversation.

SARAH: I wasn't flirting with him.

MICHAEL: I saw what kinds of looks you were giving him. Don't play dumb. You used to give me those same looks before you had me spank you in the stairwell.

SARAH: I don't like this, Michael. I don't like the side of you that I'm seeing right now.

MICHAEL: You're the one who demanded to know what was wrong! I wasn't going to say anything about it!

SARAH: I don't like jealous men.

MICHAEL: And the purpose of the conversation that you included me in was to make fun of me and to call me an Uncle Tom!

SARAH: Shhhh. Shhhh, Michael, we're at work.

(Pause.)

I'm sorry for calling you an Uncle Tom. It was all in good fun, I swear. You're actually one of the nicest guys I know.

(She kisses him on the forehead.)

Honestly, I didn't realize that we were excluding you. I really like Simon and got along with him. Is that a crime? Don't you want your girlfriend and best friend to get along with each other?

MICHAEL: You're right. Between not getting any sleep and . . . I'm stressed out. I'm sorry.

SARAH: Did you call the management company?

MICHAEL: Yes, they said that they're going to make Ted get carpeting and inspect the apartment.

SARAH: That's great to hear. Then maybe we can stop talking about this.

MICHAEL: You act like I'm doing something to you. It's not my fault that they're loud.

SARAH: You know that I don't care about the noise. What upsets me is the fact that you're constantly talking about it. If them getting carpet will make you shut up about it, then I'll be happy.

(She walks away with the stapler.)

SCENE 19

Ted's apartment is now mostly covered in carpet. He rolls one last carpet over some padding and he surveys his work in a self-satisfied manner. There is a knock on his door. Ted answers it.

TED: Hey, Bob, come on in.
BOB: Thanks.

(Bob enters.)

Hope I'm not disturbing you.
TED: Of course not. I was just doing some reading.
BOB: How do you like being a house-husband?
TED: Nothing to complain about. More men should do this.
BOB: Men didn't do that in my day. We called them sissies.

TED: I'd like to think I contribute. I wouldn't want a nanny to raise my child.

BOB: Hm. Mind if I take a look around?

TED: Of course not.

(Bob surveys the apartment, then pulls up a corner of rug, takes out a ruler, then measures the padding.)

BOB: You've even got the proper half-inch padding. What's wrong with this guy?

TED: I don't know. He's been making my life a living hell.

BOB: I wish that our building was a co-op so that we could've prevented him from moving in, I really hate troublemakers.

TED: Tell me about it.

BOB: Did you file a police report after he tried to barge into your apartment?

TED: No.

BOB: The guy tried to rape your kid, and you didn't file a police report? You should do that.

(Ted doesn't know what to say.)

I think we have to scare this guy a little.

TED: How?

BOB: I have my ways.

TED: You know, he doesn't even have carpet in his apartment.

BOB: He doesn't? How dare he file a complaint when he's not in compliance himself?

TED: Yeah, it's crazy.

BOB: Well, I'll let you get back to your reading.

TED: Talk to you soon.

(Bob exits. Ted immediately starts to roll up the carpet and pad.)

They better give me a refund on all of this. I love my hardwood floors.

SCENE 20

Michael is sitting on the floor of his apartment chanting. Above him Ted stomps around while his child rides a three-wheeler all over the apartment, making a deafening sound. Ted also has some sort of heavy-metal music playing. The result is an unbearable amount of noise.

MICHAEL: NA-MU AMI-TA-BUL
 NA-MU AMI-TA-BUL
 NA-MU AMI-TA-BUL
 NA-MU AMI-TA-BUL
 NA-MU AMI-TA-BUL
 NA-MU AMI-TA-BUL.

(There is a knock on the door. Michael can't hear it because of all the noise from above.)

NA-MU AMI-TA-BUL
NA-MU AMI-TA-BUL.

(The banging becomes so loud that it seems like someone is trying to break down the door.
 Michael opens his eyes and looks around.)

What the fuck is that?

(He jumps up and goes to the door.)

Who is it?
BOB: It's the president of the condo association!
MICHAEL: Who?
BOB: It's the president!

(Michael opens the door.)

MICHAEL: Hi.

BOB: Where on earth is all that noise coming from?

MICHAEL: It's my upstairs neighbors.

BOB: Jesus, that's loud.

MICHAEL: I told you. Have you inspected his apartment yet?

BOB: I did, earlier today.

MICHAEL: And?

BOB: He has carpet and pad covering every inch of the apartment.

MICHAEL: That's bullshit, man. Do you hear the rolling from that bike or whatever the fuck it is?! I wouldn't be able to hear that if he had carpet and pad down.

BOB: I see why you would think that, but I promise you that Ted is in full compliance with the rules.

MICHAEL: Well, can't you check again? He obviously took up the carpet and pads!

BOB: We're not checking his apartment again. We've intruded on Ted's life enough.

MICHAEL: I'm gonna file a lawsuit against Ted and the condo association if you don't go back up there right now!

BOB: Are you?

MICHAEL: I am.

BOB: You're going to file a lawsuit when you're not in compliance with the carpeting rule yourself!?

MICHAEL: I just moved in!

BOB: Doesn't matter. Rules are rules. You clearly think that everyone needs to follow the rules except you.

MICHAEL: I don't think that.

BOB: Let me ask you a question.

MICHAEL: What?

BOB: Do you like little girls?

MICHAEL: What?

BOB: Do you like to fuck little girls?

MICHAEL: No! What the fuck is wrong with you?!

BOB: This building is filled with good, friendly people. People who don't want neighbors who they have to worry about fucking their kids.

(The child has started to run all around.)

MICHAEL: I don't want to fuck kids.

BOB: Then why did you try to barge into Ted's apartment and demand to speak to his daughter?

MICHAEL: I just wanted to tell her not to run in the house. I mean, listen to that!

BOB: I have a nine-year-old granddaughter. You stay the fuck away from her!

(Bob spits in Michael's face then starts to exit.)

And get some damn carpets!

(He exits.)

SCENE 21

Michael sits alone in his apartment, drinking straight out of a bottle of whiskey. He absentmindedly watches porn on his computer. He is not masturbating, just blankly staring at the screen. His cell phone rings. He picks it up.

MICHAEL: Hi Sarah.
    Tonight?
    I don't think so. I'm really really tired, plus I think I might be coming down with a cold.
    Of course I want to see you. I just don't want you to get sick.
    No, I'm not still mad. I promise.
    I love you, too.

(He hangs up the phone.
    The lights fade and come back up again to indicate the passage of time. Michael has not moved from his position on the couch and is asleep, hugging his bottle of whiskey. Suddenly, from above, we hear running, stomping, and the sounds of a child playing. Michael wakes up. The first thing he does is take

*a long swig of whiskey. Then he takes a wash rag and runs it
under the tap. He washes his face, then under his armpits and
his crotch area. He puts on deodorant, a T-shirt, button-down
shirt, suit pants, and a jacket. He takes another long swig of
whiskey and walks out of his apartment.*
    Blackout.
    In the darkness we hear this conversation:)

You guys headed to school?
TED: Stay away from us!
MICHAEL: Can't I just walk with you for a little while?
TED: No!
MICHAEL: Hey, little girl, what's your name?
GIRL: Cindy.
MICHAEL: Cindy. That's a nice name.
GIRL: Thanks!
TED: Stop it.
MICHAEL: I'm your downstairs neighbor.
TED: Stop it.
MICHAEL: And when you run it makes me very unhappy.
TED: C'mon, Cindy, take my hand, we're crossing the street.
MICHAEL: No don't go! I'd really appreciate it if you started
    watching more TV, or played with more puzzles instead
    of— WATCH OUT!

*(We hear a car screech, then the deafening high-pitch scream of
a little girl. Then all goes silent. A few moments later we hear
the sound of sirens.)*

SCENE 22

Michael is standing in Sarah's office talking to her.

MICHAEL: . . . Ted really didn't like the fact that I was walking
    with them, so he steps off the sidewalk without looking,
    and starts to cross the street, and a car hits them.

SARAH: Oh, my God! Did you follow them into the street?

MICHAEL: No, but I continued trying to talk to them from the sidewalk.

SARAH: Well, how are they?

MICHAEL: Ted was fine, just a little shaken up . . .

SARAH: And the girl?

MICHAEL: Well, it . . . it appears that she broke both of her legs.

SARAH: You're kidding.

MICHAEL: I'm dead serious.

SARAH: That's terrible. That's terrible, Michael.

MICHAEL: Is it?

SARAH: Yes. A little child has lost her ability to walk.

MICHAEL: But, probably not forever.

SARAH: You'd really like that wouldn't you? If her back was broken and she had to be in a wheelchair for the rest of her life.

(Michael ponders this.)

MICHAEL: I mean, I wouldn't wish that on her but . . .

SARAH: You're a fucked-up and twisted individual, Michael.

MICHAEL: I don't understand why you're mad at me? You're the one who taught me about chanting.

SARAH: What does that have to do with anything?

MICHAEL: Well, you're supposed to visualize what you want while you chant, right?

SARAH: Are you telling me that you've been visualizing that little girl with broken legs while you chant?

MICHAEL: No! I would visualize a peaceful and serene apartment. But you keep telling me that God works in mysterious ways. I think that this might be God's answer to my prayers.

SARAH: I can't talk to you anymore. Get the fuck away from me.

(Michael goes back to his office.
Sarah picks up her phone and dials.)

Hey, Simon?

Yeah hi, it's Sarah.
Yeah, Michael's girlfriend.
I really need to talk to you. Do you think that we could
meet up for a drink tonight?
Great. See you then.

(She hangs up the phone.)

SCENE 23

*Michael is at a fancy restaurant with Delroy, the basketball star.
They are in the middle of dinner. Michael has an empty martini
glass in front of him.*

MICHAEL: Have you seen our waitress?
DELROY: No, I haven't seen her.
MICHAEL: I need another drink.

(Michael looks around agitated.)

Where the fuck is she?
DELROY: Chill out, man. It's cool.
MICHAEL: Bad service just really irritates me.
DELROY: There she is.

(Delroy flags her down.)

Excuse me, my friend would like another martini.
WAITRESS: Right away, sir.
MICHAEL: And my fish is overcooked.
WAITRESS: You're unhappy with the way your fish was prepared?
MICHAEL: Are you deaf?
DELROY: Michael, calm down.

(Michael closes his eyes and inhales deeply and slowly exhales.)

MICHAEL: Fish should be cooked medium-rare, and this is well-
done.

WAITRESS: We always cook Chilean sea bass all the way through.
MICHAEL: Where did your chef go to culinary school? DeVry?

(Delroy starts laughing out loud when Michael says this, even though he's kind of horrified at the way Michael has been behaving.)

WAITRESS: I'll have your food redone with the Chilean sea bass medium-rare.
MICHAEL: Thank you very much. I appreciate that.
WAITRESS: You're welcome, sir.

(The Waitress exits.)

DELROY: You're funny, man.

(Delroy laughs.)

DeVry!

(They both start laughing.)

I've never met a brother like you before.
MICHAEL: I bet that lady is going to spit in my food.
WAITRESS *(Reentering)*: And I'm not going to spit in your food. I would never do that.

(The Waitress sets the martini down and walks away.)

DELROY: She's totally going to spit in your food now.
MICHAEL *(Resigned)*: Yeah. I guess that's better than pissing in my food.

(They both laugh.)

DELROY: You're not going to be happy with that Chilean sea bass, you know.

MICHAEL: Why?

DELROY: It's still chewy at medium-rare. Chilean sea bass is a delicate fish. You have to cook it all the way through, but if you overcook it by three seconds it's ruined.

MICHAEL: Shit.

DELROY: Salmon and tuna are very tender and quite perfect when cooked medium-rare, but not sea bass.

(Michael drinks his whole martini in one gulp.)

You have quite the tolerance.

MICHAEL: It doesn't happen overnight. You have to drink excessively for years to become like me.

(Delroy laughs.)

If you want, I can show you what drinking is really about tonight.

DELROY: Sure. Why not?

*(Delroy downs his drink.
Michael shouts to the Waitress.)*

MICHAEL: We need some shots over here!

(The Waitress arrives.)

WAITRESS: Shots of what?

MICHAEL: Johnnie Walker Blue.

WAITRESS: That's going to be very expensive.

MICHAEL: I know. Bring us six shots.

(The Waitress exits.)

So, I want to talk to you about your account.

DELROY: Okay.

MICHAEL: I'm only telling you this because we're brothers, you know, black guys.

DELROY: Okay.

MICHAEL: You shouldn't be doing business at our firm.

DELROY: But it's one of the top-rated firms in the country.

MICHAEL: Yeah, I know.

(The Waitress comes back with a tray of shots and sets them down on the table.)

Thank you.

(Michael and Delroy both pick up the shot glasses.)

DELROY: Cheers.

(They clink glasses and down their shots.)

MICHAEL: This firm is fucking racist, man. There aren't any black partners. I've been there for ten years, and they still haven't—

DELROY: Mark led me to believe that you were a partner.

MICHAEL: Nope. I'm just the most senior black guy that they have.

DELROY: Wow. I'm going to have to think about that.

MICHAEL: You're a huge celebrity. You're a symbol of excellence within our culture. By being with this firm you're sending the message that big firms and large corporations can discriminate and won't suffer any consequences.

DELROY: Well, what do you suggest?

(Michael lifts two shots and hands one to Delroy.)

MICHAEL: Cheers!

(They clink glasses and down the shots.)

I've decided to start my own law firm, and I want you to be my first client. I'm sick of being kept down by the man.

DELROY: How long has *The Man* been holding you down?

MICHAEL: Well, uh, uh, my whole life I guess.

DELROY: I appreciate your ambition. You've got balls, man.

MICHAEL: Hey, you ever done coke?

DELROY: Not in years.

MICHAEL: Me either. But it would be really fun, don't you think?

DELROY: Sure, why not?

(They grab the last shots and down them.)

MICHAEL: Awesome. I know a guy.

DELROY: What about your Chilean sea bass?

MICHAEL: Fuck the sea bass!

(Shouting to the Waitress.)

Check please!

SCENE 24

Simon and Sarah have just finished having sex. Sarah is lying on top of Simon. Simon is out of breath. Sarah is ready to go again.

SARAH: I need you to fuck me again with that big dick of yours.

SIMON: Hold up, hold up, I need a few moments to recharge.

SARAH: Fine.

(She climbs off him.)

You cheat on your wife much?

SIMON: No. But we've been having a lot of problems lately.

SARAH: The miscarriages?

SIMON: Yeah.

SARAH: I'm sorry.

SIMON: It is what it is.

(Long pause.)

SARAH: I think he might have pushed her.

SIMON: Michael would never do something like that.

SARAH: Really? He seemed awfully happy about it afterwards. It made me sick to see him elated about a child getting injured.

SIMON: That child has been ruining his life. Wouldn't you be happy to see something bad happen to one of your enemies?

SARAH: First of all, I don't have any enemies. Second, a child can't be anyone's enemy.

SIMON: In this case a child is his enemy. She hasn't intentionally done anything to Michael, but she's still his enemy.

(Pause.)

Did he say that he pushed her?

SARAH: Of course not. I just have this feeling. And he's drinking again. Smelled like a whiskey factory this morning.

SIMON: He needs help.

SARAH: I've tried to help him. I'm through.

(Simon climbs on top of her. She feels his penis.)

You're sooo hard.

(She glides him into her as the lights fade to black.)

Oh, Simon. Simon!

SCENE 25

Delroy and Michael are snorting lines of cocaine in Michael's apartment.

DELROY: Wooo! This is some good stuff!

MICHAEL: Hell yeah, man. Want to listen to some Neil Young?

DELROY: Neil Young??!! That's my boy! Do you have that album, uh, with that song, uh, "Twisted Road."

MICHAEL: Of course, dude!

(Michael blasts the music and they start dancing and singing along.)

MICHAEL AND DELROY:
First time I heard "Like a Rolling Stone"
I felt that magic and took it home
Gave it a twist and made it mine
But nothing was as good as the very first time
Poetry rolling off his tongue
Like Hank Williams chewing bubble gum
Asking me, "How does it feel?"

(There is a loud banging on Michael's door.)

DELROY: Yo, man, what is that?

(Michael turns down the music.)

MICHAEL: Who is it?
TED: It's Ted.
MICHAEL *(To Delroy)*: Ted's my asshole neighbor.

(To Ted through the door.)

Hold on, Ted, I'll be right there.

(Michael and Delroy hide the cocaine.)

DELROY: Should I hide?

(Ted starts banging on the door again.)

MICHAEL *(To Ted)*: Hold on!
        (To Delroy) Why would you hide?
DELROY: I'm Delroy Johnson, and we've got a shit load of drugs
    in here. Hiding would make me feel a little better.

MICHAEL: Fine, whatever. Go hide in my bedroom.

(Delroy goes and hides.

Michael opens the door and as soon as he does Ted hits him as hard as he can in the head with a baseball bat. Michael is immediately knocked unconscious. Ted stands over him and hits him over and over again in the head with the bat. He also hits him in the legs, everywhere. Ted should hit Michael twenty to twenty-five times. It should seem extremely excessive.

Ted is out of breath and finally stops hitting Michael. He calmly surveys the apartment, then silently walks out. He closes the door behind him.

A few moments later, Delroy exits the bedroom and sees Michael lying on the floor motionless.)

DELROY: Michael?

(He goes over to Michael and checks to see whether he's alive. Delroy is not sure whether Michael is alive or dead. Delroy grabs his stuff and leaves the apartment.)

SCENE 26

Sarah is in her office texting with Simon and giggling. Mark comes over to her.

MARK: Have you seen Michael?
SARAH: No.
MARK: Where the fuck is he?!
SARAH: What happened?
MARK: You know Delroy Johnson?
SARAH: Yeah.
MARK: I asked Michael to take Delroy Johnson out to dinner last night because we were about to sign him as a client.
SARAH: All right.
MARK: Do you know what that son of a bitch told Delroy Johnson?

SARAH: What?

MARK: Michael told Delroy Johnson that this firm is racist and that he should take his business elsewhere.

SARAH: No! He wouldn't do that!

MARK: He did! If you see Michael tell him to pack his fucking stuff! He's fired!

SARAH: Don't you want to hear Michael's side of the story first?

MARK: That contract would have been worth millions of dollars.

SARAH: So, Delroy Johnson isn't going to sign?

MARK: Of course he's not signing!

(Mark starts to exit in a huff.)

SARAH: Wait a minute.

MARK: What?

SARAH: I'm gonna get him to sign.

MARK: How?

SARAH: Does it matter?

(Mark walks over to Sarah.)

MARK: If you can get Delroy Johnson to sign, you'll make partner.

(Sarah smiles.
  Mark exits.)

SCENE 27

Sarah is in Delroy's apartment.

SARAH: Thanks for seeing me on such short notice.

DELROY: Well, you made it sound like an emergency.

SARAH: It is. Michael is in the hospital.

DELROY *(Acting shocked)*: What??

SARAH: Yeah. He's in a coma. Someone tried to beat him to death.

DELROY: Oh my God.

SARAH: Yeah, and you were the last person to see him.

DELROY: Are you—are you sure about that?

SARAH: Pretty certain.

DELROY: Look, I had nothing to do with it. I didn't even GO back to his apartment.

SARAH: Is that what the security camera footage would show?

DELROY: Look, I only went back to his place for a nightcap. I have no idea what happened to him after I left.

SARAH *(Pulls a contract out of her purse)*: There aren't any security cameras, Delroy.

(Pause. They lock eyes.)

I think it's in your best interest to sign with us.

DELROY: Look, Michael told me that your firm is racist, and I don't want to be associated with a firm that doesn't support diversity.

SARAH: Michael is an alcoholic and a drug addict. The police found four grams of cocaine in his apartment. He was clearly out of his mind during your meeting. He only said that we were racist so he could poach you as a client.

DELROY: I don't know. I'm gonna have to think about this.

SARAH: There's nothing to think about. Right now, my boss and I are the only people who know that you were the last person to see Michael. What do you think will happen if the police find out about that? You're going to become a suspect, and your picture is going to be splattered across every newspaper in this country.

DELROY: How can you prevent the police from finding out? I mean—

SARAH: We'll make it look like Michael spent all evening drinking and getting high in his apartment—alone.

DELROY: But we were out in public together.

SARAH: Don't concern yourself with our methods, but I can assure you that there won't be any record of your reservation, and that every waiter and busboy will be silent about your presence there.

DELROY: You sure this is going to work?

SARAH: I promise. And trust me, if you do get charged with a crime, we're the people that you want on your side.

(Delroy nods his head gravely, then signs the contract.)

You won't regret this. I promise.

(Sarah puts the signed contract in her bag, then exits.)

SCENE 28

Michael is unconscious in a hospital bed. He's got a bandage wrapped around part of his head. He has a cast on one arm and a cast on one leg. Sarah sits by his side, holding his hand and reading e-mail on her phone. Simon enters.

SARAH: Hi, Simon.

SIMON: Hey. How is he?

SARAH: They don't think he has any internal bleeding, so that's good.

SIMON: Someone really fucked him up.

SARAH: Yeah.

SIMON: Who do you think did this to him?

(Pause.)

SARAH: Karma.

(Pause.)

SIMON: That's fucked up, Sarah. Michael doesn't deserve this.

SARAH: Doesn't he? He wished harm on a child, so harm has come to him.

SIMON: When's karma coming to get you?

SARAH: What are you talking about?

SIMON: You fucked your boyfriend's best friend? You think karma smiles upon that sort of thing?

SARAH: That's different. It's not like Michael and I are married.

SIMON: Doesn't matter. It's still wrong.

SARAH: Fuck you. You're the one sleeping around while your poor wife has miscarriage after miscarriage because something is wrong with your sperm.

SIMON: You don't know that!

SARAH: I do know that. There's something . . . you just kind of seem retarded, you know . . . not in a traditional way, but retarded nevertheless.

SIMON: Hey, I'm a dentist! A retarded person would never be able to become a dentist!

SARAH: As far as I can tell retards are the only people who are allowed to become dentists.

SIMON: You're a real bitch.

(Pause.)

SARAH: He pushed her. That's what Ted is saying.

SIMON: Well, I don't think he did.

SARAH: A change came over Michael during the past few days. He really turned into a monster.

SIMON: Okay, for the sake of argument let's say that he did push her. Let's say you're right. You have no idea what kind of pain he's been in. None of us has any idea.

SARAH: So what?

SIMON: You can't judge a person unless you've felt their pain, unless you've walked a mile in their shoes.

SARAH: Using that standard, we wouldn't be able to judge anyone.

SIMON: Exactly! All of us are capable of almost anything given the right set of circumstances.

SARAH: So, you can imagine a set of circumstances where you'd push a child into the street?

SIMON: It's hard to imagine what we'd actually do until we're in any particular situation. You probably think that you would've resisted becoming a Nazi if you lived in Germany during Hitler's reign. But I guarantee that you would've been goose-stepping and Sieg Heiling better than anyone else.

SARAH: That's not true, because I have integrity.

SIMON: Okay. Here's a really good example. I don't believe in hitting women, but right now I'm pretty close to throwing you out that window, because nothing would give me more pleasure than seeing your guts splattered all over that sidewalk out there.

SARAH: But the difference between you and Michael is that you won't actually do that.

(Simon becomes very threatening and puts his finger in her face. It looks like he's really thinking about hitting her.)

SIMON: Don't test me.

(Pause. He walks away.)

And personally I think it's wrong for you to assume that Michael is guilty! Neither one of us was there!

SARAH: The police found four grams of cocaine in his apartment. He was probably high out of his mind when he did it!

SIMON: I'm fucking sick of you judging the rest of us from your little throne.

SARAH: What are you so upset about?

SIMON: If karma did this to Michael then you're also saying that karma is the reason why my fucking wife keeps having dead babies! We didn't do anything to deserve that. No one deserves—

SARAH: Look, all I meant was that—

SIMON: I know what you meant. You meant that we all get what we deserve, that we all reap just what we sow or some shit like that!

SARAH: Simon—

SIMON: No, listen to me. No one knows what the fuck they're doing. You don't know what you're doing, I don't know what I'm doing, and our parents didn't know what they were doing! All of us are feeling our way through this world day by day, hour by hour, minute by minute, and it's all a fucking shit storm! No one can escape it! Rich, poor, good parents, bad parents, doesn't matter! For some reason we're all meant to suffer. Constantly suffer. Sometimes I feel like my head is going to explode because I can't get any relief, you know. It's amazing that we don't all commit suicide!

SARAH: You're being overdramatic.

SIMON: Am I? Michael was happy in his life before you came along.

SARAH: He was an alcoholic. I tried to save him.

SIMON: I never even heard him mention the word racism before you put the silly idea that he wasn't getting promoted because of discrimination in his head.

SARAH: I just told him the truth.

SIMON: No you didn't. I've known the man for twenty years, since we were in college. And I never heard him say that anything was racist before he met you! Why couldn't you just let him be happy?

SARAH: Well, none of it matters now anyway.

SIMON: What do you mean?

SARAH: I kind of hope that he doesn't come out of this coma.

SIMON: Why would you say that?

SARAH: If he wakes up he's fucked. He got fired from his job today.

SIMON: So what? He'll find another job.

SARAH: And the police are going to charge him with felony possession for having all of that cocaine.

SIMON: He's a lawyer. He'll beat that.

SARAH: And Ted is pressing charges against him.

SIMON: Michael should be pressing charges against Ted! I bet Ted's the one who did this to him!

SARAH: Ted would have an excellent reason if he did indeed do this.

SIMON: Michael may be in a world of trouble, but if he lives, he'll get through this. It'll be difficult, and it'll be a struggle, but with our help he'll get through this.

(Pause.)

SARAH: You're right. With our help, he'll get through this.

(Michael opens his eyes. Sarah and Simon both stare at Michael. Blackout.)

END OF PLAY

INTIMACY

PRODUCTION HISTORY

The world premiere of *Intimacy* was produced by the New Group (Scott Elliott, Artistic Director; Adam Bernstein, Executive Director) at the Acorn Theater in New York on January 29, 2014, with support from the MAP Fund (a program of Creative Capital, primarily supported by the Doris Duke Charitable Foundation), The Andrew W. Mellon Foundation, the Venturous Theater Fund and The Lark Play Development Center. The production was directed by Scott Elliott; set design was by Derek McLane, costume design was by Scott Elliott, lighting design was by Russell H. Champa, video design was by Olivia Sebestky, sound design was by Shane Rettig; the production stage manager was Valerie A. Peterson. The cast was:

JERRY	Keith Randolph Smith
PAT	Laura Esterman
JANET	Ella Dershowitz
JAMES	Daniel Gerroll
MATTHEW	Austin Cauldwell
FRED	David Anzuelo
SARAH	Déa Julien

CHARACTERS

JERRY, black, forty to sixty

PAT, Jerry's wife, white, fifty to seventy

JANET, Jerry and Pat's daughter, biracial but looks absolutely white, eighteen

JAMES, lives next door to Pat and Jerry, white, forty to sixty

MATTHEW, James's son, white, eighteen

FRED, a contractor, Hispanic, forty to sixty

SARAH, Fred's daughter, Hispanic, seventeen

SETTING

A wealthy suburb. The present.

PROLOGUE

MATTHEW: My mother died a couple of years ago. It was terrible. The most terrible part was seeing how it affected my father. He loved her so much. So did I, of course, but *his* whole reality crumbled. I really couldn't focus much on grieving for my mother 'cause I was so worried that he was going to commit suicide. Every night I would have horrifying dreams about finding my dad dead when I woke up in the morning. You know, walking down the stairs to find him hanging in the living room, or walking into the bathroom to find him in the bathtub with his wrists slit.

(Pause.)

My dad worked on Wall Street in "Financial Services." I don't really know what that means. I asked him a bunch of times, and his answers never really provided any clarity for me about his job. I do know this—my dad made a lot of money. After my mother died he just quit his job. Just left.

I was like, "Dad, you can't quit your job!" And he said, "We don't really need the money. We haven't needed the money for a while now." I don't think that we're super rich, but who knows. My dad is very, very frugal, so you can't get a sense of how much money we have by his spending habits. He always tips exactly twelve percent, which is so embarrassing. And every week he diligently takes our cans and plastic bottles to the recycling center so he can get the $3.80 or whatever it is.

(Pause.)

My mother always wanted me to be an artist. She had me start taking violin lessons at three years old, and I started playing the piano when I was five. I continued taking piano lessons until she died. It was then that I realized that I didn't have a passion for music. I love film. I love great films. I love the work of Jonas Mekas, Man Ray, Andy Warhol, Lars von Trier and Rainer Fassbinder. This is what I want to do with my life. Films make people forget themselves and transport them to a magical place. A place where they can toss off the dreariness and ordinariness of everyday life. Being a filmmaker means providing people with the catalyst to live out their greatest and deepest fantasies. Film is better than any drug in the world.

(Pause.)

I want to create something to commemorate my mother's memory. The worst thing about her dying, for me, was that I never got to say good-bye. When someone is sick for a long time, and you know that they're going to die, you have time to reconcile yourself to this fact. It makes it easier, I think. My mother just walked out the door one morning, and never came home. She once said to me, "Follow your heart, Matthew. Follow your heart, and you will always be happy."

I'm going to follow my heart. This way I'll always know that she's proud of me.

ACT ONE

SCENE 1

James, Mathew's father, is outside his house with Fred.

FRED: So, do you think that you want to move forward with these projects.

JAMES: I'm not sure.

FRED: You know that I'll give you a great price.

JAMES: It's tempting. It was her house. She decorated everything. Everywhere I look there are reminders of her. I want to make the house my own again. Besides, if I ever want to sell the place this work will be necessary.

FRED: Are you thinking about moving?

JAMES: I think about it.

(Pause.)

So, how much will all of this cost?

FRED: It's a lot of work. Granite countertops, mahogany cabinets, stainless steel appliances, radiant heating in the bathrooms, will cost you about fifty thousand dollars.

JAMES: Fifty thousand dollars! I thought that you said you were going to give me a good price!

FRED: That is a good price! It's going to cost me forty-five.

JAMES: How much would you normally charge for a job like this?

FRED: Sixty.

JAMES: Wow! You must be rich.

FRED: Hardly. You know Sarah's going to have to get a scholarship if she wants to go to a good college.

JAMES: Yeah, tuition is ridiculous. How are Sarah's grades?

FRED: Straight A's, thank God. What about Matthew?

JAMES: B's and C's.

FRED: That's too bad.

JAMES: He just doesn't apply himself to things that he's not interested in. He's not a renaissance man like Sarah.

FRED: I'm very lucky.

JAMES: So how much is the painting going to cost?

FRED: Painting every room in the house will cost fifteen thousand dollars.

JAMES: To slap some paint on a few walls!

FRED: Fine. I'll do it for twelve thousand dollars. I won't make any profit on the painting.

JAMES: It's a deal.

(Jerry and Pat approach Fred and James.)

JERRY: Hi, Fred.

PAT: Hi, James. Getting some work done?

JAMES: Yeah. I'm trying to make the place my own again.

JERRY: I can understand that. When I walk into our master suite I think—

JAMES: This is my wife's bedroom.

JERRY: Exactly! With the four-poster canopy bed and the purple walls.

PAT: You've never complained. How's your wife doing, Fred?

FRED: She works night and day.

PAT: It does seem that way. Every time I go to Walmart she seems to be there.

JERRY *(To Fred)*: Do you do any landscaping, amigo?

FRED: Yeah.

JERRY: Every spring, when the grass starts to grow again, these purple weeds overtake my yard. But it doesn't happen on James's property.

FRED: You need to use TruGreen.

JERRY *(To James)*: Is that what you use?

JAMES: Yup.

JERRY: Even in the winter?

JAMES: Yup.

PAT: Did you hear about Patrick and Jane?

FRED: No.

(James shakes his head no.)

JERRY: They're getting a divorce.

JAMES: Really?

PAT: Yup. Apparently they're swingers.

FRED: I wouldn't have pegged them for swingers.

JERRY: So, apparently Jane and Patrick were swinging with Kevin and Christina—

JAMES: Lord help us.

PAT: And Jane and Kevin started to see each other outside of the arranged swinger meeting times.

FRED: That doesn't sound so terrible. I mean, if Jane and Patrick are having sex with Kevin and Christina, then what does it matter *when* they fuck?

JAMES: I'd prefer it if you didn't cuss.

FRED: Sorry, James.

JERRY: Well, here's the kicker. Kevin got Jane pregnant!

JAMES: I hope she's planning to keep it.

PAT: Apparently they're planning to move in together to raise the kid.

FRED: So he's leaving Christina?

JERRY: They shouldn't count their chickens before they're hatched. At forty-six years old there's a high likelihood that she'll miscarry.

PAT: Or worse, the kid could have Down syndrome, and they'll have to take care of a cripple for the rest of their lives.

JAMES: Don't you think that's an insensitive thing to say?

JERRY: It's the truth.

PAT: Jerry and I had those same fears ourselves. Everyone has those fears, I think.

JAMES: See, everything worked out all right for you. We should try and see the positive in every situation.

PAT: Yes, I suppose so.

JAMES: God works in mysterious ways. One can never know the mind of the Lord. God has a plan for all of them, and He has a plan for each of us.

(Uncomfortable silence.)

FRED: Well, I really should get going.

JERRY: Us, too. We're mounting a flat-screen TV on our bedroom wall.

JAMES: You got a new TV? How big is it?

PAT: Fifty-two inches.

JAMES: Wow.

SCENE 2

Three scenes at once:
James is in his bedroom saying his morning prayers.

JAMES: Dear God, help me. I am alone. I know You are with me but I still feel alone. I have my son, and I love him more than anything, but a child can't be your sole companion in life. He doesn't want to spend that much time with me anyway.

(In another scene: Fred is having breakfast with his seventeen-year-old daughter, Sarah. They are eating cereal. She is furiously texting.)

FRED: Will you stop doing that?

SARAH: Stop doing what?

FRED: It's not polite to text while you're eating a meal with someone.

SARAH: Cold cereal isn't a meal.

(In the third scene:
   Pat is sitting with her eighteen-year-old daughter, Janet.
   Janet looks worried and forlorn.)

PAT: What's wrong?

JANET: Nothing.

. . .

JAMES: Every day, I think about ending my life. I know it would be a sin to do so, but I can't stop thinking about how wonderful that would be. All day long, memories flood back to me, and it's unbearable.

. . .

FRED: What time will you be home tonight?

SARAH: I have rehearsal until six o'clock.

. . .

JAMES: There are so many things that I would have done differently. My wife was a saint. She really was. But so many things annoyed me about her. I lived in a constant state of annoyance.

. . .

PAT: Did you and Paul have a fight?

JANET: Yes.

PAT: What were you fighting about?

JANET: I'm embarrassed to say.

. . .

JAMES: She liked to talk with her hands. Whenever we would have a conversation all I could focus on was how her hands were waving around in front of my face. And every time

she took a bite of food she would run her tongue along
the inside of her lips to make sure no bits of food were
left in there. I couldn't stand to watch her doing that, so
I would avert my eyes. I know that this is my own craziness.
I know that, and I wish that I hadn't spent so much time
being annoyed about these things, but I couldn't help it.
Every morning I would wake up and pray. I didn't know
who I was praying to then because I wasn't "born again"
yet. But I would say, "Dear God, O Eternal Force, Spirit of
the Universe, please help me not to get angry at Katherine
for moving her tongue around in her mouth or talking with
her hands. Please help me to rid myself of these character
defects."

. . .

SARAH: Will Mom be home for dinner?
FRED: No. She's working a double.

. . .

JAMES: I would say this prayer every morning and yet I would
spend half my time with her giving her hateful looks, hoping, and praying that she would stop doing these things
that annoyed me so much.

. . .

PAT: If you guys were fighting about sex then you know that
you can be absolutely honest with me and there won't be
any judgment.

. . .

SARAH: Why does Mom have to work all the time?
FRED: We need the money. You know that. Besides, your mother
and I want to have a little money in the bank to help you
pay for college.
SARAH: Relax, Dad, I know that I have to get a scholarship.
FRED: I am relaxed. Maybe you're the one who's not relaxed.
SARAH: I just don't like the fact that she has to work at Walmart.

FRED: This is exactly why you have to go to college. If you go to college, then you won't have to work at Walmart like your mother.

SARAH: It's embarrassing. People at school make fun of me because of it.

FRED: They make fun of the fact that your mother works? Everyone has to work somewhere.

SARAH: There's this stigma that anyone who works at Walmart is poor.

. . .

JAMES: And now she's gone. She's in Heaven with You. Until my life ends, I promise to spend every moment trying to perform Your will and make the world a better place. Amen.

. . .

PAT: You're a woman, and I'm a woman, and we need to be able to talk about these things. I wish that I had been able to be open with my mother about sexual matters.

(Pause.)

JANET: Sometimes I have trouble having more than one orgasm through vaginal sex.

PAT: Okay.

JANET: So after you know, a guy is finished, I still feel like I need more.

PAT: Uh-huh.

JANET: I decided to be open about this issue with Paul and he agreed to go down on me after we have sex.

PAT: Okay.

JANET: But the thing is that I like to be eaten out for like forty-five minutes after sex.

PAT: So?

JANET: He says that his tongue gets tired and that he won't do it anymore. He called me a freak and broke up with me.

PAT: You don't need a man like that around. There are plenty of men who would die to have a lover like you.

JANET: Thanks for understanding.

. . .

SARAH: I wish we lived in a town with people like us.

FRED: Our town has one of the best school systems in the state. You're going to be able to go to Harvard because of the opportunities that this town has provided you with. Next time someone makes fun of the fact that your mother works at Walmart, you make fun of the fact that their parents are doctors.

SARAH: How do I do that?

FRED: Doctors make a lot of money but they spend an awful lot of time doing disgusting things. They spend half their time looking in people's ears, mouths and noses, and when they're not doing that they're sticking their fingers in people's assholes and their vaginas—

SARAH: Dad!

FRED: What?

SARAH: That's disgusting!

FRED: It is disgusting. Their jobs are disgusting. You know who else gets paid a lot?

SARAH: Who?

FRED: Garbagemen.

SARAH: Really?

FRED: Yes. Because their job is disgusting. The more disgusting the job, the higher the pay. That's why your mother only gets paid eight dollars an hour.

. . .

PAT: You know . . . I'm proud of you for speaking up about your sexual needs. Relationships can be like a prison for a woman if she's not being tended to.

JANET: I told Dad that I'd meet him at the park. I should really go.

PAT: Gonna do some tai chi?

JANET: Yup.

PAT: How's the search for an agent going?

JANET: Oh, I didn't tell you! I found an agent to represent me yesterday.

PAT: That's wonderful, dear!

JANET: He says that he's going to start setting me up with a lot more film work!

PAT: That's fantastic! I'm so proud of you for taking initiative the way you have.

JANET: I just hope that Dad doesn't find out about it.

PAT: If he does I'll straighten him out.

SCENE 3

Jerry and Janet are in the park doing tai chi. They finish a form and stop for a moment.

JANET: Dad, are you disappointed that I'm taking the year off? You can be honest.

JERRY: Not at all. Obviously your mother and I would like to see you get a degree. On the other hand, I'm almost certain that our plumber and electrician make more money than my salary and your mother's combined.

JANET: Then why did you bother going to school for so many years?

JERRY: The pursuit of knowledge is its own reward. I never told you this, but, my freshman year roommate in college was transgender. We really didn't have a name for it then, except to call him a cross-dressing faggot. I didn't call him that of course. We weren't super close, but I did like him. Everyone made fun of him relentlessly, and I watched as he became more and more isolated and depressed. He got heavy into drugs and ended up committing suicide.

JANET: That's terrible.

JERRY: It is. His suicide really affected me, which is why I'm pursuing my third PhD in Queer Studies. I wanted to better understand how my behavior and the society at large contributed to his death.

JANET: That's really cool, Dad.

JERRY: I want you to pursue what makes you happy. I want you to be the person that you want to be. That's the most important thing in this life.

(Janet hugs Jerry. Jerry leads and they start to do another tai chi form in unison.)

JANET: I love you, Daddy.

SCENE 4

Simultaneous scenes:
    James is cutting the hedges in his front yard using manual hedge clippers. Jerry walks out onto his front porch. Jerry watches James for a moment then walks over to him.

JERRY: What are you doing?
JAMES: I'm cutting the hedges.
JERRY *(Incredulous)*: With manual hedge clippers?!
JAMES: What do you use?
JERRY: Electric hedge clippers! You're living in the stone age, man.
JAMES: I like using these. It's good exercise.

(Jerry continues to watch James cut the hedges.
    In another scene: Sarah approaches Matthew. She's really happy to see him.)

SARAH: Hi, Matthew!
MATTHEW: Oh, hi, Sarah.
SARAH: Do you mind if I have lunch with you?
MATTHEW: Uh. Um. Sure.

. . .

JERRY: Hey, let me ask you. How much does Joey charge you to cut your grass?
JAMES: Twenty-five a week.

JERRY: Huh.

JAMES: How much does he charge you?

JERRY: He just raised my rate to thirty-five. That little prick.

. . .

SARAH: So, what colleges did you apply to?

MATTHEW: I'm not going to college.

SARAH: But you sent in applications, right?

MATTHEW: I filled them out and threw them in the trash.

SARAH: That's so badass!

. . .

JERRY: I'm gonna fire him, that's what I'm going to do. Joey
sucks. He never cuts the very back of my yard.

JAMES: He's not the greatest lawn mower.

JERRY: I think the kid might be blind.

JAMES: It's not about the results. We need to encourage kids in
this community who take that kind of initiative. Joey certainly doesn't have to work. But he chooses to. I don't think
you should fire him.

JERRY: You think that I should just stand here and let him fuck
me in the ass?

JAMES: That language makes me a bit uncomfortable.

JERRY: Sorry, James. What do you think I should do?

JAMES: Have a conversation with him about the things that are
annoying you, and if he doesn't improve then you can think
about firing him.

. . .

MATTHEW: Where did you apply?

SARAH: Princeton, Yale and Harvard. UPenn, Brown and Cor-
nell are my safeties.

MATTHEW: What did you get on your SATs?

SARAH: 2300.

MATTHEW: Holy shit! You're a genius!

. . .

JAMES: Hey, uh, when do you think that you'll be done with those saw horses?

JERRY: I should be done stripping the door in two weeks, and I'll need another week for the staining. Is that okay?

JAMES: Totally. You know, I used to strip wood when I was a kid. The chemicals we used were toxic. We used to get high off the fumes. Not on purpose, of course, but we would certainly get high.

JERRY: They don't use that stuff anymore. The wood stripper I use is environmentally friendly and completely nontoxic.

JAMES: It must not work very well.

. . .

SARAH: Do you want to go to prom with me?

MATTHEW: What?

SARAH: Do you want to go to prom with me?

MATTHEW: That's like eight months away.

SARAH: So?

. . .

JAMES: Do you mind if I ask you a personal question?

JERRY: Go ahead.

JAMES: We've lived next door to each other for a long time, and well, I've always wondered, uh, your wife is a lot older than you, right?

JERRY: Yeah, Pat is ten years older than me.

JAMES: Wow.

JERRY: She was my PhD advisor when I was in graduate school at UC Berkeley.

JAMES: My wife, God bless her soul, thought that you and Pat were the same age, but that Pat wasn't aging well.

JERRY: Nope. She's just old, but I have a thing for older women. The older the better.

JAMES: You like cougars?

JERRY: Yeah, I guess you could say that.

. . .

SARAH: I like you.

MATTHEW: We don't even know each other that well.

SARAH: What are you talking about? We've known each other since kindergarten!

MATTHEW: What I mean is—

SARAH: That we don't hang out with the same people.

MATTHEW: Yeah.

SARAH: Do you already have a date?

(Pause.)

MATTHEW: No.

SARAH: I'm not going to beg.

MATTHEW: Fine. I'll go to prom with you.

SARAH: Great!

(She gives him an unexpected quick peck on the lips, then stands to leave.)

SCENE 5

Simultaneous scenes continue:
    Jerry calls from the bathroom.

JERRY: What do you think a black tarry stool looks like?

PAT: What?

. . .

SARAH: I've got to get to class.

. . .

JERRY: I said what does a black tarry stool look like?

PAT: It's probably black, like tar.

. . .

MATTHEW: Bye.

. . .

JERRY: The shit I just took looks really dark. I think I have colon cancer.

PAT: No you don't. Blood in your stool is indicative of colon cancer. So, you should be worried about seeing red, not black.

JERRY: It says here on WebMD, when blood enters your stool in the upper GI tract it turns your shit black. Would you mind taking a look?

PAT: Oh God. I'm not a doctor, you know. This doesn't look too bad. It's not black and tarry at least. It does look a little weird though. Some of it's very loose. But I wouldn't describe it as black. It's very dark brown.

JERRY: No it's black.

PAT: You're fine. Eat more spinach. But if you're really worried just get a colonoscopy. You're probably due for one anyway.

JERRY: That's a good idea. I will get a colonoscopy.

(Pat and Jerry kiss.)

How was class today?

PAT: You know, I see these eighteen-year-old girls, and it makes me wonder where the feminist movement went wrong.

JERRY: What do you mean?

PAT: These girls come to class, all dolled-up, faces caked over with makeup, sweatpants with "Juicy" written across their bottoms, and their breasts hanging out.

JERRY: What's wrong with that?

PAT: What's wrong with that? They're objectifying themselves.

JERRY: Yeah. And?

PAT: We fought so that men would value us for our personalities and ideas, and not just our vaginas.

JERRY: But wouldn't having "Juicy" written across your ass be defined as sexual liberation?

PAT: We stopped wearing makeup, we stopped shaving, we wore what we wanted, not what *Juicy Couture* told us to wear. We were independent.

JERRY: I had forgotten that you used to not shave your armpits and legs. Why did you start shaving again?

PAT: You used to complain about my hairy legs scratching you during sex. But I can say that I haven't worn makeup for over thirty years.

JERRY: And I think you're absolutely beautiful.

(They kiss.)

PAT *(Sexy)*: Why don't you turn out the lights?

JERRY: I'd rather leave them on.

PAT: But I'd rather you shut them off.

JERRY: I want to look at you.

PAT: Just turn off the fucking lights.

JERRY: Fine.

(Jerry turns out the lights.)

SCENE 6

Jerry is sitting on his front porch reading. James walks out of his house to go to his car.

JERRY: Hi, James!

(James doesn't acknowledge Jerry.)

Hi, James!

(James walks off without looking at Jerry. Pat steps onto the porch.)

PAT: Have you seen my deodorant?

JERRY: Something really weird just happened.

PAT: What?

JERRY: James wouldn't speak to me.

PAT: That's strange.

JERRY: I said hi twice, and he wouldn't even turn around.

PAT: Maybe his hearing is going. We're all getting old. Your hearing isn't so great either.

JERRY: I guess so.

PAT: Will you come inside for a moment? I need you to sign some cards.

(Pat enters the house. Jerry follows.)

SCENE 7

Matthew is masturbating while looking out his window. Janet is in her bedroom, undressing and changing into her pajamas. James is in his bedroom, on the phone with his pastor.

JAMES: Yes, it's me again, Pastor. I'm sorry for calling so late.

Oh, you're in the middle of dinner. I'll try to make it quick.

Well, do you believe in ghosts?

Yes. Yes. Of course you do. Angels and demons. Of course.

Well, I feel like my house is haunted.

By my wife's spirit.

No, it's not a good thing. It's hard for me to sleep. I always feel like there's a presence that wants me to be very uncomfortable. That's the only way I can describe it. I think she might be trying to get revenge on me.

For being so irritable while she was alive.

The only thing I can think of is to move.

An exorcism?! No, I don't think so. No. No. I think I'm going to sell this house. My wife's presence isn't the only reason I want to leave. I feel like my son will be morally corrupted if we stay in this place.

No, not by my wife's ghost.

There's an evil sexual deviant among us, and we're all in danger.

I don't want your food to get cold. I'll tell you more when I see you in person.

Thanks for your guidance, Pastor.

(James exits his room. He knocks on Matthew's door.)

MATTHEW: Who is it?
JAMES: Your father.
MATTHEW: Can you come back in a couple of minutes?
JAMES: I need to talk to you now.
MATTHEW: Okay. Hold on.

(He orgasms. There is semen on his stomach and his pajamas.)

JAMES: What are you doing in there?
MATTHEW: Hold on! Hold on!

(Matthew grabs some tissues and wipes the semen off his stomach and does his best to wipe it off his pajamas. He throws the tissues into the trash and opens his door.)

What's going on?

(James enters and looks around suspiciously.)

JAMES: You doing drugs in here?
MATTHEW: No, Dad.
JAMES: Hmm. Let me look at your eyes.

(James grabs hold of Matthew's head and looks hard into his eyes for a moment.)

Well, you don't look high.
MATTHEW: I'm not high, Dad.

(James lets go of Matthew's head.)

JAMES: Step back.

(James looks Matthew up and down. There is still some semen on Matthew's pajamas. James sees it.)

Oh, I see what you were up to.

MATTHEW: Jesus Christ.

JAMES: Don't take the Lord's name in vain.

(James looks out the window and sees Janet in the window brushing her hair.)

Oh, I see. You like that little harlot who lives next door.

MATTHEW: What's wrong with you?

JAMES: Don't get any ideas in your head about messing around with that girl. She's dangerous.

MATTHEW: Why are you referring to Janet as "that girl."

JAMES: Never you mind that. Just stay away from her.

MATTHEW: But we're the same age.

JAMES: You are not the same age. You're seventeen and she's eighteen.

MATTHEW: But she's hot!

(James slams his hand down on Matthew's desk.)

JAMES: STAY AWAY FROM HER!

(Pause.)

I'm sorry. I'm sorry.

MATTHEW: You need to get a grip, Dad.

JAMES: You're right. You're going to be going to go off to college next fall anyway.

MATTHEW: We'll see.

JAMES: You can't become a filmmaker without going to school.

MATTHEW: Great film directors don't go to school. Formal training ruins artistic inspiration.

JAMES: Name one great film director who didn't go to film school.

MATTHEW: Steven Spielberg.

JAMES: He's an exception. Name another.

MATTHEW: James Cameron, Sir Ridley Scott, Peter Jackson, David Fincher—

JAMES: Okay, okay, you've made your point.

MATTHEW: College is a waste of time and money. Parents want their kids to go to college to guarantee that they only associate with people from upper-middle-class backgrounds and marry into the right type of family. I'm not interested in any of that. I want to be with real people.

JAMES: We'll see.

MATTHEW: I'd rather you bought me a really good camera than spend your money on tuition.

JAMES: I'll think about it.

(Pause.)

Oh, by the way, we're moving.

MATTHEW: Why? I love this house.

JAMES: Houses require a lot of upkeep. Something's always leaking, and mowing the lawn, and raking the leaves . . .

MATTHEW: You hire people to mow the lawn and rake the leaves.

JAMES: But it's very expensive!

MATTHEW: Are you planning to move back to England?

JAMES: Of course not! I've lived here for almost forty years! I want to move to a condo where I won't have to worry about any of that stuff. Besides, everywhere I look, something reminds me of your mother. It makes me sad. I hope you understand.

MATTHEW: I like that there are reminders of her everywhere. It makes me feel like she's still here somehow.

(James moves to leave.)

JAMES: We all deal with loss differently. Good night.

MATTHEW: Good night.

(James exits.)

SCENE 8

Jerry and Pat are on the porch. They see a "For Sale" sign on James's lawn.

PAT: Oh. Oh my. Well, that's odd.

JERRY: Did you see it yesterday?

PAT: Nope. That wasn't there yesterday.

JERRY: They must have put it up in the middle of the night.

PAT: That is very, very strange.

JERRY: First James won't talk to me, and now their house is up for sale? Something is going on.

PAT: With Katherine dead and Matthew graduating from high school, he probably wants to downsize.

JERRY: I'm gonna get to the bottom of this.

SCENE 9

Matthew and Sarah are making out behind their school. They stop making out for a moment.

MATTHEW: Do you want to go back to my house?

SARAH: You're naughty.

MATTHEW: You're just so hot. I want to make love to you.

(Sarah laughs.)

SARAH: You don't want to make love to me. You want to fuck me.

MATTHEW: Maybe I do.

SARAH: You can't fuck me yet.

MATTHEW: Can I eat you out? Can we do something? I'm going crazy with all this kissing.

SARAH: You can fuck me on prom night.

MATTHEW: That's so far away! Please come back to my house.

SARAH: I can't go back to your house. You know that your dad just hired my dad to work on your house, right?

MATTHEW: So?

SARAH: If he caught me with you, he'd fucking kill me.

MATTHEW: Really?

SARAH: Yeah, he doesn't allow me to date.

MATTHEW: That's ridiculous!

SARAH: What can I say? I'm his little girl. He got super overprotective after I had cancer.

MATTHEW: I could see that.

(Silence.)

Are you a virgin?

SARAH: Yeah. Are you?

MATTHEW: Yeah.

SARAH: Do you want to make a pact to lose our virginity to each other on prom night?

MATTHEW: Yes.

(They kiss. Matthew is really hard. She puts her hand on his erection.)

SARAH: It looks like you have a little problem that needs to be taken care of.

(She rubs his penis through his pants.)

MATTHEW: Please keep doing that.

SARAH: I have a better idea. Let's go back to my house.

MATTHEW: You sure your dad won't be home?

SARAH: My dad won't be home until six and my mom is never home.

SCENE 10

Jerry is sitting on the toilet reading a book. After a couple of moments, farting sounds are heard. We see James walk up to the front door of Jerry's house. He bangs on the door. Jerry is startled. He doesn't know what to do. He listens closely. When no one comes to the door James rings the doorbell. Jerry jumps up, pulls up his underwear and his pants, tucks his shirt in, buckles his belt, and goes to answer the door.

JERRY: Hi, James!

JAMES: I want my sawhorses back.

JERRY: What?

JAMES: You've had them for seven months. I want my sawhorses back!

JERRY: I promise that I'll finish the doors this weekend.

JAMES *(Practically shouting)*: I want them now!

JERRY: Why are you so angry?

(Silence.)

Are you selling your house because you're angry with me?

JAMES: It's not just you. It's your family. None of you have any moral values.

JERRY: I know that we don't go to church every Sunday like you do, but I assure you that we practice secular humanism.

(He thrusts a magazine into Jerry's hands.)

What is this?

JAMES: It's a *Barely Legal*. Turn to page forty-four.

(Jerry opens the magazine. He is in complete shock.)

JERRY: Oh my God. Oh my God.

(He's having trouble breathing.)

JAMES: I don't want you or your family members crossing my property line. I don't want you to wave, or—
JERRY: But how did you get this?
JAMES: Never you mind where I got it. *You* should be arrested for reckless parenting!

(James starts to walk away.)

JERRY: Did you jerk off to her?

(James stops and turns around.)

JAMES: What?
JERRY: Did you jerk off while looking at pictures of my daughter?

(James starts to chase Jerry. Jerry runs, James is in hot pursuit.)

Yeah, I've seen you staring at her when she's in the pool, you fucking pedophile pervert!

(James catches up to Jerry and pulls him to the ground. James gets on top of Jerry and starts trying to hit him. Jerry is blocking.)

I bet you've been jerking off thinking about her since she was twelve.

(Jerry can no longer fend off James's punches and James is repeatedly hitting Jerry in the face. Jerry stops moving. He has been knocked out. James gets up and starts to walk back to his house, then he stops and stands still for a moment. He turns around and picks up the magazine. He leaves Jerry lying on the lawn. James walks calmly into his house. We hear sirens as the lights fade to black.)

SCENE 11

Jerry, Pat and Janet are at home.

PAT: Really? Nothing else happened.

JERRY: That's it.

JANET: So, James bangs on the door, demands his sawhorses back, and as you walk into our yard to retrieve them, he pulls you down, gets on top of you, and repeatedly starts hitting you in the face.

JERRY: That's right. What? You don't believe me?

JANET: It's strange, that's all.

JERRY: Well, why do YOU think he attacked me? Can you think of an explanation?!

JANET: Don't freak out, Dad! I'm on your side.

(Pause.)

PAT: I've always thought that James needed medication.

JERRY: Well, one of the neighbors called the police and they took him into custody.

PAT: Should we press charges?

JERRY: No! That would just make things worse. But I do plan on getting a gun.

PAT: A gun has never made any situation better.

JERRY: I would feel a lot safer if there were a gun in the house.

JANET: Dad's right. Mr. Williams is obviously a lunatic. I also would feel a lot safer if we had a gun in the house.

(Janet takes Jerry's hand.)

JERRY: I plan to sleep with it under my pillow.

(Janet nods her head in agreement.)

PAT: You're out of your minds! Statistics show that keeping a gun in the home increases the risk of injury and death to *the homeowner.*

JERRY: You're a professor of women's studies, you don't know anything about guns.

PAT: Did you know that the risk of homicide is three times higher in households with guns? And that a firearm in the home increases the risk of suicide by a factor of five and increases the risk of suicide with a firearm by a factor of seventeen.

JANET: You can't just go around throwing abstract statistics in our face. Dad is in real danger, and we need to do something about that.

JERRY: There's no need for us to commit to buying a gun right now. Let's just drive down to the gun store, take a look around, and try to keep an open mind.

(Blackout.)

SCENE 12

James, Pat and Janet are going into Walmart. Fred is exiting the store as they're about to enter.

PAT: Hi, Fred!

FRED: Hey, guys.

JERRY: What are you up to?

FRED: I was just bringing my wife her dinner.

PAT: That's very sweet of you.

FRED: It costs so much money to eat out.

JANET: Why can't she just bring her own meals with her?

FRED: It's really just an excuse to see her.

PAT: Well, I think it's very nice that Fred treats his wife so well.

FRED: So, what brings you guys to Walmart?

JERRY: We're buying a gun.

PAT: We're looking at guns. We're not really sure that we're going to buy one yet.

FRED: You should buy a gun. It's very important that Americans exercise their Second Amendment rights.

JANET: Are you even a citizen?

FRED: Of course I'm a citizen.

JANET: Huh.

JERRY: Do you own a gun?

FRED: I own seven.

PAT: That seems excessive.

FRED: If someone breaks into your house while you're home, that means that they are prepared to kill you if necessary. Home owners have to be willing to do the same to intruders.

PAT: You really believe that?

FRED: Liberals are primarily concerned with creating a toddler society. They want to treat the American populace like we're a bunch of children. That's why we have gun-control laws and this reprehensible welfare state.

JANET: You don't believe in welfare?

JERRY: That seems strange coming out of your mouth since, you know, you must have relatives that are—

FRED: On welfare!? I can't believe you! Why do you think that my wife works at Walmart for sixteen hours a day?! We don't believe in handouts. We're either going to make it on our own, or not make it at all.

PAT: That seems rather draconian. Surely, that philosophy doesn't apply to Sarah, right? I mean, you try to give Sarah everything that she wants, don't you?

(Fred laughs.)

FRED: It's unhealthy for a child to be given everything that they want. It gives them a false sense of entitlement when they go out into the world. I mean, look at the kids in this neighborhood.

JERRY: What are you saying?

FRED: Nothing. Nothing. You know, I really have to get back to work. It was nice seeing you.

PAT: Yes, it was nice seeing you, too.

(Fred walks away.)

What a jerk.

SCENE 13

Sarah's house. Sarah and Matthew are in bed. Sarah's legs are in the air with her thighs squeezed close together and Matthew is furiously pumping away between her legs. It looks like they are having sex but they are not. He's rubbing his penis back and forth between her thighs.

SARAH: I think we need more lube. It's beginning to hurt.

(Matthew grabs the bottle of lube and squirts more between her thighs. He begins to pump furiously.)

MATTHEW: That better?
SARAH: Yeah.
MATTHEW: Jesus, Sarah. It feels so good. Oh. Ah.

(He pumps even faster. He climaxes.)

God help me.

(He collapses. Sarah starts laughing.)

What?
SARAH: You got cum in my eye.
MATTHEW: I shot that far?
SARAH: Yeah, can you hand me a tissue or something?
MATTHEW: Sure.

(He grabs a tissue and wipes her eye.)

Sorry about that.
SARAH: It's okay.
MATTHEW: That was so intense. What do you call that again?
SARAH: Frottage.
MATTHEW: Frottage. What does that mean exactly?
SARAH: It's when you rub your body against another person's body for sexual gratification. But there's never any penetration with frottage.

MATTHEW: So, if I stick my penis between your breasts that's also frottage?

SARAH: Yup. Or if you rub your penis between my butt cheeks or even in my armpit.

(They laugh.)

MATTHEW: I liked rubbing it between your thighs.

SARAH: I liked it, too. With my legs up in the air like that, your penis was rubbing my clit.

MATTHEW: Did you have an orgasm?

SARAH: I did. I think I love you, Matthew.

MATTHEW: I love you, too.

(Pause.)

What are you going to major in in college?

SARAH: I want to be a doctor.

MATTHEW: Really?

SARAH: Yeah. I want to be like your mother. I want to help people in need like she did. So many doctors are just concerned about money. Two doctors refused to treat me before we came to your mother.

MATTHEW: Why didn't you come to her first?

SARAH: It's such a small community. We didn't want everyone to know our business, you know.

MATTHEW: Yeah, I know.

SARAH: Did your mother ever talk to you about treating me?

MATTHEW: Never. Doctors aren't supposed to talk about that stuff. I didn't even know until you lost all of your hair. That's when the rumors started.

SARAH: What rumors?

MATTHEW: That you had cancer.

SARAH: Oh. Everyone stopped talking to me.

MATTHEW: Really?

SARAH: It was a very lonely time. You stopped talking to me.

MATTHEW: We weren't really friends.

SARAH: Yeah, but you would always say hi to me in the hall. Then my hair fell out and you stopped.

MATTHEW: What do you say to a kid who's going to die?

SARAH: I wasn't going to die.

MATTHEW: We didn't know that. It was scary for everyone. It introduced everyone to the idea of their own mortality.

SARAH: And once my hair started to grow back everyone started to talk to me again.

MATTHEW: Crazy.

SARAH: It was like a light switch.

MATTHEW: I'm sorry for treating you that way. I really am.

SARAH: I forgive you.

(Pause. Jerry enters his house with a brown bag containing a magazine.)

JERRY: Hello? Hello? Anyone home?

. . .

SARAH: You should probably go. My dad will be home in twenty minutes.

SCENE 14

Jerry places the copy of Barely Legal *on the kitchen table. He stares reluctantly for a moment. He is clearly nervous. He opens the magazine and turns to page forty-four.*

JERRY: How did this happen?

(At this moment an imaginary version of Janet comes onstage completely naked.)

IMAGINARY JANET: You know exactly how it happened. You remember walking in on me masturbating to your porn when I was thirteen. You never said anything. You just tiptoed away.

JERRY: I didn't know what to do. What is a person supposed to do in that situation?

IMAGINARY JANET: Don't feel guilty. You did the right thing.

JERRY: Yes, I did believe that I was doing the right thing.

IMAGINARY JANET: That's the spirit! Daddy, do you like what you see? Do you like staring at your baby's shaved pussy? I shaved it for you, Daddy.

JERRY: Did you?

IMAGINARY JANET: All your favorite websites had pictures of young girls, probably just turned eighteen years old, with shaved pussies. It turned me on, Daddy.

JERRY: Did it?

IMAGINARY JANET: It did, Daddy. It was at your computer that day that I had my first orgasm. I had been trying to play with myself every night before, with no luck. But as I sat at your computer looking at those girls with their shaved pussies, I got really wet. I didn't know what was happening. Then I slid my hand into my panties and discovered my clit. I came in about a minute. Thanks for introducing your little girl to the ways of the world.

JERRY: I didn't mean to. I didn't mean to do that to you. I didn't know how to erase my internet browser then.

IMAGINARY JANET: There's nothing to apologize for, Daddy. I love porn. I love masturbating. I love sex. That's why I do what I do.

(Still looking at the magazine, Jerry starts to cry.)

JERRY: No. No. I'm sorry.

IMAGINARY JANET: Stop apologizing. I want you to jerk off looking at your little girl. I want you to cum just for me. I want you to cum just for me.

JERRY: No. No. I can't do that.

IMAGINARY JANET: Come on, Dad. Just touch yourself a little bit. You're not even turned on a little by your baby?

JERRY: Please Janet, don't do this to me.

IMAGINARY JANET: Come on, Daddy, you can do it.

(He starts rubbing his penis through his pants.)

That's right, Daddy. I want you to cum on my face. That's what you imagine when you look at those other girls, right?

(Jerry snaps out of it. He quickly pulls his hand away from his penis. Imaginary Janet disappears. He hears a key in the lock. He quickly hides the magazine. Janet walks into the room.)

JANET: Hi, Dad!
JERRY: Hi, Janet.

(She's drinking a fruit smoothie.)

JANET: I won't be home for dinner.
JERRY: Why is that?
JANET: I have to work late.
JERRY: But you had the morning shift today.
JANET: Uh, yeah. But someone called in sick, so I said that I would cover for them.

(He starts crying again. She pulls his head against her stomach and she strokes his head. He hugs her.)

What's wrong, Daddy?

(Jerry gets the magazine. He hands it to Janet.)

Oh.
JERRY: That's why James and I were fighting. That's why he's moving.
JANET: Oh God.
JERRY: I've been a terrible father.
JANET *(Tenderly)*: Dad, Dad, this has nothing to do with you. You've been the most wonderful father that anyone could ask for.
JERRY: I want you to stop.

JANET: I can't do that, Dad.

JERRY: You're degrading yourself.

JANET: This is a career choice just like any other career choice. I do what I do because I like it.

JERRY: You're delusional if you really believe that.

(Janet takes her father's hand.)

JANET: What would you do if you had a son who was a porn star. Would you feel different?

(Jerry ponders this.)

JERRY: It would be different. I wouldn't be as worried about him. I'd know that he wasn't being taken advantage of. You're being used and degraded.

JANET: Just because women like sex and do it for a living doesn't mean that they're oppressed. I mean, really Dad, have you ever thought about those women in the porn you watch? All of them are daughters, mothers, sisters and wives!

JERRY: Wives!? What kind of maniac would marry a porn star?! Probably the same type of man who takes his wife's last name.

JANET: Dad, you sound like a misogynist!

JERRY: Wait. Do you do film also?

JANET: I've mostly been doing magazine work, but I shot my first two films this month. I really enjoy it, Dad.

(Jerry starts to get visibly shaken up again. He's practically hyperventilating.)

JERRY: You had sex on tape? That's disgusting.

JANET: I can't deal with this right now. I've got to go get fucked on camera. I don't need your patriarchal double standards distracting me. See you later.

(She storms out. Jerry is left shaking at his kitchen table. After a few moments he goes to a cabinet in the kitchen and takes out a bottle of whiskey. He pours a tumbler full and drinks it.)

SCENE 15

James is on his knees in his dining room praying.

JAMES: Dear Heavenly Father,
I strayed from Your path and resorted to violence. I know that this is not the way. Sometimes, I have trouble controlling my anger and frustration. I am angered and frustrated that the world is not what I want it to be. My world is not what I want it to be. Help me to overcome this. Please remove this defect of character.
Please help me. Please help me. Help my house to sell quickly so that my son may be removed from the corrupting influence of the whore next door. Also, please help her to find her way in this world and to see that treating her body the way she does is pure degradation. Help her to find the pure love that my wife and I shared before she was taken away from me. And God, please, please get these contractors out of my house.
In Christ's name.
Amen.

(Matthew enters. James rises from his knees.)

Do you say your prayers every night, Matthew?
MATTHEW: If you wanted me to believe in God, then you should have raised me that way.
JAMES: I've always been religious.
MATTHEW: You only started going to church after Mom died. Your beliefs are weird, Dad, but I try to accept them.

(James places his hand on Matthew's head and starts speaking in tongues:)

JAMES: Hiji biji laka luka fiki fuki binbi minji—

(Matthew slaps James's hand off his head really hard.)

MATTHEW: Don't force your evangelical mumbo jumbo on me! Stop it, Dad!

(Silence.)

JAMES: I bought you something.
MATTHEW: What? A Bible?
JAMES: Hold on.

(James exits and comes back with a beautifully wrapped box. Matthew opens it.)

MATTHEW: A digital camera!

(Matthew removes it from the box.)

Wow! This is top of the line!
JAMES: It is.
MATTHEW: Thanks, Dad!

(Matthew and James embrace.)

JAMES: I've been thinking about what you said the other day, and I'm not going to force you to go to college if it won't make you happy. There's enough unhappiness in the world, and I don't want to add to it. Besides, if you don't go to college, then I can buy that Porsche that I've always wanted.
MATTHEW: Thanks, Dad!
JAMES: But if I agree to let you skip college then you've really got to hold up your end of the agreement.
MATTHEW: What agreement?
JAMES: You have to agree to finish two short films by the end of the year.
MATTHEW: I can do that!
JAMES: I'm going to give you forty thousand dollars to complete these projects.
MATTHEW: This is unbelievable!
JAMES: It's what your mother would have wanted.

(Matthew shakes his head up and down in silence.)

But this is it. I won't give you any more money after this. I'm just getting you started. You're going to have to make your own way in this world, just like I did.

MATTHEW: I won't let you down.

JAMES: You're a good kid. And I love you.

MATTHEW: I love you, too.

(Matthew and James hug again. The doorbell rings.)

Who is that?

JAMES: It's the contractor.

(Matthew goes to his room. James answers the door. James's demeanor has changed. He is stone cold.)

FRED: Hi, James.

(James walks into the house without saying hello. Fred follows. James looks up at his dining room ceiling.)

JAMES: What the fuck is this??!!

FRED: What?

JAMES: The trim isn't fully painted! You see that, where the dark blue meets the light blue, you can still see a little white under there!

FRED: I'll come back with a painter's brush and take care of that.

(James looks down and points to the wainscoting in the dining room.)

JAMES: And look at this!

FRED: What? It looks fine.

JAMES: Your workers didn't put a second coat of paint on the wainscoting, and they forgot to paint behind the toilet even though I asked them three times!

FRED: I'm sorry, James, I'll have the workers come back and redo it. There's no need to get this upset. Anything that you're not satisfied with I'll have redone.

JAMES: Good! I have quite the list!

FRED: I'm not making a penny on this job. I had to use five coats of paint in the living room because of the deep color you chose, and I had your old lights removed and put in new sconces for free. I'm doing this because of the kindness that your wife showed my family after—after my daughter got leukemia.

(Fred chokes up.)

Your wife practically treated my daughter for free. My daughter wouldn't be alive today had it not been for her.

(James seems genuinely affected by this. He pats Fred on the shoulder.)

JAMES: I know. I know. I'm sorry for yelling. I know that you're giving me a good deal.

(Pause.)

But does a good deal mean that I get C-results? I mean, if you tell me that getting a good deal means C- and D-work then just let me know. I can accept that.

FRED: No. And I told you that I would fix everything.

JAMES: Yes, but your workers should have done it right the first time! I'm sick of waking up at 7:30 each morning to let a bunch of dirty Mexican thieves into my house!

FRED: Did they take something?

JAMES: My toolbox is missing, my electric drill—

FRED: I'll replace them.

JAMES: The problem is that they lack proper supervision. In Mexico, they get to sit around all day, and sing and play the banjo, but here they have to really work. They need

someone to keep them focused, but you're never around.
I need you to come to my house and supervise them every
day. Can you do that?

FRED: I will.

JAMES: I hope you understand that I'm not giving you one more
cent until this work is completed to my satisfaction. I want
A+ results.

FRED: I understand.

(James moves through the house.)

JAMES: Now come look at these stairs!

(Blackout.)

SCENE 16

Fred is at home. Sarah walks through the door.

SARAH: Hi, Dad.

FRED: How was school?

SARAH: Good.

FRED: I saw you walking around with Matthew.

SARAH: Oh. Where did you see us?

FRED: I was just driving around.

SARAH: Oh.

FRED: His father's a fucking asshole, excuse my language.

SARAH: What happened?

FRED: Every time I go over there he just yells at me. I'm kind of
used to that because as a contractor people yell at you a lot,
but today he started going off about Mexicans.

SARAH: What did he say?

FRED: You know, that they're lazy and that they have no work
ethic because all they do is sit around playing the banjo.

SARAH: He actually said that?

FRED: Yup.

SARAH: That's racist, Dad. How does he know that we're not Mexican?

FRED: He knows that our family is from Honduras.

SARAH: But still. That really offends me. I'm going to talk to Matthew about this.

FRED: Don't. I shouldn't have said anything. I was just venting.

SARAH: He needs to know that his father is a racist.

FRED: Please, Sarah. It was probably a slip of the tongue on James's part.

SARAH *(Incredulous)*: A slip of the tongue?

FRED: They're good people. We can't ever forget what his wife did for us. We're indebted to your boyfriend's family.

SARAH: He's not my boyfriend.

FRED: I saw you holding hands, *and* you have a hickey on your neck.

(Pause.)

Are you having sex with him?

SARAH: No.

FRED *(Becoming slightly sinister)*: You better not be. Nobody touches my little girl in that way.

SARAH: Am I grounded?

FRED: No. But that doesn't mean that I won't break his fucking legs if I see another hickey on your neck.

(She nods her head, then goes to her room.)

SCENE 17

Jerry is drunk. He is in his living room sitting in the dark, waiting for Janet to come home. He takes swigs straight from his bottle of whiskey. Janet enters. Jerry doesn't say anything. She starts to walk to her room, then notices Jerry in the dark. She is startled.

JERRY: Hi.

JANET: Oh my God!

JERRY: Do I scare you?

JANET: No— It's just. I didn't see you there.

JERRY: How was work?

JANET: Fine.

JERRY: Did you have some nice orgasms?

JANET: I'm going to my room.

(She starts to go to her room but Jerry leaps up and restrains her.)

Let go of me!

JERRY: Not until you tell me about your day at work. You said that your job was a career choice just like any other career choice. Well, normal people sit down and talk about their day at work with their families. Now sit down.

(She sits.)

So, did he go down on you first, or did you go straight to sucking his dick?

(Silence.)

When he started to fuck you, did you start with missionary and then go to doggy style, or did the director prefer some other positions?

(Silence.)

Did he pull out and cum on your ass or on your face?

JANET: It was a girl-on-girl scene. There was no guy.

(Pause. Jerry takes a swig of his whiskey.)

JERRY: How much do they pay you?

JANET: None of your business.

JERRY: You're a whore. You have sex for money. How much do they pay you?!

JANET: I'm getting paid two thousand dollars for this film.
JERRY: Get the fuck out of my house!!!
JANET: No.

(Jerry leaps up and pulls her from the chair. He starts trying to push her out the door.)

Get off of me! Get off of me!
JERRY: You're making enough money to get your own apartment. Get the fuck out of my house, you dirty whore!
JANET: Mom! Mom! Help!

(Pat comes running down the stairs.)

PAT: What's going on here?!

(Pat breaks up the struggle.)

JERRY: Janet needs to leave the premises immediately!
PAT: Jerry, stop shouting.

(Pat grabs the bottle from him.)

JERRY: She has sex on camera for money and poses in magazines, too!

(Jerry goes and gets the magazine. He hands the magazine to Pat.)

Either she needs to stop what she's doing or she needs to find another place to live.
PAT: Jerry, you're drunk. You're sleeping on the couch tonight.
JERRY *(Incredulous)*: Did you see the magazine?!
PAT: Yes, I did. *(To Janet)* C'mon, honey. Let's go upstairs and put you to bed.

(Pat puts her arm around Janet and they walk upstairs. Jerry closes his eyes and passes out on the couch.

Janet goes into her bedroom and locks the door. At this moment Matthew's room is illuminated. He has been sitting near his window, waiting for Janet to come home for hours. When he notices her he jumps up and turns his camera on. Janet starts to undress while Matthew tapes.

Lights up on Fred in his bedroom alone. He sits down in front of a laptop and types. Suddenly a hardcore porn movie with teenage boys having sex with each other comes up on his computer screen. The sound of the film fills the theater. Fred starts to masturbate. The phone rings. Fred answers it.)

FRED: Hi, honey.

(He listens.)

The manager's making you work overnight again!? That's slave labor!

(He listens.)

I know. I know. We do need the money. I just wish that we could be together as a family more.

(He listens.)

I love you, too. See you in the morning.

(Fred hangs up the phone and starts masturbating again to the porn movie. The movie continues until the lights fade to black.)

SCENE 18

The next morning. Jerry is still passed out on the couch. Pat comes downstairs.

PAT: Wake up, Jerry!

(She goes over and shakes him.)

Wake up!!

(Jerry opens his eyes, but doesn't say anything.)

What's wrong with you? Huh? Sit up!

(He sits up. He looks woozy.)

You and I watch porn together all the time. Don't you think it's a bit hypocritical of you to condemn our daughter for doing something that you enjoy so much?

(Silence.)

I mean, Jerry, Janet is a catalyst of pleasure for millions of people. You should be proud of that. How many individuals touch people's lives in such an intimate and profound way?

(Silence.)

She's like a diplomat, or a philanthropist. Well, a movie star is what she really is. How many parents can say that their child is a movie star?

(Silence.)

Why won't you say anything?

(Jerry runs to a trash can and repeatedly vomits. Pat gets him water. He drinks.)

JERRY: I was feeling a little nauseous.
PAT: That's what you get when you start thinking you're Ernest Hemingway.
JERRY: I don't see how you can be so calm about all of this.
PAT: Everyone watches porn. If we didn't have actresses for adult films, then we wouldn't have anything to watch.

Imagine a world without pornography, Jerry. It would be a very, very bleak place.

JERRY: That's why James and I were fighting, you know. And that's why he's selling his house. He said that if we had raised our daughter right, then she wouldn't have chosen this line of work.

PAT: How did he find out about Janet's career choice?

JERRY: A copy of *Barely Legal*.

PAT: Well, I'd like to know where he got a copy of that magazine. It's not like they send it to people's houses as junk mail! He hasn't been right since his wife died in that car accident. I bet most people would thank us for having a beautiful teenage daughter that has chosen to share her body with the world. I mean, who doesn't enjoy looking at naked teenage girls?

(Pause.)

JERRY: How long have you known about this?

PAT: Since she started six months ago.

JERRY: You knew about this and you didn't tell me?!

PAT: I was afraid that you wouldn't react well, and from the look of things, I was right. But rest assured, I put an end to that *Barely Legal* stuff right after she posed for them. I informed her that *Barely Legal* is beneath her.

JERRY: So, what is she doing now?

PAT: She's working with a production company called Burning Angel. It's run by a woman and mostly women are on the staff. I support them because they're snatching pornography and eroticism from the hands of men, and turning it into something female-centric.

JERRY: Do you really think that it makes a difference?

PAT: You'll see the difference when you watch her film.

JERRY: I don't know if I can watch her film.

PAT: We've always told Janet to pursue her dreams, and we have supported her endeavors unconditionally.

JERRY: Don't you think that this is a little different?

PAT: She's eighteen years old and about to leave the nest. Now is not the time to turn our backs on the parenting style that we raised her with. Besides, she'll feel completely alienated and alone if we don't support this decision, and I'm afraid . . . I'm afraid . . .

JERRY: Of what?

PAT: That she'll push us out of her life and we'll never see her again if we reject the path that she's taken.

(They stare at each other. Blackout.)

SCENE 19

The sound of a car driving very fast down the street. We hear it screech as it turns into James's driveway. We hear a car door slam, then we see James walk into his house with a huge smile on his face. Matthew is in the living room on his computer.

JAMES: Wanna see my new car?

MATTHEW: You bought a new car?

JAMES: Yeah, I bought a Porsche.

MATTHEW: Are you going to go to jail?

(Pause.)

JAMES: Why would I go to jail?

MATTHEW: For beating the shit out of Mr. Davis on his front lawn.

JAMES: I didn't think you knew about that.

MATTHEW: Dad, this town is tiny. Everyone at school is referring to you as Rocky.

JAMES: Oh.

MATTHEW: Why did you do it, Dad? People are saying that you're crazy. I don't like it.

(Long pause.)

JAMES: I discovered that Janet, well, she's an adult entertainer, and I feel that what she does is deeply immoral and perverse, and that's why Jerry and I got into an altercation.

MATTHEW: Why do you care about what Janet does for a living?

JAMES: Because I don't want you around that type of corrupting influence. What would your mother say if she knew that we were living next door to a porn star?

MATTHEW: Honestly, I don't think that Mom would care. I actually think she would have supported Janet.

JAMES: Did you already know that Janet—

MATTHEW: Of course! She's the most popular girl in the neighborhood! I'm totally in love with her. Everyone is. I have all her magazines upstairs! The question is, how did *you* find out about it?

JAMES: Well, I've been very lonely since your mother passed—

MATTHEW: So you've been jerking off to *Barely Legal*.

JAMES: The flesh is weak, Matthew. It's sinful, I know. I'm not proud of it. I'm going to try to stop.

MATTHEW: Stop what?

JAMES: Sometimes, I go on the internet and I can't stop. I go from website to website for hours.

MATTHEW: Dad, everybody does. The world isn't what you think it is anymore. Lots of regular people are even making their own porn. Have you ever heard of a site called XTube or a site called YouPorn?

JAMES: No.

MATTHEW: Those are sites where anyone can upload their homemade porn videos. Millions of people have uploaded videos. Lots of couples at my school have, and I'm pretty sure there's one of my chemistry teacher, but I can't prove it.

JAMES: I've been trying to protect you, but you've already been corrupted. I can't accept what you're saying, Matthew. And I'm disturbed to find that you have all of that whore's magazines upstairs in your room! I'm confiscating them!

MATTHEW: Why?! So you can jerk off to them!? I'm not giving you the magazines. You're a fucking hypocrite, and you need to go to therapy. You *really* need to go to therapy. You've been out of your fucking mind since Mom died. You're not going to go to hell for jerking off while thinking about your next door neighbor's daughter. That fraudulent religion has turned you into an idiot! You should give in. Be free. Accept that she's beautiful, and that she has chosen to share her tight teenage body with us. She *wants* you to jerk off thinking about her! She *wants* you to! Jerk off and be merry!

(Matthew exits. James kneels to pray.)

JAMES: God. I am alone. I have no friends. I have no one to confide in but You. Something happened to me today. My son told me that I needed to go see a therapist, but I don't need to go see a therapist. I only need You, gracious Lord. So, what happened to me was this: I drove my Porsche down to the lake, and I got out and sat by the water. There was a mother and her young son feeding geese bread crumbs. The mother was about twenty-five years old. She was slender. She was wearing tight black spandex pants. I could see every curve of her luscious bottom, and her pink thong was peeking out from the top of her pants. She reminded me of my wife. She reminded me of my youth. My wife and I used to take our son down to that very lake. And as I stared at her slender body, and the sun streaming through her light blond hair, suddenly the beauty of the world was upon me. All of its beauty. It enveloped me. All of the people. All the beautiful people. And I realized that the world was a place worth living in. There is joy. There is still joy to be had. There is beauty amongst the leafless trees, their branches reaching towards the sky in the midst of winter. Towards You. Towards Heaven. There is joy amidst the anguish, anxiety, and sorrow. I want to live. I want to truly be a part of the world again. Help me to do this, Lord. Help me to be free again. Help me to break my addiction to masturbation.
Amen.

(James starts to sing a hymn: "Arise, He Calleth Thee":)

Weary, lonely, sad, forsaken,
Humbled to a station low,
Sat a hopeless blind man begging,
By the road to Jericho.
Soon he heard the noise of footsteps,
As of waters rolling nigh;
For the Galilean Prophet
With the throng was passing by.

Then arise, He calleth thee,
Sick or suff'ring, blind or lame!
Jesus healed in Galilee,
He is evermore the same.

When he heard that it was Jesus,
Who had healed the sin-sick soul,
Then he called aloud for mercy,
That he, too, might be made whole.
But the multitude rebuked him,
Saying he should silent be;
Yet he only called more loudly,
"Have compassion, Lord, on me!"

Paused the Master for a moment—
"Bring him hither unto Me."
Someone ran to bear the message:
"Come, arise, He calleth thee!"
Oh, what words of cheer and comfort!
What today could sweeter be
To the weary, sick, and suff'ring—
"Come, arise, He calleth thee"?

Then as he approached the Master,
Healing virtue to receive,

Jesus said, "Thy faith hath saved thee,
Be it as thou dost believe."
And the blind man's eyes were opened,
He had proved the promise true;
Ye, who still in sickness languish,
Lo, the Master calls for you.

ACT TWO

SCENE 1

Matthew and Sarah are in bed. Sarah is lying on her stomach.
They have obviously just finished engaging in sexual activity.

MATTHEW: I think I like sticking my dick in between your butt cheeks better than I like sticking it between your thighs.
SARAH: Yeah?
MATTHEW: Yeah. It was amazing when you would flex your butt muscles while I was thrusting.
SARAH: I'm glad you liked it.

(Pause.)

Your cum is getting cold on my back. Will you rub it in?
MATTHEW: Sure.

(He rubs his semen into her back.)

SARAH: Thanks. I think all of the semen that you've been shooting on me has done wonders for my skin.

MATTHEW: Yeah?

SARAH: Semen contains protein, zinc and vitamin E. I don't have zits on any of the places that you've shot your semen. We've always got to remember to rub it in. I don't like when it dries and gets all crunchy on my skin.

MATTHEW: I'll remember.

SARAH: Next time we do it I want you to cum on my face. I have a few zits on my cheek.

MATTHEW: No problem.

(Pause.)

Your dad has been giving me some pretty hardcore stares whenever he sees me at the house.

SARAH: He said that he was going to break both of your legs if he saw another hickey on my neck.

MATTHEW: He knows that we're seeing each other?

SARAH: Yup.

MATTHEW: Why didn't you tell me?

SARAH: I didn't want you to worry.

MATTHEW *(Looking at her neck)*: Shit! I think you have a hickey forming!

SARAH: Oh it's not that bad. My hair will cover it. What do you think of Mexicans?

MATTHEW: What do you mean?

SARAH: You know, what do you think of Mexicans? Like the workers in your house?

MATTHEW: I don't think about them very much.

SARAH: Do you think that they're lazy and play the banjo all day?

MATTHEW: What are you talking about?

SARAH: My dad said that your dad is racist against Mexicans.

MATTHEW: It's a generational thing. If a black person does something strange our parents are like: "Must be because they're black." I don't really think about race.

SARAH: I do.

MATTHEW: Really?

SARAH: Yeah. It's hard for me not to notice the fact that I'm not

white. White people don't have to have a constant awareness of race. They can just walk around without people
staring at them and feel comfortable in their own skin. *You
only become aware of race when you feel threatened by a
black guy.*

MATTHEW: That's not true. I don't feel threatened by black guys.

SARAH: Are you telling me that you don't feel a little anxious
when you see a group of black teenagers walking towards
you at the mall.

MATTHEW: Okay. Maybe I feel a little anxiety then.

SARAH: See! But that's your only race awareness. You're only
aware of it when you feel threatened. I think most white
people mean well, but that they don't realize the small
things that they do.

MATTHEW: You're talking in generalities. Give me a concrete
example.

SARAH: People are always staring at me.

MATTHEW: That's because you're beautiful.

SARAH: I can feel people noticing my non-whiteness. I think
that white people have a fascination with minorities that
makes them want to stare as hard as they can whenever one
comes along.

MATTHEW: You're being ridiculous! You're practically white!
Maybe that's true for darker-skinned people, but most Hispanic people are white!

SARAH: Not Mexicans.

MATTHEW: No, not Mexicans. You can tell someone is Mexican
if they're short, dark and have a banjo under their arm.

(He laughs.)

SARAH: Shut up!

*(He starts to tickle her. She laughs. She keeps brushing up
against him as he tickles her. He's erect again.)*

You keep poking me!

MATTHEW: Sorry. You're so sexy that he keeps springing back to life.

SARAH *(Grabbing his penis)*: Wow. You're rock hard. I want you to fuck my breasts so that you can cum all over my face. I need to get rid of this acne.

(He gets into position as the lights fade to black.)

SCENE 2

Jerry and Pat are sitting on their bed. They are watching one of Janet's movies. Jerry looks uncomfortable.

PAT: It's all right, Jerry. You just need to accept the situation and relax.

JERRY: It's hard for me to watch.

PAT: That's because you're resisting the experience. Stop thinking, "I'm watching my daughter have sex" and replace that thought with, "I'm helping my daughter to further her career."

JERRY: Okay.

(Pause. Jerry takes a deep breath.)

PAT: That position is good.

JERRY: It is.

PAT: When her knees are pulled up like that we can see how well-toned her buttocks are.

JERRY: Indeed. Lots of women have flabby asses. Even some thin girls who do porn. But not my little girl.

PAT: Nope. Not her.

JERRY: See, what's happening now—I don't know—it just doesn't look real.

PAT: You think she's faking?

JERRY: Yeah, I think she's faking.

PAT: It's not entirely her fault though—

JERRY: I agree.

PAT: I mean, that girl isn't even licking her clitoris. She's licking the lips, but how's anyone supposed to cum with someone doing that?

(Pause.)

JERRY: This is starting to look more real.

PAT: How can you tell?

JERRY: From the way she's breathing.

PAT: Her breathing has become—

JERRY: There she goes!

PAT: Oh, that's beautiful. Isn't our daughter beautiful?

JERRY: Now that was a real orgasm.

PAT: She came for real because that girl started to lick her butthole while sliding her finger in and out of her vagina.

JERRY: Indeed.

(Pause.)

Do you like having your butthole licked?

PAT: I do.

JERRY: Who's licked your butthole?

PAT: You have. Sometimes you do it by accident if it's really dark in the room. One time I had my butt up in the air and you were giving me oral sex from behind, and you licked my butthole for like fifteen minutes. I think you were doing it by accident, but it was actually the most intense orgasm that I ever had.

JERRY: Can I tell you a secret?

PAT: What?

JERRY: I was doing it on purpose.

PAT: Really?

JERRY: Yup. I always lick your anus on purpose. It's never an accident. I'm actually kind of obsessed with it, but it embarrasses me that I like it so much, so I pretend that I'm doing it by mistake.

PAT: Why does it embarrass you?

JERRY: I don't know. I guess I thought you would judge me, or think less of me, if you knew that I had an obsession with licking buttholes.

(Pat lifts up her skirt and lays back.)

PAT: Lick my asshole, and make sure to get your tongue in there good.

(Jerry pulls Pat's underwear aside and starts to lick her ass.)

Oh, Jerry, this is the best. Oh God. I can't believe that we waited this long to—Oh God. OH. OH. JESUS. YES.

(Janet walks through the door. Janet's video is still playing in the background while Jerry performs analingus on Pat. Janet looks genuinely confused and horrified.
She stares at them for a moment. Pat is moaning as her orgasm consumes her.)

JANET: What are you doing?!

(Jerry lifts his head up.)

JERRY *(Calmly)*: Sorry, Janet. We got a little carried away.

JANET: You're watching my movie while having sex?! Ewww!

PAT: It's not what it looks like, dear. Your father has had a change of heart.

(Jerry nods in agreement.)

JERRY: I don't have a problem with your career choice anymore, Janet. I see the hypocrisy of my behavior and I apologize.

JANET: Really?

JERRY: Really. Your mother and I were watching your movie because we're proud of you. We want to support you in every way that we can.

PAT: We're very proud of you, but we think that there's room for improvement.

JANET: What do you mean?

PAT: Come sit down and we'll show you.

(Janet reluctantly sits down.)

JANET: Okay.

JERRY: Where's the remote?

(Pat hands the remote to Jerry.)

PAT: Here it is.

JERRY: Thank you. I'm going to rewind for a little bit. You see, your mother and I think that some of your orgasms seem more real than others.

PAT: We don't think it's entirely your fault though.

(Blackout.)

SCENE 3

Janet is at Matthew's house.

JANET: What the fuck is wrong with you?!

MATTHEW: What?

JANET: You've been videotaping me.

MATTHEW: How did you find out?

JANET: Those videos that you uploaded onto YouPorn! How could you do that?!

MATTHEW: I'm sorry.

JANET: It'd be one thing if you were just peeping into my window. That's natural. But to videotape me and upload it onto the internet . . . That's messing with my livelihood!

MATTHEW: I'm sorry.

JANET: I feel really, really violated. Especially by the video of me— of me uh—

MATTHEW: Masturbating in your bed.

JANET *(Vulnerable)*: Yeah. How could you?

(Pause.)

I know you may think it's weird that this bothers me, given my line of work, but you have to understand that when I'm on camera I'm acting. I still have a private self and I feel like you've stolen that from me.

MATTHEW: Janet, when I was watching you masturbating, for the first time in my life I truly felt at peace. I wanted to share that feeling with people. I wanted other people to experience what I experienced while watching you.

(Pause.)

JANET *(Genuine)*: I'm touched. I really am. But do you think that people are actually experiencing what you experienced when they watch that video?

MATTHEW: I would like to think that they are. There is something divine about sexual arousal. True sexual arousal. In most porn movies you can tell that the women are just faking it. But when you see a woman who is genuinely sexually aroused, there is divinity in that. *That* video shows you absolutely unmasked. You know, if you could learn how to reveal your truest self while you're performing, I think you might become the most famous performer who ever lived.

JANET: What are you suggesting?

MATTHEW: I'm going to delete the video. But I haven't just been taping you out of some lurid interest. I'm going to be a film-maker. I convinced my dad to buy me an expensive camera and to give me forty thousand dollars to make a film. My dad wants me to make two short films. But instead I'm going to make one feature-length. And I want you to be the star.

JANET: Really?

MATTHEW: While I was taping you that morning, masturbating in your bed, I had an epiphany. I think that making porn is my calling. I've been watching porn since I was eleven and I've always loved it, but I've also always had this deep feeling inside that I could do it better. Like the porn films in the seventies.

JANET: What do you mean?

MATTHEW: In the seventies, pornography was viewed as an art. They wrote scenes, and performed them, and the images were more genuinely arousing. We were watching the actors connect. We were watching their souls connect. Most porn today focuses on close-ups of dicks pounding vaginas or anuses. It's very unsexy and clinical. And frankly I think it's a little dirty. Of course it wouldn't be a porn movie if you didn't have the money shot. All porn movies have to have that. But I do think that we degrade ourselves a little when we reduce sex to simple anatomy. That's why I want you to star in my film. I feel like I can see your soul. You're my muse, Janet.

(James enters.)

MATTHEW: Hi, Dad.

JANET: Hi, Mr. Williams.

(James runs his eyes all over Janet's body. Janet is wearing a shirt that exposes her cleavage and a short skirt. He stares at her breasts and her legs. It is very awkward. His breathing is labored.)

MATTHEW: Dad, are you all right?

(James continues to stare at Janet. He can't pull his eyes away. He just stands there with a huge erection, breathing very heavily.)

JAMES: You need to put some clothes on, young lady. Your breasts are falling out of your shirt and your skirt is so short that I can almost see your . . . Have some self-respect. You look like a damn harlot.

(His erection is bigger than ever. She tries to pull her skirt down a little lower and cover her breasts with her shirt.)

MATTHEW: That's really rude, Dad.
JAMES: It's the truth. She makes life hard for everyone.
JANET: I'm sorry that my clothing offends you.
JAMES: Excuse me.

(He exits to his bedroom.)

JANET: I should probably go.

(She starts to get up.)

MATTHEW: That's probably not a bad idea. He's acting weirder than normal.
JANET: I want to finish this conversation though.
MATTHEW: Really?
JANET: Yeah, it sounds like a really interesting idea.
MATTHEW: Want to get together tomorrow after school?
JANET: Yeah.

(We hear James make a series of very loud sexual noises from the bathroom.)

JAMES *(Offstage)*: OH. OH GOD. HEAVEN HELP ME. OH GOD. YOU STUPID BITCH!

(James has climaxed and all goes silent.)

JANET: What the fuck was that?
MATTHEW: Maybe he's on the phone.

(Janet stares at Matthew incredulously. James walks out of the bedroom. He is completely distraught.)

What's wrong, Dad?
JAMES: I can't stop.

JANET: Can't stop what?

JAMES: I can't stop doing what you want me to do.

JANET: I don't want you to do anything.

JAMES: Yes you do. Don't lie. You know why you pose in those magazines. You know what you want me to do.

JANET: Don't look at those magazines if they make you this distraught. I don't want to make anyone feel badly.

JAMES: I made a resolution yesterday to stop all that, and I did. I didn't masturbate yesterday. It was the first time that I've gone a day without masturbating in probably two years.

MATTHEW: Dad, stop.

JAMES: It's the truth. And I felt so good about not masturbating yesterday. I didn't look at any pornography yesterday, and I haven't looked at any today. But then I walk through the door and you're sitting here in the flesh. Sitting here . . . I can't fight myself anymore, Janet. You're so beautiful. And I know it's a sin. I know it's a sin, but your thighs look so wonderful. Your breasts. Your hair. Your youth. And I couldn't resist going to my bedroom and masturbating. I'm addicted. I feel like I can't leave the house. I can't turn on the TV. I can't go anywhere without seeing scantily clad women who want me to masturbate while thinking about them.

JANET: You know, Mr. Williams, maybe your addiction to masturbation comes from your lack of human connection.

JAMES: Maybe.

JANET: How long have you had this problem?

JAMES: Since my wife died. I mean, it's not like our sex life was that great, but it was sufficient, and I loved her. But after she died something was awakened in me. I had never been into porn before. But after she was gone there was nothing to stop me from staying up all night . . .

JANET: It sounds like a big part of your problem is loneliness. You have to learn how to productively fill the time that you used to spend with your wife.

JAMES: How am I supposed to find a girlfriend at my age? I was nineteen when I got married. I was a virgin. I really don't know anything about dating.

MATTHEW: Mom took your virginity?

(James nods yes.)

JANET: And you've never been with another woman?

(James shakes his head no.)

Have you ever kissed another woman?

(He's embarrassed. Janet kisses James deeply on the lips. It is a long French kiss. Matthew looks on with confusion. Blackout.)

SCENE 4

Jerry and Pat are standing on their porch talking.

JERRY: What do you think about selling our house?
PAT: Where would we go?
JERRY: I'd like to retire to a beach house on the coast of Portugal.
PAT: That sounds nice. But I wouldn't want to be that far away from Janet.
JERRY: Janet's an adult now and she's making enough to support herself. At some point we have to stop basing our decisions around our child.
PAT: Can we keep an apartment here?
JERRY: I have a better idea. We give Janet a hundred thousand dollars for a down payment on a house. And we help her pick it out. That way Janet has a nice place to live after we move, and we'll have a really nice place to stay whenever we come to town.
PAT: I like that idea!
JERRY: We'll find one of those old houses that has a carriage house in back, and we'll live in the carriage house so that we can each have our own space.

PAT: Then we can spend the summer and spring here, and the fall and winter in Portugal. I love it!

(James approaches Jerry and Pat's porch. Jerry pulls out a handgun and points it toward James.)

JERRY: Stop right there, motherfucker!

(James stops.)

PAT: What are you doing, Jerry?

(James continues to walk toward the porch.)

JERRY: Stop right there or I'm gonna blow your head off.

(James stops again.)

JAMES: I'm not here to hurt you, Jerry. Put that gun away.
JERRY: I'm not putting the gun away.
JAMES: It's not even real!
JERRY: What?
JAMES: Anyone who knows anything about guns can tell the difference between a BB gun and a real gun.
JERRY: It's a *pellet* gun you idiot.
JAMES: I came over here to apologize. I'm really sorry, Jerry. I was wrong to say the things I did, and to beat you up. Janet's actually a very lovely person. I was wrong to judge her based on her profession and I was wrong to judge you based on her actions. I mean, none of us can really control what our kids do.

(Jerry lowers the gun.)

JERRY: I appreciate that.
PAT: Yes, we appreciate that.
JERRY: So, uh, have you gotten any bites on your house?

JAMES: I've gotten a couple of lowball offers. They were offering cash. People think that if they offer cash then they can rob you blind.

JERRY: What's the lowest you would take?

JAMES: Probably six hundred and fifty thousand. I just spent a ton of money doing renovations.

JERRY: Are they done? I still see Fred and his workers over there almost every day.

JAMES: That's because those Mexicans can't seem to do anything right the first time.

PAT: Yeah, we've had some problems with our lawn people.

JAMES *(To Jerry)*: You fired Joey?

JERRY: Yeah. He told me to go fuck myself after I gave him that talk.

JAMES: At least you tried.

PAT: So anyway, the new lawn people. Mexicans. Are supposed to come every Saturday, but sometimes they come on Sunday or not at all.

JERRY: You never know whether those people are going to show up or not.

JAMES: Tell me about it. And they're ungrateful. My wife and I had Mexican women clean our house. And you know, we'd pay them about fifty dollars each for a day's work. That seems fair, right?

JERRY: That seems more than fair to me.

JAMES: And do you know that after only a year of service they had the nerve to ask for a raise. We were paying $6.25 an hour. Minimum wage was only $5.85. When I said no they told this sob story about how they each had you know, like, five to seven kids and how they couldn't make ends meet and my wife just had to cut them off. She told them that since they were illegal immigrants they should be thrilled that we were paying them as much as we were!

PAT: She was right!

JERRY: Your wife was a good woman.

PAT: We miss her very much.

(Pat gives James a hug.)

We'd like to have you and Matthew over for dinner some-
time.

JAMES: That sounds nice.

SCENE 5

Janet is at Matthew's house.

MATTHEW: Sorry about my dad's behavior the other day.
JANET: There's nothing to apologize for. I actually think he's cool.
MATTHEW: He's weird and perverted, Janet.
JANET: So are you.
MATTHEW: I'm not weird and perverted!
JANET: You secretly videotape me while I undress and masturbate!
MATTHEW: *You* said that that was only natural!
JANET: It is natural! Everything that people do comes naturally!
That's my point. He always shows his truest self and I love
that about him.
MATTHEW: You barely know him.
JANET: I've known him my whole life! Your father is like a help-
less, wounded animal. It makes me want to wrap my arms
around him and nurse him back to health. He's doing the
best he can to survive. Have some compassion for him.

(Matthew nods his head.)

MATTHEW: I'll try.

(Pause.)

So anyway have you thought more about our film project.
JANET: I'm in.
MATTHEW: This is awesome!

JANET: So what did you have in mind?

MATTHEW: We need to do something that's never been done before.

JANET: Everything in porn has been done before.

MATTHEW: Not everything.

JANET: I draw the line at double anal penetration.

MATTHEW: I want to make a film that's all frottage. Two hours of nonstop frottage. In case you're not familiar, frottage is when—

JANET: I know what frottage is. I like this idea. I like it a lot. We're going to make a frot film! Who's going to be my co-star?

(Pause.)

MATTHEW: Well, uh. You know, I was thinking that. Uh. I'm going to be your co-star.

JANET: That's not happening, Matthew. If we're going to undertake this endeavor together then our relationship must remain professional.

MATTHEW: Suppose I found someone else to produce the film. Could I be your co-star then?

JANET: I want your father to be my co-star.

(Matthew laughs.)

I'm serious.

MATTHEW: What? What the *fuck* is wrong with you? How can you expect me to watch my father repeatedly ejaculate all over you?

JANET: I don't know, but you're going to have to find a way to deal with it. You can talk to my parents if you want. They watch my films and critique me.

MATTHEW *(Full shout)*: Fine! If you want my dad to be in the film then I want your parents to be in the film. How do you like that?

(Pause.)

JANET: You know, that's actually a great idea. We could make a neighborhood porn film. I don't think that that's ever been done before.

MATTHEW: We can call it "A Frot in the Neighborhood." Do you think that your parents would do it?

JANET: I actually think that they would. Who else could we get?

MATTHEW: I can ask Sarah.

JANET: She'd be great. What about your father?

MATTHEW: Janet. I have to draw the line at my father. He might take the money away.

(James enters.)

JAMES: I heard shouting. I'm trying to meditate.

MATTHEW: Sorry, Dad. We'll keep it down.

JANET: We were fighting about you.

JAMES: Why?

MATTHEW: Don't do this, Janet.

JANET: Matthew has decided to make a porn film with the money that you gave him and I'm going to be the star.

(Pause.)

JAMES: That's not what I expected you to do with the money. But I commend your creativity.

MATTHEW: Thanks, Dad. I thought you were going to freak out.

JAMES: You know, after the interaction that Janet and I had the other day, something changed. I can't quite describe it, but it's as if the sun is shining within my soul again. I used to wake up every morning and ask God: "Why can't these days be different than they are?" I would sit around wishing that I was someone else. Wishing that the circumstances of my life were different. But now I've embraced the realities of my life, and I love living.

JANET *(To James)*: I want you to be my co-star.

JAMES: Me? Really?

SCENE 6

Matthew has just come home from school. Fred is in Matthew's house painting alone.

MATTHEW: Hi, Mr. Alverez.
FRED: Hi.

(Matthew looks around.)

MATTHEW: Where's your crew?
FRED: I let them go home early. It's such a nice day.
MATTHEW: It is a nice day.
FRED: Why aren't you with my daughter?
MATTHEW: What?
FRED: It's such a nice day. I thought you would be in the park sticking your tongue down my daughter's throat and giving her hickeys.
MATTHEW: I'm really sorry about that.
FRED: No need to apologize. Everyone gets horny. And teenagers are hornier than most.

(Matthew is very uncomfortable.)

MATTHEW: Uh, yeah.
FRED: You better not get her pregnant though. I'll fucking kill you.
MATTHEW: We haven't had sex, I swear.
FRED: Good. Good. I'm happy to hear that. But it surprises me, given how handsome you are. I'm surprised that my daughter is able to resist.
MATTHEW: Uh. Um.
FRED: Can you get me a glass of water? I'm really thirsty.

(Matthew exits. He brings back a tall glass of water and hands it to Fred. Fred starts to drink, then pretends to lose his balance, purposefully spilling the water all over his pants.)

Damn! Spilled it all over my pants!

MATTHEW: I'll get you a towel.
FRED: Thanks.

(Matthew exits to get a towel. Fred takes off his pants. He's wearing men's G string underwear. Matthew reenters.)

MATTHEW: What are you doing?
FRED: It's uncomfortable to walk around in wet pants. I figured that I would take them off for a moment.

(Matthew hands Fred the towel. Fred starts to wipe off his crotch area.)

MATTHEW: You're wearing a thong.
FRED: I find them to be more comfortable than regular underwear. Besides, I like to look sexy for my wife. Do you like what you see?

(Long pause.)

MATTHEW: I do like what I see.
FRED: Really?
MATTHEW: Yeah. You've got a beautiful body, and a pretty big cock. I think it would look great on film.
FRED: You want to film me?
MATTHEW: Yeah.

(Fred pulls down his underwear.)

FRED: Come over here and put my cock in your mouth.
MATTHEW: See, the thing is. Uh. That I'm not gay.
FRED: Neither am I.
MATTHEW: That may be the case, but uh.
FRED: Roman men weren't gay but they had sex with young boys all the time. Being attracted to you doesn't negate the attraction that I have for my wife.
MATTHEW: I'll make you a deal. You can touch me, but only on film.
FRED: What do you mean?

SCENE 7

Matthew and Janet are watching Deep Throat.

JANET: I can't believe I've never seen this before.

MATTHEW: Isn't it amazing?

JANET: Yeah, this is like a real movie.

MATTHEW: There's a real plot here, and not a dumb one either.

JANET: Her clit being in the back of her throat is a brilliant plot-driving device.

MATTHEW: It is, isn't it?! I'd really like to do something like this.

JANET: What do you mean?

MATTHEW: I want there to be a real storyline, that actually has some depth.

JANET: That would be awesome! What are you thinking?

MATTHEW: So, here's what I'm thinking. The story centers around your character, Lily, a Christian girl who was home-schooled by her parents and knows nothing about sex. When she goes off to college she breaks her leg, and one of her professors takes pity on her and decides to come to her dorm room so she can have private tutorials and not get behind on her schoolwork. During one of these meetings she asks him about feelings that she's been having, and she's introduced to the world of frottage. This lights a fire within her but she's determined to keep her secret life of frottage a secret. When she goes home to visit her parents she discovers that she's not the only family member who shares her love of frottage. It's in their DNA.

JANET: Wow.

MATTHEW: And I want to shoot the whole thing with a handheld camera as an homage to Lars von Trier's *Breaking the Waves*. I want the audience to feel something visceral. And in his film the audience was actually nauseated by the effect of the shaky handheld camera. Though we're professionals, by using this device we'll be able capture the mise-en-scène of an amateur porn film.

JANET: I love it

MATTHEW: All my friends are about to go off to college, which has been bringing up a lot of complicated feelings for me. I see this movie as a way to explore the potential isolation and struggle to connect what everyone leaving home for the first time fears.

SCENE 8

Matthew is on the phone with Sarah.

SARAH: That's awesome.

MATTHEW: I have to tell you something. And I need you not to freak out.

SARAH: Okay.

MATTHEW: Well, when my father first gave me the money, I considered making some stupid indie film just like everyone else. But my mother always told me to follow my heart. And I realized that porn is what I really wanted to make. My mother would be deeply disappointed with me if I didn't follow my passion.

SARAH: Who's in it?

MATTHEW: Janet. My next-door neighbor. She's a porn star.

SARAH: Oh right, the girl with the black father who looks absolutely white. Do you have a thing for her?

MATTHEW: No, no! Of course not. This is strictly professional.

SARAH: Are you going to have sex with her in the film?

MATTHEW: How could you even ask me a question like that? *I love you.* I mean, truth be told, she wanted me to be her co-star, but I said no because you know, you're my girlfriend and I didn't want to do anything to jeopardize that.

SARAH: That white-black slut tried to get you to sleep with her? I'll kill that bitch!

MATTHEW: You shouldn't be angry with her. There's no sex in the film.

SARAH: No sex?

MATTHEW: It's all frottage.

SARAH: Aww. That's sweet, Matthew. Are you doing that in honor of our relationship?

MATTHEW: Of course I am. I wouldn't be making a film this unique had I not met you. I need to find a few more people to be in the film.

SARAH: Do you have people in mind?

MATTHEW: Well, I was hoping that there could be a couple of scenes between you and me. You and me expressing our love to each other for the whole world to see.

SARAH: I don't know, Matthew. What if my father finds out?

MATTHEW: Trust me, your father isn't going to be a problem. Besides, there's money.

SARAH: How much?

MATTHEW: I'm paying the actors three thousand dollars each.

SARAH: Three thousand dollars! Holy shit!

MATTHEW: Being a movie star pays very, very well.

SARAH: And you and I, we would only be with each other?

MATTHEW: You're the only girl that I'm going to be with in the film.

(They kiss.)

SCENE 9

Sarah enters her living room.

SARAH: Dad, I need to talk to you about something.

FRED: Okay.

SARAH: It's about your attraction to Matthew.

FRED *(Alarmed)*: I'm not gay!

SARAH: I'm not concerned about that, Dad. I know that you look at gay porn.

FRED: How do you know? I always erase my internet browser.

SARAH: Erasing your internet browser doesn't erase searches that you make within google.

FRED: Matthew promised that he would let me talk to you first.

SARAH: Matthew got concerned because he's shooting your scenes tomorrow, and you still hadn't told me.

FRED: I was going to tonight.

SARAH: You're a lot cooler than I thought. I really respect the fact that you're doing this. You know that I'm in the film, too, right?

FRED: Yes. Matthew and I talked all about it. I told him it's fine as long as there's no penetration. As long as your virginity remains intact.

SARAH: Thanks, Dad. I'm worried about Mom finding out.

FRED: Don't worry about your mother. She won't find out. She barely knows how to use a keyboard. Besides, she's a lot cooler than you think.

SARAH: What do you mean?

FRED: Your mother and I weren't always legit. You have to swear to secrecy about what I'm going to tell you.

SARAH: I swear.

FRED: Your mother used to be a prostitute.

SARAH: What?!

FRED: And I was her pimp.

SARAH: Jesus Christ!

FRED: And we got busted. Your Mother only served thirty days in jail, but I did two years.

SARAH: How could you pimp-out Mom?

FRED: Your mother was a prostitute when I met her. I was one of her clients. I became her pimp because I wanted to protect her. We didn't get married until after I got out of prison, and we vowed to turn our lives around.

SARAH: So, you don't think that she'll be mad?

FRED: You see a lot of weird stuff when you're a prostitute. A lot weirder than what we're doing.

SARAH: Are you sure that you're not gay? It's fine with me if you are.

FRED: I promise you that I'm not gay. I'm attracted to both men and women. I get to have sex with a woman all the time, so my fantasies tend to be about men.

SCENE 10

The setting is a girl's bedroom. There should be stuffed animals and stuff like that. Matthew is standing behind a camera. Sarah is standing next to him. They are both wearing regular clothes. Janet is dressed in porn-schoolgirl gear: white stockings, short plaid skirt, a white button-down shirt that's barley buttoned. One of Janet's legs is in some sort of leg brace. James is dressed like a professor: tweed jacket, white button-down shirt, and khakis.

MATTHEW: Dad, I just want you to know that, uh, this is really weird and awkward for me. And I, uh, you know, I'm glad that you're doing the film, I guess, but this is going to be hard for me to watch.

JAMES: I promise not to disappoint you, Son.

MATTHEW: We're serving a greater purpose. Sometimes, as artists, we have to do things that make us very, very uncomfortable, but the best artistic expression often comes from those moments of struggle, and offers us the greatest rewards.

(Janet and James nod their heads in agreement. James gets into place.)

Camera.

SARAH: Rolling.

MATTHEW: Action.

(James knocks on the door. Janet wakes up, startled.)

JANET: Who is it?

JAMES: It's Professor Thompson.

(Janet walks over to the door with the aid of two crutches and opens it.)

JANET: Sorry, Professor, I forgot that we were meeting today. I really appreciate you meeting me in my dorm room since I have a broken leg.

JAMES: It's no problem at all. Being a history professor is like being a doctor.

JANET: It's very similar.

JAMES: Indeed it is. Doctor's take the Hippocratic oath.

JANET: What's that?

JAMES: In the Hippocratic oath doctors swear to practice medicine ethically and to do everything to save a person's life. And as a professor it is my duty to educate students no matter the cost. If a student is injured and can't come to class, then I must go to her dorm room and give her a history lesson. Do you understand?

JANET: I think so.

JAMES: Today, I'm going to lecture you about the first King of England and how England became a united country.

JANET: That sounds great.

JAMES: The first King of England was William the Conqueror. He reigned from 1066–1087. He united the kingdom by—

JANET: Professor, my vagina feels funny.

JAMES: Funny good, or funny bad?

JANET: I don't know. Can you take a look?

JAMES: It is my duty.

(James puts his hand under Janet's skirt. He quickly pulls his hand away. He looks upset.)

MATTHEW: Cut! Did you forget your lines?

JAMES: No.

JANET: What's wrong?

JAMES: It's been so long since I touched a woman. I've never touched a woman other than my wife.

JANET: You've just got to relax. Pretend that the camera isn't there. Let me help you.

(She takes his hand and guides it under her skirt. She places his hand on her vagina.)

That feels nice, James.

JAMES: It does? For real?

JANET: Yes, I love the feel of your hands on my body. Can you feel how wet I am?

JAMES: Yes.

JANET: That's because of my genuine attraction to you.

(They kiss.)

Are you ready to go on with the scene?

JAMES: I feel so happy when I'm with you. I'm ready.

MATTHEW: Rolling!

JAMES: You're very aroused. When a woman gets aroused then her vagina gets wet. The only way to get rid of that funny feeling is to have an orgasm.

JANET: Can you help me?

JAMES: I can. Lie down in the bed on your side.

JANET: Okay.

(James helps her onto the bed.)

JAMES: Now, take one of your stuffed animals and put it between your legs, right next to your vagina.

JANET: Do I need to take my underwear off?

JAMES: There's no need for that. That would be immodest.

JANET: What now?

JAMES: Rub the stuffed animal back and forth between your legs.

JANET: Okay.

(Janet starts to rub the stuffed animal back and forth between her legs.)

What were you saying about William the Conqueror?

MATTHEW: I'm coming in for a close-up.

(He starts to rub himself while he tries to lecture her.)

JAMES: I was saying, um. You see, William the Conqueror was related to Edward the Confessor. But Edward was childless so—

JANET: Do you want to stick your pee-pee into my vagina?

JAMES: No, Lily. No. I don't want to make a baby.

JANET: I don't want to make a baby either.

JAMES: I'm going to teach you about something called frottage. Take off your shirt. And your bra.

JANET: Okay.

(She takes off her shirt and bra. James then climbs on top of her and he and Janet start to tenderly make out.)

MATTHEW: No kissing! Stick to the script.

(James unbuckles his pants and pulls them down along with his underwear.)

JAMES: I'm sorry. Now lift up your arm.

(She does. He puts his penis in her armpit.)

Good. Now lower your arm.

(She does.)

Hold it tight so that enough friction for my penis is created. Now add the stuffed animal.

(He starts to thrust.)

JANET: Am I doing a good job?

JAMES: You're doing a great job. Your armpit is nice and sweaty. Oh. Oh. It feels so wet. Oh God. It's better than any pussy. Your armpit hair gently tickling me. The musty smell of your armpit sweat . . . I love it. I'm getting close.

JANET: Me, too.

(He starts to thrust violently fast, then stiffens as he begins to orgasm.)

MATTHEW: Okay let it go.

(Both orgasm together.)

Cut. That was perfect!
JAMES: That was amazing, Janet.

SCENE 11

Sarah and Janet are manning the camera. Fred is dressed in a cardigan and khakis. Matthew is just wearing boxer shorts.

MATTHEW *(To Sarah and Janet)*: You know what you're doing with the camera?
JANET: Yes.

(Sarah gives a thumbs-up.)

MATTHEW: Great. So, the scene is going to start with me under the covers in bed. Fred, you'll be sitting on the edge of the bed next to my head.

(Matthew gets under the covers. Fred gets into place next to him.)

Sarah, you might want to . . .
SARAH: Oh yeah, I think it's time for me to get a coffee.
MATTHEW: You know, I'm supposed to have an erection the whole time that he's reading the story, but I don't have one right now. So, I'll use this flashlight. But I'm going to need a fluffer later, so I'll text you.
SARAH: Okay.

(Sarah exits.)

MATTHEW: Camera.
JANET: Rolling.

MATTHEW: Action!

(While Fred is reading he is constantly getting distracted by Matthew's penis under the covers.)

FRED: Good night window, good night tree, good night carpet, good night bees, good night radiators, and good night lamps, good night toy box, good night facts. On to dreamworld you will go, where anything can happen, yes you can even be like Aladdin! So, good night to the light and every sound in the land. It's time to go to sleep now, so close those eyes, and clasp those little hands.

MATTHEW: Thanks for reading me a story, Uncle Fred.

FRED: Any time, Little Matthew.

MATTHEW: Will you read me another one?

(Fred looks at Matthew's erection sticking straight up under the covers.)

FRED: It doesn't seem like you really want me to read you another story.

MATTHEW: What do you mean?

FRED: You have an erection, Matthew. Certainly you know what an erection is.

MATTHEW: Yes, I do.

FRED: Have you tried playing with yourself?

(Matthew nods his head yes.)

What do you think about when you masturbate?

MATTHEW: I think about you, Uncle Fred. Is that wrong?

FRED: It's not wrong, Matthew. It's only natural. There are many ways to masturbate. Do you want Uncle Fred to show you a new way?

MATTHEW: Yes.

FRED: You can't tell your parents though.

MATTHEW: I promise.

(Fred takes off his shoes and socks. He then peels the covers back.)

FRED: Your penis looks nice and strong. Just like your father's.

(Fred then sits in a chair next to the bed and puts his feet on either side of Matthew's penis. He jerks Matthew off with his feet. They stare into each other's eyes.)

How does that feel?

MATTHEW: I think I'm about to cum, Uncle Fred.

Cut.

Okay so now I'm going to have to get Sarah to fluff me to the point of being ready to ejaculate and then right before I cum you will put your feet around my dick and then I'll splice everything together to look like I came from your foot job.

FRED: Am I that disgusting to you?

MATTHEW: You don't disgust me. I'm very open-minded. However, my penis feels differently.

FRED: This isn't right.

MATTHEW: What isn't?

FRED: When I agreed to do this you promised that we were going to have a genuine intimate moment. What you're doing is making me feel bad about myself.

MATTHEW: I'm not trying to make you feel bad. It's just . . . I'm not gay and being with a man is making me extremely uncomfortable.

FRED: You haven't even tried. As far as I can tell you've completely closed your mind off to the experience.

MATTHEW: Well, what do you suggest that we do?

FRED: Let me do what Sarah was going to do.

MATTHEW: Okay.

(Fred starts to give Matthew a blowjob.)

That does feel good.

(Fred stops so that he can speak.)

FRED: A man knows the penis better than any woman ever could.

(Fred starts to blow Matthew again. The pleasure that Matthew is experiencing is obvious.)

MATTHEW: Okay. Okay. I'm about to nut.
JANET: Rolling!
MATTHEW: Action.

(Fred quickly puts his feet around Matthew's penis and starts jerking him off again. Janet checks her phone, then starts texting.)

FRED: So, what did you think?

(Matthew kisses Fred.)

Whoah. Hey. I thought you said no kissing.

(Matthew and Fred kiss again.)

MATTHEW: I don't care. I need to get closer to you. Camera!
JANET: Rolling!

(Fred and Matthew make out as the lights fade to black.)

SCENE 12

Pat and Jerry's house. Matthew is behind the camera. Matthew and Janet are giving Jerry and Pat instructions.

MATTHEW: First of all, I really want to thank the two of you for doing this. I'm super excited for your scene because it's unlike anything else in the movie. You'll notice that your scene in the script is completely blank.
JERRY: I was wondering about that.
MATTHEW: That's because I want you to improvise your scene.

PAT: What?!

JANET: Matthew and I didn't tell you beforehand because we didn't want you to overthink it.

MATTHEW: We want you to be completely natural and honest. So, in this scene, Janet's character, Lily, is interviewing her parents in an effort to unearth whether her love of frottage is truly embedded in her DNA. But what's fascinating is that we have you, Janet's real parents, playing the roles of Lily's parents. This scene really drives home the question of: "Does art imitate life? Or does life imitate art?"

JERRY: Can you talk a little more about how to improvise a—

MATTHEW: Just do what comes naturally. Rolling!

JANET: Mom, have you and Dad ever engaged in frottage?

PAT: When we started dating sometimes your father liked to, uh, stick his penis between my breasts. Besides that, no.

JERRY: That's not true. After you had the abortion we were—

JANET: You had an abortion?

PAT: It was a complicated situation. Your father and I were secretly dating at the time. I was his PhD advisor. There would have been a scandal and I didn't have tenure. I would have lost my job.

JANET: Wow. I didn't know that you and Dad had a secret romance.

PAT: We did. And of course I regretted that abortion with all my heart. We had so much trouble getting pregnant with you. It took three years, and all sorts of fertility treatments.

JERRY: You're our little miracle.

PAT: You are.

(Pause.)

JANET: Anyway. Frottage.

JERRY: Right. So, you're not supposed to have sex for like three or four weeks after having an abortion, and I was super horny. For the first couple of weeks your mother was being fairly generous with the blowjobs, but she lost interest in that. So, one day we were lying in bed, and I started finger-ing your mother. After that I went down on her. After she had an orgasm I was really really horny and it was clear that your mother wasn't going to reciprocate.

PAT: He wasn't being sensitive to my feelings.

JERRY: I was young!

PAT: Having an abortion is traumatic.

JERRY: So, anyway, I laid down behind her and I was trying to stick my dick in her pussy but your mother made me stop. Then I tried to stick it in her ass, but she wouldn't let me do that either.

PAT: Anal sex hurts!

JERRY: How would you know? You've never even tried!

JANET: You and Mom have never had anal sex?

JERRY: Never.

JANET: Orgasms from anal sex can be much stronger than ones from vaginal sex.

JERRY: So, anyway, I rubbed my dick against her pussy and her thighs created the proper friction and I came all over the place.

JANET: Mom, would you be willing to lose your anal virginity on camera with Dad?

MATTHEW: Frottage only!

JANET: Shut up, Matthew! Mom, would you be willing to do that? I think everyone would love to see that.

JERRY: It would make me very happy.

(He grabs her hand and holds it lovingly.)

PAT: All right. If this will make my husband and my daughter happy, then yes, I'll do it.

JANET: Thank you, Mom.

(Janet gives Pat a hug.)

PAT: But no close-ups of my asshole getting stretched!

(Pat and Jerry have anal sex as Matthew films them. Pat and Jerry kiss afterward.)

MATTHEW: That was beautiful.

JANET: It was.

MATTHEW: When we began this artistic endeavor I thought it was about frottage. But after being with all of you, and witnessing the emotional and transformative breakthroughs that we've gone through together, I now see what my film is really about. It's about intimacy. It's all about intimacy.

SCENE 13

Matthew, James, Pat, Jerry, Fred, Sarah and Janet have just finished watching the film.

MATTHEW: Hey, guys, I'd really love to shoot a behind-the-scenes group interview for the DVD release. How does that sound?

FRED: I'd be okay with that.

(Everyone nods in agreement. Matthew pulls out a camcorder and starts recording.)

MATTHEW: We're here together two months after shooting the film *Intimacy* and we have the cast here to talk about their experiences making the film. *(To the cast)* Pat and Jerry, tell your fans how shooting *Intimacy* affected you?

PAT: I'm so happy. I'm so happy that we made that film.

JERRY: Me, too. Pat and I rarely have vaginal sex these days because—

PAT: The orgasms I have from anal sex are better than anything I've experienced. I feel like I'm twenty-one again.

JERRY: I feel the same way.

(They kiss.)

MATTHEW: Fred?

FRED: I was totally transformed by the whole experience. I feel like I got to openly express myself for the first time in my life. It's such a joy to be able to show the world who you really are. Thanks for giving me the opportunity to be a part of this, Matthew.

MATTHEW: You're welcome.

SARAH *(To Fred)*: And I feel like our relationship has grown so much. I mean, before this, we only talked about superficial things, and now I feel like I can talk to you about anything.

FRED: I love you, Sarah. And I'm so happy that you accept me for who I truly am. Thank you for that.

SARAH: You're welcome. I love you too, Dad.

FRED: Jerry and Pat have really inspired me. I think that I'd like to make a porno with your mother.

JAMES: Do you think she'll go for that?

FRED: Why not? She likes porn.

MATTHEW: How about you, Dad?

JAMES: It would be impossible for me to describe how I feel. But I'll say this: I think that I've finally gotten over your mother's death. I think that she would be proud of me for what I've done. And I think that she would be proud of you, too.

MATTHEW: I think you're right.

JANET: I'm in love with you, James.

JAMES: What?

JANET: I'm in love with you. I haven't been able to stop thinking about you ever since we kissed that day at your house. The vulnerability that you showed made me want to protect you, and be your shield against all the sorrow in the world. I love you. And I want to be with you.

(She gets down on one knee and takes out a box with a ring in it. She opens the box.)

Will you marry me?

SARAH: Oh my God!

(Pause.)

JAMES: Yes. I will marry you, Janet. I've loved you for as long as I can remember.

JERRY: This is cause for celebration!

PAT: I think we have some champagne!

(Pat exits and reenters immediately with glasses already filled with champagne and hands them out.)

MATTHEW: I'm so happy for you, Dad!

(They hug.)

FRED: Are you going to start calling Janet "Mom" now?

(Everyone laughs.)

JANET: I think that would be appropriate.

MATTHEW: Okay, Mom.

(Everyone laughs again.)

PAT: Let us raise our glasses to Janet and James, two of the finest people in this neighborhood. Let us wish them peace and happiness as they begin their life together.

(They clink glasses and drink.)

FRED: I'm a licensed minister, you know.

JAMES: You are?

SARAH: Yeah, Dad got ordained online through Universal Life Church so that he could perform my cousin's wedding.

PAT: Could you perform the ceremony right now?

FRED: I don't see why not.

JERRY: But James doesn't have a ring for Janet.

PAT: She can use my ring.

(Pat takes off her wedding ring and hands it to James.)

JERRY: Pat!

PAT: I'll get a new one.

JAMES: This is wonderful!

JANET: Thank you, Mom!

FRED: Okay everyone, gather 'round.

(Fred gets in between James and Janet. Janet and James face each other with Fred in between. Everyone else forms a semicircle around them.)

Do you, James Williams, take Little Janet to be your lawfully wedded wife, to have and to hold, in sickness and in health, as long as you both shall live?

JAMES: I do.

FRED: Do you, Little Janet, take James Williams to be your lawfully wedded husband, to have and to hold, in sickness and in health, as long as you both shall live?

JANET: I do.

FRED: You may kiss the bride.

(Janet and James kiss tenderly. Everyone claps.)

JAMES: When do you want to move in?

JANET: You're not going to sell the house?

JAMES: Not anymore. I want to make it our home.

MATTHEW: What about me?

JAMES: Oh, I think that you're going to make enough money to get your own place after our film is released. Besides, don't movie directors need to move to Hollywood?

PAT: Any time that you get sick of Janet and James you can come stay at our place.

MATTHEW: Really?

JERRY: Of course. You're family now. We're your grandparents.

PAT: You can have Janet's room after she moves out.

MATTHEW: Thanks, Grandma.

(Pause.)

SARAH: You never told us how *you* felt about making the film, Matthew.

MATTHEW: Well. I discovered my bisexuality.

SARAH: I guess that doesn't surprise me. The scene between you and my dad looked very genuine and realistic.

MATTHEW: It was. Are you okay with that?

SARAH: Okay with you being bisexual or being with my dad?

MATTHEW: Both.

SARAH: I'm going off to college in the fall, so I'd rather not be trapped in a monogamous relationship. I've been reading a lot about polyamorous relationships, and I think that I could really get into that.

MATTHEW: I like this polyamorous relationship idea.

SARAH: And if it makes you and my dad happy to be together, who am I to stop it. We all love each other. What's wrong with that?

(Matthew and Sarah kiss, then Fred gives Sarah a kiss on the head. Matthew, Sarah and Fred have a group hug.)

JAMES: So, Sarah, have you gotten accepted to any colleges yet?

SARAH: Matthew didn't tell you?!

MATTHEW: I forgot.

FRED: She got a full scholarship to Princeton!

JANET: That's amazing! I'm so happy for you!

PAT: That is wonderful, dear.

JERRY: You deserve it.

PAT: I have to go to the bathroom.

(Pat exits.)

JANET: So, what are you going to major in?

SARAH: I'm going to be pre-med. I want to become a doctor just like Matthew's mom.

MATTHEW: I think Mom would really be proud of the film.

JAMES: I know she's smiling down on us from Heaven.

(Pause. Pat reenters.)

PAT *(To Jerry)*: There's no hot water in the bathroom.

JERRY: Damn hot water heater has been acting up lately. We probably need a new one. There's another thousand dollars down the drain.

FRED: Don't worry, I'll replace it for you, and I'll give you a really great price.

JERRY: How much?

FRED: Eight hundred dollars.

JERRY: That doesn't seem like a good deal to me. How about six hundred dollars?

FRED: You're really cheap, you know that?

PAT: He's always been that way. You'd think that he was a Jew.

FRED: Well, he certainly is trying to Jew me over!

(Everyone laughs except Jerry.)

JERRY: You know, I might be Jewish. They have those Jews in Ethiopia.

JANET: I'm not sure that they have the cheap gene. I mean, they don't have any money to be cheap with.

(Everyone laughs.)

MATTHEW: That's true.

SARAH: You're all racist. I don't know what's wrong with you.

FRED: It's not racist if it's true. *(To Jerry)* I'll replace the hot water heater for seven hundred dollars.

JERRY: Deal.

(Fred takes out a banjo and plays "La Cucaracha." Everyone sings and dances as the lights fade.)

END OF PLAY

LECTURE ON
THE BLUES

PRODUCTION HISTORY

Lecture on the Blues was written to be performed in conjunction
with "Blues for Smoke," an exhibition at the Whitney Museum
of American Art in New York, on April 27 and 28, 2013. It was
directed by Jim Simpson. The cast was:

SECURITY OFFICER	Frank Harts
ACTOR	Jeff Biehl
PLANT I	Cameran Hebb
YOUNG LADY	Tedra Millan
MAN I	Adam Lebowitz-Lockard
MAN 2	Eric Folks
MAN 3	Jimmy Dailey
WOMAN I	Lily Padilla
GUARD	A real Whitney guard

CHARACTERS

SECURITY OFFICER, black
ACTOR, white
PLANT 1, white
YOUNG LADY
MAN 1, white
MAN 2, white
MAN 3
WOMAN 1, white
WOMAN 2, white
GUARD

AUTHOR'S NOTE

Lecture on the Blues was performed at the Whitney Museum in conjunction with their "Blues for Smoke" exhibit. When guests visiting the museum entered the lobby, we had an actor dressed as a Whitney Museum security guard loudly announcing that he had seen a dress rehearsal of the "Lecture," and that it was the most amazing thing he had ever seen. He would also go up to individuals in the lobby and even down to the restaurant in the basement to encourage people to go up and see the "Lecture" if they really wanted to learn something about the blues. So, patrons encountering him fully believed that he was an eccentric security guard at the Whitney. Even some of my friends, who knew that they were coming to see a performance, remarked to me: "Can you believe this guy?! You can't get a better endorsement than that."

The audience was then seated in the video gallery on the fourth floor. It was set up like a lecture hall: a podium at the front and about ten rows of chairs. Most audience members fully expected that they had sat down to watch a normal lecture. There was nothing on the posters outside the lobby or inside the Whitney to suggest that the audience was about to watch a performance. The poster simply said:

Thomas Bradshaw
A Lecture on the Blues
1:30 and 4:00 P.M.

Then a white actor, Jeff Biehl, entered and began his lecture. I was surprised and amused to find out later that some members of the audience actually thought it was me standing up there delivering the lecture. They thought this even though he said his name was Jeff Biehl and that Thomas Bradshaw "claims" that he wrote the script.

I staged six audience plants, who were part of the acting troupe "The Bats" from The Flea Theater. Audience members would interact with the plants, especially Plant 1, trying to get her to stop interrupting the "Lecture."

I thought this play might be hard to read without some context. I hope I've done a sufficient job of setting things up.

—TB

PROLOGUE

A Security Officer stands by the elevator bank on the first floor of the Whitney Museum.

SECURITY OFFICER: Ya'll should really check out Thomas Bradshaw's lecture on the blues in the video gallery on the fourth
floor. That shit is off the hook. I was on the fourth floor,
you know standing guard, and I saw the dress rehearsal.
I'm telling you, if you want to learn somethin' about the
blues GO CHECK THAT OUT! The exhibit itself is
pretty good. But I'm tellin' you, THIS IS GREAT!

*(This is repeated in one fashion or another to many people as
they wait for the elevator.)*

THE LECTURE

In the video gallery a lectern is set up. The audience waits. An Actor, dressed in a tweed jacket, looking very intelligent and knowledge-able, enters with an air of self-importance, and stands behind the lectern. The Security Officer stands in the back of the room.

ACTOR: My name is [actor's name]. You may have seen me in shows such as [name shows that actor has been in]. It is true that I am primarily known as one of the most well-known stage actors in New York City, well, in the country really— but I am also an expert on the blues. I have been listening to the blues most of my life, and been a living embodiment of the blues through my life experience. Now, Thomas Bradshaw will claim that this has been highly scripted, but in truth, much of it is improvised, and what text there is, I pretty much handed to him on a silver platter.

SECURITY OFFICER: I don't remember that from the dress rehearsal.

ACTOR: Can you try to remain quiet?

SECURITY OFFICER: Sorry. Sometimes I accidently speak out loud when I'm talking to myself in my head.

ACTOR: I understand. I have a sister who has Tourette's syndrome. So anyway, when I was a kid there was always music playing in our house. The music of B.B. King, Etta James, Muddy Waters, Ray Charles and Billie Holiday always seemed to fill my ears. Inevitably, I always had one of their songs stuck in my head.

(The Actor laughs to himself.)

Billie Holiday was always reserved for Saturday nights. My mother and father would slow dance in the living room, then go up into their room, lock the door and blast the song "Night and Day."

(He laughs to himself again.)

I was only a child so I didn't realize what was going on. My mother would moan so loud that you could hear it over the music. I thought that she was trying to sing along but couldn't remember the words.

(He closes his eyes and imitates his mother's orgasm sounds:)

Oooh oooh uh yeah baby!

(He laughs a little more.)

That's one of the only clear memories that I have of my mother, slow dancing with my father in the living room, and moaning at the top of her lungs behind a closed door. You see, she died when I was only seven years old. Now here's the only other clear memory that I have of my mother: she picked me up from school one afternoon and we pulled up to a four-way stop sign near my house. As we entered the intersection, a car ran the stop sign to our left and smashed into my mother's side of the car. I wasn't hurt, but I vividly remember her bleeding from her mouth and ear. Her last words were: "I love you. Be a good boy for your father."

(The Actor pauses and wipes his eyes.)

I'm sorry. I don't usually talk about that. I never talk about that in fact, but I feel it's relevant. Moving on, let's talk about the blues.

The blues isn't just about being sad. The blues has primarily been associated with African-American artists, though I would make the argument that some of the best blues artists of all time are white men—but I digress—I'll get to that in a moment.

The blues originated from the pain and frustration that African-Americans had to endure in this country because of slavery, and then the institutionalized racism, referred to as Jim Crow, that followed. I think that LeRoi Jones, now

Amiri Baraka, summed it up best in his play *Dutchman*.

(The Actor glares at the Security Officer, who is now sleeping against the wall.)

Excuse me, am I boring you?

(The Security Officer remains asleep.)

Hey! Security Officer!

(He wakes up.)

Your job is to stay awake and protect the art, not sleep during my lecture.

SECURITY OFFICER: Sorry. I went to the club last night. Was out until four in the morning. Brought this girl home who had a big ol' booty—

ACTOR: We don't need to hear about the details of your evening. Just stay awake and keep your mouth shut. Okay?

SECURITY OFFICER: Okay.

ACTOR *(To the audience)*: I'm sorry about that. Clearly the Whitney isn't all that rigorous in their hiring process for security guards.

So, anyway, in his play *Dutchman*, LeRoi Jones writes—

(The Actor pulls out a copy of Dutchman.*)*

This passage is from page thirty-four in case anyone has a copy and wants to follow along.

(The Actor starts talking in a heavy black dialect, which is nothing like his own. He acts out the text in an animated way. In between the sections of quoted text he goes back to his lecturer persona.)

"I'll rip your lousy breasts off! Let me be who I feel like being. Uncle Tom. Thomas. Whoever. It's none of your business. You don't know anything except what's there for you to see. An act. Lies. Device. Not the pure heart, the pumping black heart. You don't ever know that. And I sit here, in this buttoned-up suit, to keep myself from cutting all your throats. I mean wantonly. You great liberated whore! You fuck some black man, and right away you're an expert on black people. What a lotta shit that is. The only thing you know is that you come if he bangs you hard enough . . ."

Skipping ahead.

"Old bald-headed, four-eyed ofays popping their fingers . . . and don't know yet what they're doing."

And in case you don't know, "ofay" is a derogatory term for a white person, used by black people.

"These ofays say, 'I love Bessie Smith.' And don't even understand that Bessie Smith is saying, 'Kiss my ass, kiss my black unruly ass.' Before love, suffering, desire, anything you can explain, she's saying, and very plainly, 'Kiss my black ass.' And if you don't know that, it's you that's doing the kissing.

"Charlie Parker? Charlie Parker. All the hip white boys scream for Bird. And Bird saying, 'Up your ass, feeble-minded ofay! Up your ass.' And they sit there talking about the tortured genius of Charlie Parker. Bird would've played not a note of music if he just walked up to East Sixty-Seventh Street and killed the first ten white people he saw. Not a note! . . ."

Moving on.

"A whole people of neurotics, struggling to keep from being sane. And the only thing that would cure the neurosis would be your murder. Simple as that. I mean, if I murdered you, then other white people would begin to understand me. You understand? No. I guess not. If Bessie Smith had killed some white people she wouldn't have needed that music. She could have talked very straight and plain about the world. No metaphors. No grunts. No wiggles in the dark of her soul. Just straight two and two are four.

Money. Power. Luxury. Like that. All of them. Crazy niggers turning their backs on sanity. When all it needs is that
simple act. Murder. Just murder! Would make us all sane."

(The Actor closes the book and rests it on the lectern.)

In case you couldn't tell, the character that I was reading is
supposed to be black, and he's talking to a white woman on
a train. It's powerful stuff. Very powerful.

Now, I know what I think that passage means, but I'd
like to know what some of your interpretations are.

(The Actor calls on a white female, Plant 1.)

Yes, young lady.

PLANT 1: First of all, I'd like to say that that reading sounded
racist to me.

ACTOR: What was racist about that?

PLANT 1: I felt offended as a white person, 'cause I felt like I was
being attacked.

ACTOR: I was just quoting a passage from a play—

PLANT 1: I don't care. I felt offended.

ACTOR: Okay, well, maybe you can explain to all of us why you
feel offended.

PLANT 1: That passage is promoting a black revolutionary
agenda which calls for the destruction of the white race.
I also don't appreciate your appropriation of the African-
American idiom. And if you can't understand that, then
you're a retard.

ACTOR: Okay. I can understand that. But just so you know, I'm
not retarded. And I take offense to your use of the word
retard. But I'm gonna let that go. I'd still like you to answer
the question about what you think the passage means.

PLANT 1: Sure. I think the passage is pointing out that African-
Americans have violent impulses that need to be channeled.

SECURITY OFFICER: What did she say? What did you say?

PLANT 1: You heard me.

SECURITY OFFICER: If anyone else makes a comment like that, I'm gonna show all ya'll what a violent impulse really looks like.

PLANT 1 *(Stands and points at the Security Officer)*: I feel threatened. Now I feel threatened!

SECURITY OFFICER: You need to sit your skinny white ass down before I break you in half.

PLANT 1: That offends me! You're offensive! After the show I'm going to find the head of security and get you fired!

SECURITY OFFICER: I am the head of security, bitch!

PLANT 1: I just want you to know, you're behaving like an illiterate, uneducated monkey.

ACTOR: That's enough! That's enough! Obviously this type of material arouses a passionate response. But that's only natural when you finger the core of the American experience, and really get its juices going.

(Plant 1 sits.)

I knew it was a mistake to open this up to the audience. I'm just going to give my interpretation of that passage.

The blues is about the internalization of hundreds of years of unspeakable horrors and trying to create something beautiful out of that. It's an effort on the part of the artists to not be burdened themselves. An effort to cast off the burden of oppression and be free. They find freedom through the music.

(The Actor nods his head solemnly.)

All for our enjoyment. They did it all for our enjoyment.

Now, I'm a white man. I don't really know what it's like to be oppressed. Oh sure, whenever one of my black friends mentions slavery, I bring up the fact that one of my distant ancestors was a serf in England six hundred years ago, but in my heart of hearts I know that the two can't be compared.

When the subject of slavery comes up I also mention that I'm one-sixteenth Cherokee Indian—I mean Native

American. 'Cause we all know what the Native Americans, my ancestors, had to endure.

And of course, as a white man, I now worry about reverse racism when it comes to my child. I have a young child. He's only five, but because of Affirmative Action for minorities, it's possible that my son won't be able to get into a good college. Now don't get me wrong. I'm a liberal. I'm a Democrat. I love Affirmative Action, but I do worry that it will make it harder for a white man to get into college as a result of all the women and minorities that they let in because of Affirmative Action.

But I digress. The blues. All right. Here we go. Now, I'm gonna name who I think are the greatest blues artists of all time.

Number one: Bob Dylan.

Number two: Led Zeppelin.

Number three: well, I'm not gonna name who that is. Instead, I'm going to do something very special for you. I belong to a boutique Christian sect where we channel the dead. We usually only do this during religious ceremonies, but I'm going to make an exception, and do it for you right now. The ghost of the third greatest blues artist is going to take over my body and speak through me. I couldn't get Bob Dylan or Robert Plant to come here today, so we have to settle for this.

(The Actor lights two candles. He then does an elaborate ritualistic dance. He closes his eyes and starts to violently shake all over. He then opens his eyes. He surveys the audience.)

Wow. Small crowd. Really small crowd. Where am I?

SECURITY OFFICER *(Sarcastically)*: The Whitney Museum.

ACTOR: Thanks, brother.

SECURITY OFFICER: Hmph!

ACTOR: I'm Jimi Hendrix. No one has ever channeled me before. It's strange to be back.

(He looks at his hands.)

A little weird to be a white guy, though.

So anyway, since I'm here, I want to set some things straight about the night of my death. I know there's all this talk about me being a part of the original 27 Club. You know, Jim Morrison, Janis Joplin and me. Of course later Kurt Cobain joined. But I'm here to say that I don't belong in that club. I didn't die of a heroin overdose! I wasn't doin' no heroin! I loved drugs, but heroin is no fun! That's no way to party! I loved to do acid. Acid will make you crazy, but it won't kill you.

Now, I was an insomniac. I had a lot of trouble winding down at night, so I would drink some wine and take some sleeping pills. Well, they came out with this new sleeping pill Vesparax that I had never taken before. I had built up a tolerance to barbiturates, so I used to take more than the prescribed dosage of any given pill. The Vesparax label said to only take half a pill, so I took nine. But you know, that's not what killed me. What killed me was drinking a shit-load of wine on an empty stomach. I started to vomit while I was sleeping, and didn't wake up because of all those sleeping pills, and choked to death. Not as sexy as dying of a heroin or cocaine overdose, I know, but it's the truth.

(Notices a Young Lady in the audience.)

Stand up.

YOUNG LADY: Me?

ACTOR: Yeah. You're a real fox, you know that? Stand up. I want to see you.

(She laughs and blushes. Then she stands up. He looks her up and down.)

I wish I had my guitar. I would write you the greatest love song. Turn around.

(She turns around.)

Lord, I miss women. The things I would do to you.
(To the Young Lady) Have you heard any rumors about my escapades when I was alive?
YOUNG LADY: I've heard some things.
ACTOR: Like what?
YOUNG LADY: Like, I heard that you used to have three women in your bed at once.
ACTOR: That's the truth. Sometimes I would have five or six women.
YOUNG LADY: Really?
ACTOR: I'm a man. A real man. I know how do things. You know what I mean?
YOUNG LADY: I think so.
ACTOR: When I'm with my women. I make sure all of them cum, and cum real good, before I experience that sacred release. It is sacred you know. That's one of the things you learn after you die. Sex is really the only religious act. It makes God happy.

(Pause.)

You getting wet?
YOUNG LADY: Uh. Uh. I'm embarrassed to say.
ACTOR: It's okay, baby. I know that you are. Take off your shirt.
YOUNG LADY: No, you take off your shirt.

(He takes his shirt off.)

ACTOR: Come over here. Let Jimi love you, baby.

(The Security Officer starts to rub his penis through his pants. He says things like, "Yeah. That's right. Now this is what I call art."
The Young Lady walks over to the Actor and they start to make out in front of the audience. He takes off her shirt. She stands there in her bra. They start to make out some more and he starts to take off her pants.)

PLANT 1: Stop treating her like she's a sex object, Jimi Hendrix.

YOUNG LADY: But I like what he's doing.

SECURITY OFFICER: Yeah, let them finish!

PLANT 1: It doesn't matter whether you like it or not. You can't let some spirit degrade you publicly like this!

YOUNG LADY: But I don't feel degraded!

PLANT 1: You don't think it's degrading to get fucked in front of a roomful of people?

YOUNG LADY: This is a once in a lifetime opportunity. Jimi picked me over everyone else! You're just jealous!

PLANT 1: It's women like you that set us back. You're the reason why we get paid less than men, and why men in this country still think they can rape women.

SECURITY OFFICER: I'm sick of your feminist bullshit!

(He grabs Plant 1. They struggle.)

PLANT 1: Get off of me, you misogynist! The only reason you're doing this is because you hate women!

(The Security Officer drags her into the hallway as she screams.)

Let me go, you stupid nigger!

SECURITY OFFICER: Now that's offensive!

(He hits her, then drags her just outside of the door and slams the door behind him. He turns to the Actor.)

And I'm sick of you pretending to be Jimi Hendrix.

(He starts to walk toward the Actor.)

ACTOR: Please don't hit me.

SECURITY OFFICER: And stop trying to take advantage of this poor girl.

(To the Young Lady) Put your clothes back on! This isn't a strip club. This is the Whitney Museum. Have some respect for the institution.

(The Security Officer grabs the Young Lady and puts her back in her seat. The Actor falls down. He looks like he's having a seizure. The Actor wakes back up. He stands.)

ACTOR: Where's my shirt! Who took my shirt!?

SECURITY OFFICER: Don't pretend like you don't remember, you pervert. You tried to rape that girl in front of everybody!

YOUNG LADY: It wasn't rape. I liked it! And it wasn't him. It was Jimi!

(Plant 1 reenters the theater with two women and two men.)

MAN 1: Where's the man who said the bad thing about feminism?

PLANT 1: He's right there.

SECURITY OFFICER: She called me a nigger!

MAN 1: We don't care.

MAN 2: After you said that bad thing about feminism we don't care about racism anymore. You insulted our wives, sisters and daughters.

SECURITY OFFICER: You don't care about the fact that black people were slaves for almost four hundred years?

WOMAN 1: I think that's an exaggeration.

SECURITY OFFICER *(Laughs; to Man 2)*: You probably took your wife's last name when you got married.

WOMAN 1: So what if he did? That's what progressive couples are doing these days.

SECURITY OFFICER *(Laughs some more)*: That's the gayest shit I've ever heard. Your husband's a faggot!

MAN 3 *(From the audience)*: That's offensive to gays!

PLANT 1 *(Takes out a switchblade and opens it)*: We're gonna castrate you for saying negative things about our super-progressive politics!

MAN 3: I'll hold him down.

SECURITY OFFICER: I need backup on the fourth floor at the Tom Bradshaw thing. There's an attempted castration in progress.

(They chase the Security Officer out of the video gallery.)

ACTOR: I don't know what the fuck is going on here, but I came here to talk about the blues, and that's exactly what I'm gonna do.

C'mon, let's go up to the gallery for a brief tour. I want to make some observations about the pieces on display up there.

(The audience leaves the video gallery and they are taken up to the "Blues for Smoke" exhibit.)

Okay, everyone. We're gonna take the stairs. If you're too old or something then you can take the elevator. Make sure you've got your bags and cell phones 'cause we're going to wrap things up up there.

(The Actor leads the audience out and up the stairs. He says something like this while he's leading them into the gallery:)

I'm so sorry about that interruption. I thought things were really going well until those rude people and that incompetent security guard had to ruin everything.

Watch your step. We don't want the Whitney to get sued 'cause you don't know how to walk like a normal human being.

(They all enter the gallery.)

So this is interesting. *(Referring to a horizontal sculpture on the floor)* This here looks like it's part of the exhibit but it's really just a part of the natural makeup of the building. You can even walk on it.

(The Actor starts to walk on it. A real Guard stops him.)

GUARD: Actually that is part of the exhibit. Please don't walk on that, sir.

ACTOR: Oh. *(Beat)* So as you can see there are a bunch of piano lids here. I think this is really clever.

(He points to a coal sculpture.)

That's coal.

(He points to a train and train tracks.)

And that's a train. Can anyone guess the meaning?

(He sees if anyone has an answer.)

This is about John Coltrane! Get it!

(He starts to lead people into the next room.)

The piano lids are very heavy. They represent the weight of oppression that blacks and therefore blues artists felt. It's great that Obama's president now because that means that racism doesn't exist in this country anymore. *(Beat)* Now this room is all about abstraction.

(He walks over to a series of grid drawings.)

Can anyone guess what these have to do with the blues?

(He lets some people guess.)

Wrong. The answer is absolutely nothing. It's amazing what passes for art these days.

(He points to a painting on the far wall.)

Now this is my favorite. I'm gonna tell you all about this.

(He walks over to the little sign next to the painting and starts to slowly read. He realizes the sign is about a shopping cart and circle sculpture.)

Oh, my bad. This is about that shopping cart with the circle around it. Uh. Yeah I think that has something to do with homelessness and how it's bad. It's a very conceptual piece.

(He leads the group into the next room.)

(Pointing) Those two works are by white German artists. I have no idea what those pieces are doing in the exhibit. Last time I checked the Germans didn't like the blacks or Jews very much.

(Gestures to a series of suitcases lined up on the floor) These suitcases are a metaphor for the Great Migration. At some point blacks migrated from the South to the North 'cause they were sick of being slaves, and because there were manufacturing jobs in the North. This represents that journey.

(He looks at a painting with different people outside an apartment building.)

This painting is about the experience of blacks in the ghetto. Us white people think of the ghetto as being a bad place, but look at how much fun they're having! That guy right there is a pimp. And probably a drug dealer, too. And that woman is some kind of ho. She represents the concept of the baby mama within black culture.

Oh, wait a minute. Those people at the bottom look like Latinos. I can tell by the fact that those guys are playing the maracas. Latinos love maracas in their music. I'm gonna have to rethink this one.

(The Actor reads a sign about "being a nigger" out loud, then he says:)

I think that one's self-explanatory.

(He leads the group into the next room and points at a coatrack sculpture.)

There's a coatrack if anyone wants to hang their jacket up.

(He looks at a painting on the wall, confused.)

Uh. Hmmm.

(He walks over to a collection of Prospero poems and drawings.)

Now I have a special connection to these pieces. These were drawn by my niece and nephew who are in first and third grade. Aren't they great?

(He points at a painting on the far wall of a chapel room.)

That says Otis Redding right there. I'm gonna tell you a story about him.

(He walks into the chapel and stands behind a lectern.)

Otis Redding was one of the greatest blues musicians of all time. Maybe the fourth greatest blues musician, behind Bob Dylan, Led Zeppelin and Jimi Hendrix. The night before Otis Redding died he recorded a rough cut of his most famous song "Sitting on the Dock of the Bay," then he died in a plane crash the next day. He was twenty-six years old. Can you believe that? He didn't even record all the verses of the song, and still it's a song that we all love. He never got to experience the success and fame that would come from that song. He's like JFK or Abraham Lincoln. The unfulfilled potential of these great men. If that isn't the blues I don't know what is.

(He leads the audience in singing "Sitting on the Dock of the Bay" by Otis Redding.
    Pause. He looks around the chapel.)

All of this red leather. Must be some sort of church where they practice BDSM.

Moving on.

(He leads them into the next room and reads out loud from a couple of posters on the wall.)

Those are self-explanatory.

(He leads them into the next room.)

Now this is a painting of James Baldwin, America's first gay black icon.

And that over there is a portrait of a tree that they used to lynch black people.

And there is a portrait of Thomas Bradshaw. *(Points to a painting of a young musician by Beauford Delaney)* It really looks like Thomas, doesn't it? Pretty fancy to have your portrait in a museum.

(The Actor backs out of the room.)

Well, that concludes my lecture and tour. I hope you learned something about the blues today. I am an official tour guide for the museum and am allowed to give private tours. At your house even. I'd be happy to come back home with you and, uh, continue my lecture in exchange for dinner. We could put on some records and I'll explain the nuances of the music. Anyone want to do that?

(He looks around.)

Okay, well, uh, we also accept tips. I'm gonna pass around this basket, and you can contribute what you think I deserve. That's what they do in the black church, you know. They pass around a basket and put money in it for God.

(The Actor is about to pass the basket around when the Security Officer enters.)

ACTOR: Hey man, did they castrate you?

SECURITY OFFICER: Those fools tried, but I managed to get the knife away from them. I considered castrating *them* but I realized that those two guys had already been castrated by those women, if you know what I mean.

(He laughs. Then he becomes very serious.)

Why are you up here in the gallery?

ACTOR: I'm giving a tour.

SECURITY OFFICER: You're not a docent! You're not allowed to give tours!

ACTOR: Well, I did! And there's nothing you can do to stop me now.

SECURITY OFFICER: I've had it with you! Leave the museum!

ACTOR: No! These people are about to give me money!

SECURITY OFFICER: They're not allowed to give you money! Leave!

ACTOR: No!

(The Security Officer forcibly removes the Actor from the gallery. As he is being dragged out, the Actor yells:)

There's another show at four P.M. Tell your friends!

END

JOB

PRODUCTION HISTORY

Job was commissioned by Soho Repertory Theatre, and was first produced by the Flea Theater (Jim Simpson, Artistic Director; Carol Ostrow, Producing Director) in New York City on September 19, 2012. It was directed by Benjamin H. Kamine; set design was by Aaron Green, costume design was by Ashley Farra, lighting design was by Jonathan Cottle, sound design was by Jeremy S. Bloom; the production stage manager was Courtney Ulrich. The cast was:

JOB	Sean McIntyre
SARAH	Cleo Gray
JOSHUA	Jaspal Binning
MATTHEW	Edgar Eguia
RACHEL	Jennifer Tsay
GOD	Ugo Chukwu
SATAN	Stephen Stout
JESUS	Grant Harrison
DIONYSUS	Eric Folks
ESTHER	Marie-Claire Roussel
JONAS	Adam Lebowitz-Lockard
ANDREW	Bradley Anderson
DAVID	Jimmy Dailey
MIRIAM	Layla Khoshnoudi
JOSEPH	Alex Coelho
JEREMIAH	Ivano Pulito
SON 1	Abraham Makany
SON 2	Chester Poon

MESSENGER	Timothy Craig
NEW WIFE	Nicolle Medina
YOUNG WOMAN	Christin Eve Cato

CHARACTERS

JOB

SARAH, Job's wife

JOSHUA, their son

MATTHEW, their son

RACHEL, their daughter

GOD

SATAN

JESUS

DIONYSIS

ESTHER

JONAS

ANDREW

DAVID

MIRIAM, David's daughter

JOSEPH

JEREMIAH, Joseph's son

SON 1, Job's son

SON 2, Job's son

A MESSENGER

SETTING

Ancient Israel. 537 B.C.

NOTE

It is possible to double-cast the roles so that only eight actors are needed.

SCENE 1

Job is in his house with Rachel, his daughter. He sits in a throne-like chair. Job's sons, Matthew and Joshua, enter with Jonas.

JOSHUA: Father, we caught this man stealing bread from the market.

MATTHEW: The shopkeeper was an old man who couldn't run very fast, so we apprehended him, returned the bread to the shopkeeper, and brought him to you.

JOB: Have my sons given an accurate account of your crime?

JONAS: Yes, sir.

JOB: Why did you steal bread from the market?

JONAS: I don't have any money, sir, and I have two small children to feed, with another on the way.

JOB: What do you do for a living?

JONAS: I'm a shoemaker, sir, but work has been slow lately. I didn't know what else to do.

(Jonas gets on his knees.)

Please pardon me. I beg your forgiveness.

JOB: Stealing is a sin. What's your name?

JONAS: Jonas.

JOB: I don't ever want to hear of you stealing again, Jonas. It defiles the word of God. If you're ever in need of food again, come to my house and you will be provided for.

JONAS: Thank you, Job. You are a wise and righteous man. Thank you for your kindness and generosity.

JOB: Rachel, fetch Jonas five loaves of bread and some cheese.

RACHEL: Yes, Father.

(Rachel leaves and returns with the food. She gives the food to Jonas.)

JONAS: Thank you.

JOB: You may go back to your family now, Jonas. If you're ever caught stealing again, I will cut off both of your hands.

JONAS: Yes, sir. I understand, sir.

(Jonas leaves.)

JOB: Matthew, was there anyone else waiting to see me when you came in?

MATTHEW: Yes, Father. There is a widow who wishes to have a word with you.

JOB: Send her in.

MATTHEW: Yes, Father.

JOB: Joshua, take the oxen out to graze.

JOSHUA: Yes, Father.

(Matthew brings in the widow Esther. She kneels.)

JOB: What is your name?

ESTHER: Esther.

JOB: Why have you come to see me?

ESTHER: My husband died a week ago and his brother came and demanded that I marry him. When I refused he threw my newborn child and me off of our property.

JOB: Why did you refuse him? It is the custom for a widow to marry the brother of the deceased.

ESTHER: This is true. But I am still in mourning for my dead husband, and I feel that it is a sacrilege against his memory to remarry so soon after. They say that you're the wisest and most righteous man in the land, so I came to seek your counsel.

JOB: My heart goes out to you and your child. Even though you have rebuked custom, I don't believe that you have sinned against God. Therefore, you will come and live with us.

MATTHEW: I'll go and make her a bed in the stable.

JOB: You will do no such thing. She is a woman. Not an animal! She will sleep in the house with us. Make up a bed in one of the spare rooms.

MATTHEW: Yes, Father.

ESTHER: Thank you, great Job.

JOB: I'll see you at dinner.

MATTHEW: Follow me.

(Esther exits with Matthew.)

RACHEL: She seems like a righteous woman.

JOB: She does. I want you to make her feel at home. Treat her as if she were your sister.

RACHEL: I will, Father.

(Shouting is heard in the background.)

What's that noise?

(Joshua enters, practically dragging a man. A girl who is badly injured enters with him.)

ANDREW: Let me go! I haven't done anything! Let me go!

JOB: What's the meaning of this, Joshua?

JOSHUA: I was letting the oxen graze in the field when I saw this man in the distance attacking this young girl. He was hitting her in the face and ripping off her clothes.

ANDREW: He's lying! That little slut was coming on to me! She was swaying her butt back and forth and even showed me her breasts. She was begging for it!

JOB: Silence! You'll have your turn. Keep going, Joshua.

JOSHUA: Forgive me, Father. I wasn't fast enough. When I reached them the girl was unconscious and he was raping her. I tried to pull him off but he wouldn't stop. Finally, I knocked him in the back of the head with my cane and the villain ceased attacking the innocent girl. We fought and I knocked him unconscious. Then I threw some water on the girl's face and woke her up, helped her get her clothes back on, and brought them to you.

JOB: Girl, what's your name?

MIRIAM: Miriam, sir.

JOB: How old are you?

MIRIAM: Thirteen.

JOB: Is what my son said true? Did this man attack you?

MIRIAM: Yes, sir.

JOB: What were you doing alone in the field?

MIRIAM: I was letting my father's goats graze.

JOB: You must no longer go into the fields alone. There are too many heathens around. Do you understand?

MIRIAM: Yes.

JOB: Rachel, tend to Miriam. Wash her, give her some clean clothes and let her rest. I'll contact her father.

ANDREW: Can I say something, Master Job?

JOB: Yes.

ANDREW: Your son's not telling the whole story! First of all, I was not raping her. She was beggin' me for it. She likes it rough is all. And after he knocks me off of her he got on top of her and had his way with her, too! So if you're going to punish me then you've got to punish him also!

JOSHUA: This man is a vile liar and a heathen! I would never do such a thing!

ANDREW: You did! You did, too!

JOSHUA: I did not!

ANDREW: Did too! You raped her!

JOB: Silence. I believe you, Joshua. I know that you would never do such a thing. As for you, what is your name?

ANDREW: Andrew, sir.

JOB: As for you, Andrew, not only have you defiled the honor of an innocent girl, you have attempted to slander my son's good name with your false accusations. You have offended God with your gross iniquities, and therefore must be stoned to death.

Matthew! Matthew! Come down here.

(Matthew runs in.)

MATTHEW: Yes, Father.

JOB: You and Joshua must tie this man up in the field. He is to be stoned to death for his iniquity. I am going to summon the girl's father so that he can have the honor of throwing the first stone.

SCENE 2

God is alone, sitting on the floor with his legs crossed. He is deep in meditation, bathed in white light. Satan enters but does not say anything. A full minute passes. Then God opens his eyes and turns around.

GOD: Oh, hi Satan. I didn't know you were there.

SATAN: I didn't want to disturb you.

GOD: You could never disturb me! You know that you're always welcome here.

(They hug.)

How is everything?

SATAN: Very good. And how are things with you?

GOD: Can't complain. *(Shouting)* Jesus! Dionysis! Your uncle's here!

(Jesus and Dionysis enter.)

DIONYSIS: What, Dad?
GOD: Your Uncle Satan is here.
JESUS: Hi, Uncle Satan.

(Jesus hugs Satan.)

SATAN: Hi, Jesus.
DIONYSIS: How are you?

(Dionysis hugs Satan.)

SATAN: Good. Good. It's good to see you.
DIONYSIS: You, too.
GOD: Jesus, why don't you go get us some wine.
JESUS: Yes, Father.

(Jesus exits and comes back with wine and some wineglasses. Jesus hands out the wineglasses and pours everyone wine.)

GOD: Let's not all stand here like a bunch of idiots! Let's sit.

(They all sit.)

So, Satan, what have you been up to?
SATAN: Oh you know, walking to and fro, to and fro, back and forth along the earth.
GOD: How is everything down there?
SATAN: Oh you know, the usual.
GOD *(Laughing)*: I know how things are when you're there. Death, destruction, lying, cheating and stealing!

(Everyone laughs.)

DIONYSIS: This wine tastes a little bitter, doesn't it?
JESUS: Yes, it does.

DIONYSIS: I think maybe it's turned into vinegar.

GOD: Dionysis is right. Jesus, fetch us another bottle. And get us some new glasses will you.

JESUS: I got the bottle last time. Why can't Dionysis do it?

DIONYSIS: You wouldn't have wine if it weren't for me!

(Jesus and Dionysis are about to fight.)

GOD: Stop it, boys! Jesus is right, you go get the bottle, Dionysis.

DIONYSIS: Yes, Father.

(Dionysis exits and then comes back with a new bottle of wine and some glasses. He fills everyone's cup except Jesus'.)

Fill your own.

(Jesus fills his own cup.)

GOD: You think that they would have outgrown that by now.

SATAN: Give them another couple of thousand years. I'm sure they'll grow out of it.

GOD: You're right. It took us, what, half a million years to outgrow that sort of thing?!

(They laugh.)

SATAN: It wasn't quite that long.

GOD: So anyway, did you see my servant Job while you were down there on earth?

SATAN: Yes, in fact, I did.

GOD: He's incorruptible, isn't he?

SATAN: I wouldn't say that.

GOD: You mean to tell me that you've seen Job engaging in iniquity?

SATAN: No, I haven't seen Job engage in a single sinful act. However, how do you expect a person to act when you've given them everything? He has two sons and one daughter who are in excellent health. You've given him seven thousand sheep, three thousand camels, five hundred yoke of oxen, and you've made him the richest and greatest man in the east!

GOD: So what? Isn't that what I promised man? That if you fear God and shun evil then you shall be rewarded? He fears me and shuns evil, so I reward him.

SATAN: Yes, but wouldn't you agree that it is much easier for a man to be righteous when things are going well for him than when things are not going well for him.

GOD: I suppose that's true.

SATAN: All I'm saying is that if Job faced some adversity I doubt that he would continue to be the righteous man that he is today. As a matter of fact, I guarantee that he'll curse you to your face if his material possessions are taken away.

GOD: What do you think about this, Jesus?

JESUS: Uncle Satan has a point.

GOD: Dionysis?

DIONYSIS: I agree with Jesus.

GOD: Okay, Satan. I give you permission to introduce adversity, hardship and calamity into Job's life. All that he has is in your power, only do not cause him any physical harm.

SATAN: Your wish is my command, dear brother. I'll be back soon to report on our wager. Good-bye, Jesus.

(Jesus and Satan hug.)

Good-bye, Dionysis.

(Dionysis and Satan hug.)

Good-bye, dear brother.

(God and Satan hug.)

SCENE 3

Job; his children; Miriam; her father, David; and Job's wife, Sarah, are celebrating and drinking wine after stoning Andrew to death. Everyone is dancing. Job clinks his glass for a toast.

JOB: The villain is dead!
ALL: The villain is dead!
JOB: Praise God!
ALL: Praise God!
JOB: Let us thank the Almighty for bringing justice to Miriam and her father, and for punishing the wickedness of the sinful Andrew.
ALL: Here here!

(Everyone drinks.)

JOB: Let us make a burnt offering to the God of Israel for the fairness and justice that he bestows.
ALL: Here here!
JOB: Rachel, go fetch a healthy lamb for us to slaughter.
RACHEL: Yes, Father.

(She leaves. She returns a moment later with a lamb.)

JOB: Let's go outside and make a bonfire!
ALL: Yaaaay!

(Everyone exits, dancing.
Matthew and Rachel reenter with Satan following. Joshua and Rachel are laughing.)

RACHEL: What did you want to talk to me about?
JOSHUA: As your older brother I wanted to discuss your chastity.
RACHEL *(Laughing)*: You're drunk. I'm going back outside.

(She tries to leave but he grabs her arm.)

JOSHUA: I'm serious, Rachel. Have you been chaste?
RACHEL: Of course I've been chaste. Now let me go.

(She tries to leave but he grabs her again.)

JOSHUA: There have been rumors that you offered up your chastity to a shepherd named Ezekiel.
RACHEL: That's nonsense, Joshua! You're drunk. You should go to sleep.

(She tries to leave but Joshua grabs her and kisses her. She pushes him away.)

What are you doing?!

(He kisses her again and she pushes him away forcefully.)

Stop, Joshua! I'll tell Father! You're acting possessed!
JOSHUA *(Distraught)*: *You* must have been possessed when you destroyed this family's honor by ruining your chastity.

(He strangles her to death. Then he lifts up her dress and his robe and starts to have sex with her corpse. Satan watches silently.)

You should have respected your chaste treasure. You should have respected your chaste treasure!

(He has an orgasm. Matthew enters.)

MATTHEW *(Horrified)*: What's going on here?
JOSHUA: I— I— Well—
MATTHEW: Rachel! What's the meaning of this? Rachel?

(He realizes that she's dead.)

Oh, Rachel. My poor sister.
(To Joshua) What have you done?!

(Matthew grabs a ceramic water jug and hits Joshua in the
face with it. It shatters everywhere. Joshua falls to the ground.
   Matthew then breaks a broomstick over his leg. He takes the
top of the broom and sodomizes Joshua with it. He pushes the
broomstick up as far as he can. Joshua makes sounds of extreme
pain.)

How does it feel, Joshua?! How do you like it?! How do you
like it?!

(Job enters with the crowd. Everyone gasps. Then they are all
silent and in shock.
   Matthew stops when he sees them. He is still for a moment.
Then he takes out his knife and slits his brother's throat. Job
grabs his chest and gasps. Matthew runs out of the room.
Everyone is in shock.)

SCENE 4

Job is sitting alone in his throne-like chair. Sarah sits silently by his
side. Job has a stone look on his face. A messenger enters.

JOB: What news do you have for me?
MESSENGER: Your son, Matthew, was found dead in the field.
   He took his own life.

(Pause.)

JOB: Thank you.

(The messenger exits. Job's grief is internalized. He's beyond
shock.)

(Softly) Oh God, why hast thou forsaken me? Why hast thou forsaken me? I have been a righteous and faithful servant who has risen above all iniquity and obeyed your will. Why hast thou forsaken me?

SARAH: How can you still have faith in God after what's happened?

JOB: You must not lose faith, Sarah. God is good and God loves us. I know he has a plan.

SARAH: If he does have a plan then it's an evil plan. Either God doesn't exist or he's a malicious God.

JOB: Don't blasphemy God's name, Sarah. We must have complete trust and faith in him and more will be revealed. Look at all he's given to us.

SARAH: Look at all he's taken away!

JOB: We can't get too attached to earthly possessions, Sarah.

SARAH: Are you saying that our children were nothing but earthly possessions?

(Pause.)

God made a contract with the righteous. It said that if we followed his word than we would be rewarded.

JOB: We have been rewarded. We must accept God's will for us no matter what that is.

SARAH: What about our children? Why did he take away our children?

JOB: Maybe our children were being punished for their sins. Have you thought about that? Maybe our children were being punished for *their* iniquity.

SARAH: I don't accept that. I think that you're an idiot!

JOB: God sees all, Sarah. God is a just God. Our children must have deserved the punishment that God inflicted.

SARAH: You're a goddamn idiot! Our children were innocent! I know they were!

JOB: The Lord giveth, and the Lord taketh away. Blessed be the name of the Lord.

SARAH: Fuck you and fuck God!

JOB: I can't love a woman who curses God.

SARAH: And I can't be with a man who refuses to defend our children.

(Pause.)

Fuck God. Do you hear me? Fuck God. Fuck God.

JOB *(Almost in a whisper)*: Stop saying that.

SARAH *(Moving closer to him, threatening)*: Why don't you make God stop me? Huh? Why doesn't *your* God stop me if he's so powerful?

FUCK YOUR GOD!

JOB *(Cowering and covering his ears)*: You're going to Hell!

SARAH: I'd rather be in Hell!

(She spits on Job and exits.
Job gets on his knees and reaches out to God.)

JOB: Why hast thou forsaken me?

(Pause.)

May the day perish on which I was born,
And the night in which it was said,
"A male child is conceived"
May that day be darkness;
May God above not seek it,
Nor the light shine upon it.
May darkness and the shadow of death claim it;
May a cloud settle on it;
May the blackness of the day terrify it,
As for that night, may darkness seize it;
May it not rejoice among the days of the year,
May it not come into the number of the months.
Oh, may that night be barren.
May the stars of its morning be dark;
May it look for light, but have none,
And not see the dawning of the day;

Because it did not shut up the doors of my mother's womb,
Nor hide sorrow from my eyes.
Or why was I not hidden like a stillborn child,
Like infants who never saw the light?
There the wicked cease from troubling,
And the weary are at rest.
Why is light given to him who is in misery,
And life to the bitter of soul,
Who long for death, but it does not come,
And search for it more than hidden treasures
And are glad when they can find the grave
Why is light given to a man whose way is hidden,
And whom God has hedged in?
For my sighing comes before I eat,
And my groanings pour out like water,
For the thing I greatly feared has come upon me,
And what I dreaded has happened to me.
I am not at ease, nor am I quiet;
I have no rest, for trouble comes.
As long as my breath is in me,
And the breath of God in my nostrils,
My lips will not speak wickedness,
Nor my tongue utter deceit.

(Pause.)

I will go sacrifice another lamb to honor you and glorify
your name.

SCENE 5

Jesus and Dionysis are alone.

DIONYSIS: Why are they always sacrificing lambs? Why do they
think we like that?
JESUS: Because of something Father said a long time ago.

DIONYSIS: Does Father really like it when they slaughter lambs?

JESUS: He loves it! You've never noticed how he gets? He does that weird dance.

(Jesus imitates the dance.)

DIONYSIS: Oooh, that's why he's always dancing like that.

JESUS: I hope Father sends me to earth one day so that everyone will praise me and burn animals in my name.

DIONYSIS: I'd like that, too. What would you do if he sent you to earth?

JESUS: I'd perform magic tricks like walking on water and I'd rise from the dead. What would you do?

DIONYSIS: I'd show everyone how awesome getting drunk is! I'd make them drink wine by the gallon, and I'd make women run around naked in the woods and do perverted things.

JESUS: What kinds of perverted things?

DIONYSIS: Anal sex, blowjobs and all sorts of lesbian activity.

JESUS: You're disgusting!

DIONYSIS: You're a show-off!

JESUS: I'm a show-off?! You tell everyone you meet about how you invented wine!

DIONYSIS: I did invent it! If you had something to be proud of you'd brag about it, too!

JESUS: You act like you invented alcohol! We were all getting drunk long before you invented wine! Whiskey has four times the alcohol content of your watered-down shit!

DIONYSIS: Father likes it!

JESUS: Father just drinks it to humor you!

(Satan enters.)

SATAN: Hello, boys.

DIONYSIS AND JESUS: Hi, Uncle Satan.

SATAN: Is your father around?

DIONYSIS: Yeah.

JESUS *(Yelling off)*: Dad! Dad!

GOD *(From off)*: What?

DIONYSIS: Uncle Satan is here to see you.

(God enters doing his burnt-offering dance.)

SATAN: Why are you doing that dance?

GOD: Job just honored me with a burnt offering!

SATAN: And it makes you that happy?

GOD: Don't think I didn't see you dancing after that little mur-
der/incest situation happened yesterday.

SATAN: Touché.

DIONYSIS: Yeah, we all saw you dancing.

JESUS: It was pretty funny.

(Jesus imitates Satan's dance. They all laugh.)

SATAN: Can we get some wine in here?

DIONYSIS *(Aside, to Jesus)*: See, Uncle Satan likes it, too. And
when I go to earth, the humans are going to love me for it!
(To everyone) I'll go get some.

GOD: Excellent.

(Pause.)

So, hardship, calamity and unspeakable horrors have befallen
my servant Job, and yet he remains righteous and faithful
and refuses to curse my name.

SATAN: This is true.

GOD: Hah! I win!

SATAN: Well, I don't know if you win just yet.

GOD: What do you mean?

SATAN: Things could still be a lot worse for Job.

GOD: His children were sodomized and murdered in front of
him!

SATAN: Yes, but that's all external. Destroy a person's physical
well-being, and their true colors will shine through.

GOD: Boys, what do you think?

JESUS: I think that Uncle Satan has a point.

DIONYSIS: I agree.

SATAN: I guarantee that he'll curse your name if his health is destroyed.

GOD: I guarantee that he won't.

(Pause.)

You may destroy his health, only don't kill him.

SATAN: Understood.

GOD: Good-bye, brother.

(Satan and God hug.)

SATAN: Good-bye.

(Pause.)

Good-bye, boys.

JESUS AND DIONYSIS: Good-bye, Uncle Satan.

(They both hug Satan at the same time.)

SCENE 6

Joseph and his son, Jeremiah, are alone at their house. Joseph has one hand. The other has been chopped off.

JOSEPH: Have you heard about Job?

JEREMIAH: No. What happened?

JOSEPH: His children murdered each other and his wife left him.

JEREMIAH: They murdered each other?

JOSEPH: Yeah, apparently Joseph murdered Rachel and then raped her.

JEREMIAH: He had sex with her after she was dead?

JOSEPH: Yup.

JEREMIAH: That's sick. I'm not sure that constitutes rape though.
JOSEPH *(Laughing)*: Yeah. I guess she didn't fight back.

(They laugh some more.)

And then Matthew caught Joshua in the act, stuck a broom-
stick in his ass, and slit his throat.
JEREMIAH: Hah! What goes around comes around.
JOSEPH: Indeed. You reap just what you sow.

(Pause.)

That's what that motherfucker gets! Chopping off my hand
for trying to feed my family!
JEREMIAH: Clearly God's punishing Job for his sins.
JOSEPH: Do you see what this means?
JEREMIAH: What?
JOSEPH: His children are dead so he no longer has any protec-
tion. He's all alone.
JEREMIAH: What do you plan to do?
JOSEPH: I was thinking that we could throw a bucket of scalding
hot water in his face and then gouge out his eyes.
JEREMIAH: That's sounds like a just punishment for his sins.
The Lord sayeth: "An eye for an eye. A tooth for a tooth."
JOSEPH: Indeed. This is God's will.

SCENE 7

*Job is sitting on his throne all alone looking miserable. After a few
moments, Joseph and Jeremiah enter carrying a large ceramic vase,
which contains scalding hot water.*

JOB: Who goes there?
JOSEPH: It is I, Joseph.
JEREMIAH: And his son, Jeremiah.
JOB: Why have you come to see me?

JOSEPH: We heard about your misfortune and have come to wash your feet.

JEREMIAH: You see, we are thankful for your infinite justice, great Job. For only chopping off one of my father's hands when he clearly deserved to have both chopped off.

JOB: You are a clear-headed and insightful young man. I predict that fortune will shine upon you.

JOSEPH: He's a good lad. Take off your sandals so we can get started.

(Job leans over to take off his sandals and Jeremiah throws the scalding hot water in Job's face. Job screams.)

JOB: My face! My face!

(Job falls to the floor and Joseph and Jeremiah each gouge out one of his eyes. Job lets out a bloodcurdling scream. Satan watches from the side. He does a dance.)

JOSEPH: This is for *your* iniquity, Job! God is punishing you for your hubris and pride!

JEREMIAH: *Your* children were killed because of *their* iniquity. We have one more present for you.

JOB: No more. Please. Have mercy on me. Enough. Please.

JOSEPH: When have you ever shown mercy to anyone?

JOB: I— I—only chopped off one of your hands instead of both. You said so yourself.

JOSEPH: Do you really think anyone would be grateful because you only chopped off one of their hands?! You chopped off my hand for trying to feed my family, and now I can't work anymore! Now I can't work anymore! I beg for food and my son, Jeremiah, works as a farmhand. Do you know how humiliating that is! How humiliating it is not to be able to support your family? No. No. We will not have mercy on you.

(Pause.)

Lift up his robe, Jeremiah.

(Jeremiah lifts up Job's robe. He's naked underneath.)

JOB: What are you doing?!

JOSEPH: I would do this myself but I ONLY HAVE ONE HAND! Castrate the sinner Job for *his* iniquity.

(Jeremiah takes out his knife.)

JOB: Please! Please! God help me!

(Jeremiah and Joseph both laugh.)

JOSEPH: He thinks God is going to help him. God didn't save me from you, and he's not going to save you from me.

(Jeremiah castrates Job. He screams.)

I'm going to feed you to my dog. She likes meat.

(Jeremiah and Joseph laugh.)

I'm glad we finally got you off that throne.

JEREMIAH: What did you think? That you were a king?

(They laugh some more as they casually walk off, leaving Job in a pool of his own blood.)

SCENE 8

Job is back on his throne. Esther is wrapping bandages around his eyes. Blood is seeping through.

ESTHER: Poor, poor Job.

(She kisses his forehead.)

Who did this to you?

JOB: Sinners.

ESTHER: Rest assured. God will punish them.

JOB: God has turned against me even though I am righteous.

ESTHER: God would never turn against anyone.

(Pause.)

Do you know what today is, Job?

JOB: I've lost track of time.

ESTHER: It's the first day of Passover!

JOB: I can't believe that I forgot!

ESTHER: Eat some matzo. It'll make you feel better.

JOB: I'd forgotten about Passover because of my grief. How could I have forgotten about the exodus of our people from Egypt?

ESTHER: God will forgive you.

(She hands him some matzo and he eats. Miriam and her father, David, enter.)

Hello, Miriam. Hello, David. What brings you here?

DAVID: We wanted to comfort our dear friend Job.

MIRIAM: And celebrate the first day of Passover with him since he no longer has any family.

ESTHER: You are truly compassionate and God-fearing people.

JOB: Esther? Who's there?

DAVID: It is I, David.

MIRIAM: And his daughter Miriam.

DAVID: We've come to celebrate "The Festival of Unleavened Bread" with you. How are you, brother?

JOB: My soul is weary. Let us go to the Second Temple and begin the Korban Pesach.

DAVID: Are you sure that you're well enough to go to the temple?

JOB: It's just up the road.

MIRIAM: I'll lead him, Father.

JOB: Esther, will you go and fetch a wild goat for the sacrifice?

(Esther exits.)

DAVID: I've brought a bucket of lamb's blood to put on your lintels and door posts.

(David starts to smear the lamb's blood on Job's door.)

JOB: You're a good friend.

(Pause.)

After Cyrus allowed us to return from the Babylonian captivity we made a burnt offering to the God of Israel of twelve bulls, ninety-six rams, seventy-seven lambs, and twelve male goats as a sin offering. That was a great day. I'm tempted to sacrifice the rest of my animals as an offering to God. Maybe then he'll smile upon me.

DAVID: That's not a bad idea.

MIRIAM: I didn't know that you were one of those who returned from Babylon.

JOB: Indeed I was. When I returned I helped to build the second temple with my own hands. Do you know what happened to the first temple?

MIRIAM: That's an easy question. It was destroyed by the Babylonians!

JOB: That's right!

DAVID: That was a pretty easy question. Ask her something more difficult.

JOB: All right. Who built the first temple?

MIRIAM: King Solomon.

JOB: Good! And what did the first temple replace?

MIRIAM *(Thinking)*: I don't know.

DAVID: C'mon Miriam, we were talking about this last week.

(She thinks.)

MIRIAM: I can't remember.

JOB: Hah! I finally got you! The first temple replaced the Tabernacle of Moses, and the Tabernacles of Shiloh, Nov and Givon, as the central focus of the Jewish faith.

MIRIAM: Now I remember!

(Esther returns empty-handed.)

ESTHER: I have terrible news.
JOB: What's happened?
ESTHER: Your whole flock is gone?
JOB: My whole flock? I had seven thousand sheep, three thousand camels, five hundred donkeys, three hundred lambs, and one hundred wild goats. They're all gone?
ESTHER: They're all gone.
JOB: What could have happened to them?
ESTHER: I fear that they've been stolen since your children are gone and can no longer look after them.
JOB: I have nothing.
DAVID: Miriam, go fetch one of our wild goats for the Korban Pesach.
MIRIAM: Yes, Father.

(Miriam exits.)

DAVID *(To Job)*: Let me help you up.

(He helps Job out of his throne.)

JOB: I need a staff.

(Esther gets a staff and hands it to him.)

Thank you.

(Miriam returns.)

MIRIAM: Are we ready?
JOB: We're ready.

SCENE 9

The next day. David, Miriam, Esther and Job are at Job's house.

JOB:

When I lie down, I say, "When shall I arise and the night
  be ended?"
For I have had my fill of tossing till dawn,
My flesh is cracked and breaks out afresh.
My days are swifter than a weaver's shuttle.
And are spent without hope.
Oh, remember that my life is a breath!
My eye will never again see good.
The eye of him who sees me will see me no more;
While your eyes are on me, I shall no longer be.
As the cloud disappears and vanishes away,
So he who goes down to the grave does not come up.
He shall never return to his house,
Nor shall his place know him anymore.
Am I a sea or a sea serpent,
That you set a guard over me?
When I say, "My bed will comfort me,
My couch will ease my complaint,"
Then you scare me with dreams
And terrify me with visions,
So that my soul chooses strangling
And death rather than my body.
I loathe my life;
I would not live forever.
Let me alone,
For my days are but a breath.
What is man, that you should exalt him,
That you should set your heart on him,
That you should visit him every morning,
And test him every moment?

Will you not look away from me, and let me alone till
    I swallow my saliva?
Have I sinned?
What have I done to you, O watcher of men?
Why have you set me as your target,
So that I am a burden to myself?
Why then do you not pardon my transgression,
And take away my iniquity?
For now I lie down in the dust,
And you will seek me diligently,
But I will no longer be.

DAVID: Are you finished?

JOB: What?

DAVID: How long can you go on like this? You're being a real
windbag.

JOB: What? Are you saying that I don't have a right to cry out
to God and seek an answer for the injustice and suffering
that I've endured?

DAVID: I'm saying that maybe you haven't suffered any injustice.

JOB: I am a righteous man. Get out of my house if you don't
believe me.

ESTHER: I agree with David.

JOB: You, too?

ESTHER: Your sons sinned against God and he has punished
them for their iniquity. God wouldn't have caused so much
sorrow and heartbreak in your life without just cause. God
does not punish without reason. You should evaluate your
life and change your ways.

JOB: What would all of you have me do?

MIRIAM: Repent.

JOB: Who's that?

MIRIAM: Miriam.

JOB: You're against me, too?

MIRIAM: I'm not against you, but I know that God is just. You
must repent and God will restore your former life.

JOB: I will not repent. I have nothing to repent for. I am not a sinner.

My soul loathes my life;
I will speak in the bitterness of my soul.
I will say to God, "Do not condemn me;
Show me why you contend with me.
Does it seem good to you that you should oppress,
That you should despise the work of your hands,
And smile on the counsel of the wicked?"

DAVID: I can't take this anymore.
JOB: Then leave!
DAVID: I will! Is there any more of that goat left?
ESTHER: Yes, I'm starving.
MIRIAM: Me, too!
DAVID: Let's go back home and eat.
JOB: I'm hungry, too.
DAVID: God will feed you.

(Miriam, David and Esther exit with the rest of the goat. Pause. Job goes back to talking to God.)

JOB:
Why then have you brought me out of the womb?
Oh that I had perished and no eye seen me!
I would have been as though I had not been.
I would have been carried from the womb to the grave.

(Joseph and Jeremiah quietly enter and walk over to Job. They tip his throne so that he falls to the floor helpless. They laugh and walk off. Job continues his speech.)

Are not my days few?
Cease! Leave me alone, that I may take a little comfort,
Before I go to the place from which I shall not return,
To the land of darkness and the shadow of death,

A land as dark as darkness itself,
As the shadow of death, without any order,
Where even the light is like darkness.

SCENE 10

Jesus, Dionysis and God are alone.

DIONYSIS: Who farted?
JESUS: It's coming from your direction.
DIONYSIS: I didn't fart. I think Dad farted. His fart is flowing
    past me to you.
GOD: I didn't fart.
DIONYSIS: C'mon, Dad.
GOD: I didn't. I really didn't. I would admit it if I did.
JESUS: I think you farted, Dionysis. Whoever smelt it dealt it.
DIONYSIS: It wasn't me!
JESUS: Yes it was!

(Dionysis stands up, ready to fight.)

DIONYSIS: No it wasn't!

(Jesus stands, also ready to fight.)

JESUS: Yes it was! You farted!

(Jesus lunges at Dionysis and they struggle. God breaks it up.)

GOD: Stop it, you two. I mean it. You've got to start acting like
    adults.

(Pause. Job's words are audible for a moment.)

JOB *(Offstage)*:
    I put on righteousness, and it clothed me;
    My justice was like a robe and a turban.

GOD: Do you hear that?

JOB *(Offstage)*:
> And I was feet to the lame.
> I was a father to the poor,
> And I searched out the case that I did not know.

(Job's words fade out.)

GOD: He's whining an awful lot isn't he?

DIONYSIS: He has been whining an awful lot. It's been keeping me up at night listening to the dreadful sound of his voice.

JESUS: Maybe we should put an end to his suffering. After all, he hasn't done anything wrong.

GOD: You're right. Jesus, will you fetch Satan for me?

JESUS: Yes, Father. Wait. Where is he?

GOD: He's over there making that volcano erupt.

JESUS: Oh, I see him.

(Jesus exits.)

GOD: I'm thinking about sending you to earth, you know.

DIONYSIS: Really?! Where?

GOD: I'm thinking about sending you to Greece.

DIONYSIS: The Greeks are awesome!

GOD: Yes, I was also thinking that—

(Satan enters with Jesus.)

SATAN: What do you want? I was busy.

GOD: I wanted to talk to you about Job.

SATAN: Why do you only hang out with Dionysis and Jesus? Where are all of your other sons?

GOD: Dionysis and Jesus are my favorites. My other sons always make a mess of my private quarters when I let them in. You're more than welcome to visit with them. They're right through that door.

SATAN: Not now. Maybe later.

GOD: So anyway, I want to talk to you about my servant Job.

SATAN: What about him?

GOD: Though you have slaughtered his family, scalded his face and gouged out his eyes, he refuses to curse my name. He holds fast to his faith. Do you agree?

SATAN: I agree. He has refused to curse your name. I was wrong.

GOD: He reminds me of my servant Abraham, who was willing to sacrifice his only son to prove his faith.

SATAN: They *are* very alike. What do I owe you?

GOD: It was a gentleman's wager. Don't worry about it. It takes a real man to admit when he's wrong. I'm proud of you, Satan.

SATAN: And I'm proud of you.

GOD: I hope that Jesus and Dionysis get along as well as we do when they get old.

(Job's voice can again be heard.)

JOB *(Offstage)*:
But now they mock at me, men younger than I,
Whose fathers I disdained to put with the dogs of my
    flock.
Indeed, what profit is the strength of their hands to me?
And now I am their taunting song,
Yes I am their byword.
They abhor me, they keep far from me;
They do not hesitate to spit in my face.

(Job's voice fades out.)

GOD: Oh, I can't take any more of that whining! Dionysis, get me my mask!

DIONYSIS: What for?

GOD: I'm going to go to earth to talk to Job.

(Dionysis gets God's mask and God puts it on. The mask should be a black traditional theater mask. It should be ominous and

*frightening. God's voice should be projected over a loudspeaker
when he talks to Job directly. It should reverberate through the
whole theater.)*

Thank you. See you later.

(He exits Heaven and reveals himself to Job.)

Who is this who darkens counsel
By words without knowledge?
Now prepare yourself like a man;
I will question you and you shall answer me.
Where were you when I laid the foundations of the earth?
Tell me, if you have understanding.
Who determined its measurements?
Surely you know!
Or who laid its cornerstone,
When the morning stars sang together,
And all the sons of God shouted for joy?
Or who shut in the sea with doors,
When it burst forth and issued from the womb;
When I made the clouds its garment,
And thick darkness its swaddling band;
When I fixed my limit for it,
And set bars and doors;
When I said,
"This far you may come, but no farther,
And here your proud waves must stop!"
Have you commanded the morning since your days began,
And caused the dawn to know its place.
That it might take hold of the ends of the earth,
And the wicked shaken out of it?
Have you entered the springs of the sea?
Or have you walked in search of the depths?
Have the gates of death been revealed to you?
Have you comprehended the breadth of the earth?
Tell *me*, if you know all this.

Where is the way to the dwelling of light?
And darkness, where is its place.
That you may take it to its territory,
That you may know the paths to its home?
Have you entered the treasury of the snow,
Or have you seen the treasury of hail,
Which I have reserved for the time of trouble,
For the day of battle and war?
By what way is light diffused,
Or the east wind scattered over the earth?
Who has divided a channel for the overflowing water,
Or a path for the thunderbolt,
To cause it to rain on a land where there is no one,
A wilderness in which there is no man;
To satisfy the desolate waste,
And cause to spring forth the growth of tender grass?
Can you lift up your voice to the clouds,
That an abundance of water may cover you?
Can you send out lightnings, that they may go,
And say to you, "Here we are!"
Shall the one who contends with the Almighty correct
    Him?
He who rebukes God, let him answer it.

JOB:

    Behold, I am vile;
    What shall I answer You?
    I lay my hand over my mouth.
    Once I have spoken, but I will not answer;
    Yes, twice, but I will proceed no further.

GOD:

    Now prepare yourself like a man;
    I will question you, and you shall answer me!
    Would you indeed annul my judgment?
    Would you condemn me that you may be justified?
    Have you an arm like God?

Or can you thunder with a voice like His?
Then adorn yourself with majesty and splendor,
And array yourself with glory and beauty.
Disperse the rage of your wrath;
Look on everyone who is proud, and humble him.
Look on everyone who is proud, and bring him low;
Tread down the wicked in their place.
Hide them in the dust together,
Bind their faces in hidden darkness.
Then I will also confess to you
That your own right hand can save you.
Who then is able to stand against me?
Who has preceded me, that I should pay him?
Everything under Heaven is mine.

JOB:

I know that You can do everything.
And that no purpose of Yours can be withheld from You.
You asked, "Who is this who hides counsel without
    knowledge?"
Therefore I have uttered what I did not understand,
Things too wonderful for me, which I did not know.
Listen, please, and let me speak;
You said, "I will question you, and you shall answer me."
I have heard of You by the hearing of the ear,
But now my eyes see You.
Therefore I abhor myself,
And repent in dust and ashes.

GOD:

You speak words of wisdom.
Open your eyes, Job, your sight has been restored!
Do you feel the growth in your groin? Your manhood has
    been given new life!

(Job opens his eyes and can see again.)

JOB: Thank you, mighty Lord.

GOD: David!

(David, Miriam and Esther all run in.)

DAVID: Yes, Lord!

GOD: My wrath is aroused against you and your two friends, for you have not spoken of me what is right, as my servant Job has.

DAVID: How were we supposed to know?

GOD: Silence!

Now therefore, take for yourselves seven bulls and seven rams, go to my servant Job, and offer up for yourselves a burnt offering; and my servant Job shall pray for you. For I will accept him, lest I deal with you according to your folly; because you have not spoken of me what is right, as my servant Job has.

DAVID: Yes, Lord.

(David, Miriam and Esther exit.
God returns to Heaven and takes off his mask.)

GOD: How was that?

SATAN: You were in rare form today.

JESUS: I haven't seen you like that since you gave Moses the Ten Commandments.

DIONYSIS: What are you going to do with him now?

GOD: I'm going to send him a new wife, and they'll have six children, twice as many as he had before. He's also going to receive far more wealth. I'm going to give him fourteen thousand sheep, six thousand camels, one thousand yoke of oxen and one thousand female donkeys.

SATAN: Why do all that?

GOD: To make Job an example to all men. To show that if you are righteous and have faith in me, then you will be rewarded.

JESUS: How long will you let him live?

GOD: One hundred and forty more years. He will see his children and grandchildren prosper for four generations. He will die old and full of days. That will be his reward for the trials that he has endured.

SCENE 11

Job is sitting on his throne in expensive and elaborate robes. His new wife is next to him. Two of his sons enter with Jonas, who is struggling.

JOB: What has this man done?

SON 1: We caught him stealing a cow from our flock.

JONAS: Yes, master Job, it is true. But I only did it because you told me that if I was ever in need then I should come to you.

JOB: I remember you.

SON 2: He ran as fast as he could when he saw us.

JOB: Why would you run if you didn't think that you were doing anything wrong?

JONAS: I was scared.

JOB: I told you to come to me if you were ever in need, not to steal animals from my flock!

JONAS: But you have so much.

JOB: That's not the point. You have acted against God's will, therefore you will be punished. I told you that if I ever caught you stealing again then I would cut off both of your hands.

JONAS: Please, please, have mercy on me. I have a family to feed!

JOB: Get my butcher knife.

(Son 1 leaves and comes back with a butcher knife.)

Thank you. Tie his hands together and hold him down.

(They tie his hands and hold them down over a table.)

JONAS: Please, please Job. Don't do this. I have a family to support.

JOB: This is God's will.

(Job lifts up the butcher knife and as he swings the knife down to cut off Jonas's hands the lights cut to black.)

END OF PLAY

SOUTHERN PROMISES

A SLAVE'S ROAD TO FREEDOM

Inspired by
The Great Escapes: Four Slave Narratives

PRODUCTION HISTORY

Southern Promises was developed through IRT Theater's Artist in Residence Program. The world premiere of *Southern Promises* was produced at Performance Space 122 (Vallejo Gantner, Artistic Director) in New York on September 7, 2008, with support from the Immediate Theatre Company and Queens Theatre in the Park as part of B.O.B. (PS 122's Best of Boroughs Program Commission). It was directed by Jose Zayas; set design was by Ryan Elliot Kravetz, costume design was by Carla Bellisio, lighting design was by Evan Purcell; the production stage manager was Teddy Nicholas. The cast was:

ISAIAH/MAN #1	Peter McCabe
ELIZABETH	Lia Aprile
DAVID	Jeff Biehl
JOHN	Hugh Sinclair
BENJAMIN	Erwin E. A. Thomas
CHARLOTTE	Sadrina Johnson
PETER/IMAGINARY SLAVE	Derrick LeMont Sanders
DOCTOR/MAIL CLERK/MAN #2	Matt Huffman

CHARACTERS

ISAIAH, the master of the plantation, thirty-two

ELIZABETH, his wife, twenty-eight

DAVID, Isaiah's brother, thirty

JOHN, Elizabeth's brother, a minister, thirty-two

BENJAMIN, a loyal slave, thirty-two

CHARLOTTE, Benjamin's wife, a light-skinned mulatto slave, she should look almost white, thirty

PETER, a slave, Benjamin's friend, thirty-seven

IMAGINARY SLAVE

DOCTOR

MAIL CLERK

MAN #1

MAN #2

CASTING NOTE

The role of Man #1 can be played by the same actor who plays Isaiah. The roles of Doctor, Mail Clerk and Man #2 can be played by the same actor. The role of Imaginary Slave should be played by the same actor who plays Peter. A total of eight actors are needed.

SETTING

A small plantation in Louisa County, Virginia, forty-five miles from the city of Richmond. The year is 1848.

NOTE

Some of the language in the play is taken verbatim from *The Great Escapes: Four Slave Narratives*. Two examples are the exchange between David and Elizabeth in Scene 4 and the last monologue of the play. That speech is how Henry Box Brown ends his own slave narrative.

SCENE 1

Isaiah is on his death bed. He has rheumatism and tuberculosis. He is in the midst of a coughing fit. Elizabeth is at his side.

ELIZABETH *(Stroking his head)*: How are you feeling, dear?

ISAIAH: The rheumatism seems better, but I can't manage this cough. Beth, I'm scared.

ELIZABETH: About what?

ISAIAH: I think I'm going to die tonight.

ELIZABETH: Hush your mouth. You are not going to die under my watch, Isaiah. You're a good man and you've led a good Christian life, therefore you have nothing to fear. God will heal you and sustain you.

ISAIAH: Even the holiest of men must eventually die.

ELIZABETH: You quit this morbid talk. You hear me?

(Isaiah has another violent coughing fit.)

ISAIAH: I had my lawyer change my will last week.

ELIZABETH: What do you mean?

ISAIAH: I'm going to free all of our slaves after I die.

ELIZABETH: Your fever must be rising. I'm going to call the doctor.

(She starts to leave the room and he grabs her arm.)

ISAIAH: Listen to me, Beth. I have had a lot of time to ponder this since I've been bedridden, and I've come to the conclusion that the abolitionists are right. I have come to believe that slavery is a mortal sin and a blight upon our civilization. In order to cross the gates of Heaven my slaves must be emancipated.

(Elizabeth is silent.)

I know this is hard for you to hear, but trust me, Beth. It is God's will.

(He has another coughing fit.)

Will you promise me that you will see to it that our slaves are freed upon my death?

(Long pause.)

ELIZABETH: I promise.

(They kiss.)

ISAIAH: You have given me the best years of my life. I love you.

ELIZABETH: I love you, too.

ISAIAH: Will you fetch Benjamin? I wish to have a word with him.

ELIZABETH: Of course.

(She leaves the room and comes back with Benjamin. The master and he grew up together.)

BENJAMIN: You wanted to see me, Massa?

ISAIAH: Come close, Ben.

(Benjamin goes to Isaiah's bedside. Isaiah has another coughing fit.)

BENJAMIN: Do you want me to fetch you some water?
ISAIAH: No. Just hold my hand and stay with me.

(Benjamin takes Isaiah's hand.)

How's your wife?
BENJAMIN: Sarah's well, Massa. She's awful sad about your illness. All the slaves is sad. You's the kindest massa a slave could ever hope for.
ISAIAH: Do you remember when we were children, Ben? How we used to catch june bugs by that creek at the edge of the plantation.
BENJAMIN: I sure do, Massa. Those was some good times.

(Isaiah starts to laugh.)

ISAIAH: And how we used to scare my sister Mary half to death by jumping out of the bushes when she'd be walking up the road from town.

(They both laugh.)

You know, Ben, I've always thought of you as a brother. I want you to know that.
BENJAMIN: I'm honored, Massa. I've always loved you.

(Isaiah kisses Benjamin's hand.)

ISAIAH: I've decided to emancipate you after I die.
BENJAMIN: What? What do you mean by emancipate?
ISAIAH: It means that you're going to be free, Benjamin. You, your wife, and all my other slaves.
BENJAMIN: I don't know what to say, Massa. Thank you! Thank you! You's a saint. Gabriel and Saint Peter will welcome you at the gates of Heaven.

ELIZABETH: I think your master needs to be left alone now to get his rest, Benjamin.

BENJAMIN: Yes, of course, Missus.

(He starts to leave. Elizabeth stops him at the door.)

ELIZABETH: Benjamin, I don't want you to repeat what the master told you just yet. I don't want the other niggers to get too excited. After all, with God's help the master might live another few years.

BENJAMIN: Yes, ma'am.

(Benjamin exits.)

ISAIAH: Will you bring in our son, Beth? I wish to see him before I go to sleep.

ELIZABETH: Of course, dear.

(Elizabeth goes into the hallway and calls to Charlotte.)

Charlotte? Charlotte?

CHARLOTTE *(Offstage)*: Yes, ma'am.

ELIZABETH: Will you bring Isaiah Junior? Your master wishes to see his son.

(Charlotte enters with Isaiah Junior in her arms. She brings him to the master's bedside.
The lights fade to black.)

SCENE 2

The sound of funeral bells. Word has traveled the plantation that Isaiah is dead.
Benjamin's wife, Charlotte, is alone, weeping. Benjamin enters. He says nothing at first.

BENJAMIN: I guess you heard that Massa's dead.

CHARLOTTE *(Softly)*: Yes. He was a good man. He treated us so well. What will become of us now?

BENJAMIN: What do you mean?

CHARLOTTE: Suppose Mistress sells us? We may never see each other again. Suppose we get bought by an unkind massa who whips us for every little thing. Aren't you afraid?

BENJAMIN: I have to tell you something.

CHARLOTTE: What?

BENJAMIN: You have to swear to secrecy.

CHARLOTTE: I swear.

BENJAMIN: I'm just as sad as you are that Massa's dead. You know he was like a brother to me. But while he was on his deathbed, God bless his soul, he told me that we was gonna be free after he died.

CHARLOTTE: Free?

BENJAMIN: Yes. He said that we was gonna be free. It's in his will.

(Charlotte drops to her knees.)

CHARLOTTE: Hallelujah! Praise the good Lord! Do you know what this means, Benjamin? It means that we can start a family.

BENJAMIN *(Overjoyed)*: I know!

CHARLOTTE: I always wanted to have a baby with you, but I ain't wanted to bring no baby into this world if it gonna be born a slave. I'd rather kill my own child than have it grow up in bondage. Now we can have a baby that'll be born free! Hallelujah!

(They start to kiss and take off each other's clothes. Then Charlotte stops suddenly.)

Are you sure?

BENJAMIN: Sure about what?

CHARLOTTE: That we're gonna be free.

BENJAMIN: Yes. Don't worry. Now lay back so that we can start a family.

(They giggle. She lays back and he enters her. They have sex as the lights fade to black.)

SCENE 3

Elizabeth is alone. Benjamin enters.

BENJAMIN: You wanted to see me, ma'am?

ELIZABETH: Yes, Benjamin, I have an urgent matter that I must discuss with you.

BENJAMIN: What is it?

ELIZABETH: You haven't told any of the slaves about the conversation that you and your master had on his deathbed, have you?

BENJAMIN: No, ma'am.

ELIZABETH: Your master had a high fever and was delirious when he told you that you would be free. You will not be freed. It is God's will that you remain on this plantation until your dying day. Do you understand?

BENJAMIN *(Hesitant. Heartbroken)*: Yes, ma'am.

ELIZABETH: Good. Now take off your shirt.

BENJAMIN: Why, ma'am?

ELIZABETH: Your place is not to ask me questions. Take off your shirt, nigger.

(He takes off his shirt.)

Now take off your pants.

(He hesitates. Then takes off his pants. He is completely naked.)

Very good, Benjamin. Now lift up my dress and climb on top of me.

BENJAMIN *(Very hesitant. Almost crying)*: But, ma'am. My wife.

ELIZABETH: If you don't do as I say I'll have you whipped until your blood runs like a river! Now lift up my dress and climb on top of me, nigger!

(He lifts up her dress and climbs on top of her.)

You know what to do, Benjamin.

(He enters her and she lets out a moan. He starts to move back and forth inside her.)

Faster, nigger! Faster!

(He pounds into her as hard as he can. She has an orgasm. He has an orgasm a few moments later. They are still. Benjamin is guilt-ridden.)

Now go fetch me some coal. The furnace in the kitchen is running low.

(Benjamin pulls out of her and gets out of the bed. Elizabeth pulls her dress back over her legs. Benjamin puts on his clothes. Elizabeth sits up and watches him leave.)

SCENE 4

Elizabeth and her brother-in-law, David, are in the parlor of her house.

DAVID: How are you holding up, Beth?

ELIZABETH: It's very difficult to manage now that Isaiah's gone. I miss him so much.

DAVID: We must find comfort in the fact that he's at home with Jesus now.

ELIZABETH: That is a comfort. But he was so young. Our son probably won't even remember him when he grows up.

DAVID: God works in mysterious ways. We must not question God's will.

ELIZABETH: Yes.

DAVID: How is my nephew?

ELIZABETH: He's very healthy. I thank God for that.

DAVID: Isaiah's spirit lives on in him.

ELIZABETH: Indeed.

DAVID: So, Elizabeth, how are you going to go about setting your slaves free?

ELIZABETH: What?

DAVID: Isaiah told me that he willed his slaves to be set free after he died.

ELIZABETH: I was not aware that Isaiah had corresponded with you about that matter.

DAVID: Indeed he did. He asked me to see to it that his wishes were executed properly.

ELIZABETH: I have no patience with people who set niggers at liberty. It is the very worst thing you can do for them. It is true that my dear husband just before he died willed his niggers free. But I and all our friends know very well that he was too good a man to have ever thought of doing such an unkind and foolish thing, had he been in his right mind. Therefore I had the will altered as it should have been in the first place.

DAVID: Do you mean, Beth, that willing the slaves free was unjust to yourself, or unkind to them?

ELIZABETH: I mean that it was decidedly unkind to the servants themselves. It always seems to me such a cruel thing to turn niggers loose to fend for themselves, when there are so many good masters to take care of them. I care nothing for the niggers, on my own account, for they are a great deal more trouble than they are worth, I sometimes wish that there was not one of them in the world, for the ungrateful wretches are always running away.

DAVID: If they are so much trouble, then why not set them free and release yourself from the burden of caring for them?

ELIZABETH: There is no good reason why property should be squandered! If my son and myself had the money for those valuable niggers, just see what a great deal of good we could do for the poor, and in sending missionaries abroad to the poor heathen, who have never heard the name of our Blessed Redeemer. My dear brother who is a Christian minister has advised me to sell every blessed one of them for what they will fetch, and go live in peace with him in New York.

DAVID: Your brother being a good Christian minister, it's strange he did not advise you to let the poor Negroes have their liberty and go North.

ELIZABETH: It's not at all strange, David, it's not at all strange. My brother knows what's best for niggers; he has always told me that Southern niggers were much better off than the free niggers in the North. In fact, I don't believe there are any white laboring people in the world who are as well off as the slaves.

DAVID: You are quite mistaken, Beth. For instance, my great-aunt before she died, emancipated all her slaves, and sent them to Ohio, where they are getting along well. I saw several of them last summer myself.

ELIZABETH: Well, freedom may do for your aunt's niggers, but it will never do for mine; and plague them, they shall never have it!

DAVID: What about Benjamin? Won't you at least free him? Isaiah and I grew up with Benjamin and feel a strong bond towards him.

ELIZABETH: I will not free Benjamin, but I won't sell him either. I plan to bring him to New York to serve me.

DAVID: I see that I cannot change your mind, so I will take my leave of you. It was lovely to see you, Beth.

ELIZABETH: It was a pleasure to see you, David. Take care of yourself.

(He exits.)

SCENE 5

Three weeks later. David and Elizabeth's brother, John, have shown up unannounced. They knock. Benjamin answers the door.

BENJAMIN: Hello, Master David. Hello, Reverend John. Do you want to see the Mistress?

DAVID: Yes, Benjamin, may we come in?

BENJAMIN: Of course. You can wait in the parlor, and I'll fetch her.

JOHN: Thank you, Benjamin.

*(Ben shows them into the parlor then goes to find Elizabeth.
Elizabeth enters a few moments later.)*

ELIZABETH: What on earth are you two doing here? John, why
   aren't you in New York?

JOHN: There's an urgent matter that we wish to speak to you
   about, and we thought it would be better done in person.

ELIZABETH: Nothing's wrong I hope!

JOHN: No. No. Quite the opposite.

DAVID: You see, Elizabeth, I have come to ask your hand in
   marriage.

ELIZABETH: How dare you make such a proposal? Your brother
   has barely been in the ground a month.

JOHN: I know that this all seems sudden, but I think that this is
   a very good idea.

DAVID: You see, Elizabeth, I've been in love with you for a very
   long time, but I couldn't express my feelings because you
   were married to my brother. Now that he's gone I thought
   that I should make my feelings known.

ELIZABETH: It was your idea for me to go to New York, John.
   Have you changed your mind?

JOHN: I think it's best for your son that he grow up with someone who can be a real father to him.

ELIZABETH: You could be a father to him!

JOHN: It wouldn't be the same. I have obligations of my own.
   Besides you're a young woman. Surely you don't plan to stay
   single forever. If you marry a man who has no relation to your
   son, how will your son be treated? Stepparents are notori-
   ously cruel to their stepchildren. If you marry David you
   know that he will love Isaiah Junior as his father would have.

ELIZABETH: You make excellent points, John. And I wouldn't be
   averse to marrying David except for the fact that he's an
   abolitionist! Do you know that he had the audacity to tell
   me to free my slaves!

DAVID: John and I have had several conversations regarding this
   matter. If you agree to marry me, then I won't object to you
   keeping the slaves.

ELIZABETH: Not objecting will not be enough. If we marry you will be master of this plantation. And as master you must not show these niggers one ounce of kindness. Kindness ruins those animals.

DAVID: I understand. I am willing to do anything to secure your love.

JOHN: So are we agreed? Will you marry David?

ELIZABETH: I will.

JOHN: Excellent! I'll perform the ceremony this evening.

SCENE 6

David, John and Elizabeth are finishing breakfast. They are fairly drunk. They like to drink mint juleps during breakfast before they have morning mass and say their prayers.

JOHN: I'm glad that you've seen the light, David! Abolition is the worst thing for these niggers! And I know firsthand. Abolishing slavery in New York in 1827 ruined every last one of those niggers. They have no idea what to do with themselves! They drink all day and look for white women to rape at night. New York has become the devil's land. I think that I might come to live down here in Georgia permanently. I feel that God's great spirit permeates this land.

DAVID: Benjamin! Charlotte! Come clean these dishes and get ready for morning mass.

(Benjamin and Charlotte enter and start cleaning the dishes. Elizabeth goes to pour herself another mint julep but the jug is empty.)

ELIZABETH: My Lord! It looks like we'll have to make another jug of mint julep before morning mass.

DAVID: Excuse me.

(David gets up and grabs Charlotte's butt as he exits.)

JOHN: Mass will begin in ten minutes.

(He exits.)

BENJAMIN: Do you want me to finish making that julep for you,
Missus?

ELIZABETH: Thank you, Benjamin.

*(She exits. Benjamin finishes making the mint julep, then he
and Charlotte pass the jug back and forth, drinking deeply.)*

CHARLOTTE: We're gonna have to mix some more or else they'll
notice.

*(Benjamin makes another batch of mint julep in the same jug
and then exits.)*

SCENE 7

*Charlotte and Benjamin enter mass being held in the parlor of the
house. When Benjamin enters, he fills John, David and Elizabeth's
glasses with mint juleps. He then sits down in a chair and puts the
jug down on the table next to him. John reads from the 88th Psalm.*

JOHN:

I call to you, O Lord, every day;
I spread out my hands to you.
Do you show your wonders to the dead?
Do those who are dead rise up and praise you?
Is your love declared in the grave,
Your faithfulness in Destruction?
Are your wonders known in the place of darkness,
Or your righteous deed in the land of oblivion?
But I cry to you for help, O Lord;
In the morning my prayer comes before you.
Why, O Lord, do you reject me and hide your face
from me?
From my youth I have been afflicted and close to death;

I have suffered your terrors and am in despair.
Your wrath has swept over me;
Your terrors have destroyed me.
All day long they surround me like a flood;
They have completely engulfed me.
You have taken my companions
And loved ones from me;
The darkness is my closest friend.

Amen.

ALL: Amen.

JOHN: Let us bow our heads and pray for our dear departed brother, Isaiah. Let us pray in silence.

(They all bow their heads except Benjamin. He takes the jug of mint juleps and starts to drink it. It spills out the sides of his mouth. He goes to put the jug back but accidentally knocks it onto the floor. Everyone looks up.)

DAVID: What on earth, Benjamin?!

BENJAMIN: I'm—I'm—sorry, Massa.

JOHN: See, David! This is what comes from being kind to niggers! They think they can drink your mint julep and rape your women! Now there's only one way to reprimand this nigger. You must resort to the lash.

BENJAMIN: No, Massa, please.

JOHN: Have you ever been whipped before?

BENJAMIN: No reverend, Massa Isaiah was very kind.

DAVID: That's going to change today, Benjamin.

ELIZABETH: Is this really necessary?

JOHN: Don't let your wife meddle in men's affairs.

DAVID: You're the one who told me that I couldn't show an ounce of kindness.

ELIZABETH *(Pleading)*: Yes, David, I did, but this is Benjamin. David, you grew up with him.

DAVID: Stay out of this, woman. John, have the overseer tie Benjamin up to the whipping post.

(John starts to drag Benjamin outside.)

BENJAMIN: No, Massa! Please! Please! I won't do it no more!
JOHN: Stop that infernal racket! He that converteth a sinner
from the error of his ways shall save his soul from death.
DAVID: He's right, Benjamin. This is God's will.

*(John continues to drag Benjamin out. David follows. Soon we
hear David whip Benjamin ten times. Each time Benjamin lets
out an excruciating scream.)*

SCENE 8

David is alone in his study writing. Charlotte enters.

CHARLOTTE: You wanted to see me, Massa?
DAVID: Yes. How's Isaiah Junior doing?
CHARLOTTE: His fever is still very high.
DAVID: Have you been bathing him with a cold washcloth?
CHARLOTTE: Yes, sir. Every quarter of an hour.
DAVID: Send Benjamin for the doctor and then come back
straight away.

(She leaves for a couple of moments, then reenters.)

CHARLOTTE: Where's Mistress?
DAVID: She and John are playing croquet with some of the
neighbors.
CHARLOTTE: Do she know how sick little Isaiah is?
DAVID: She needed to take her mind off things for a while.

(Pause.)

Shut the door, Charlotte.

(Charlotte shuts the door.)

Do you love Benjamin?

CHARLOTTE: With all my heart!

DAVID: Many people believe that niggers don't have feelings, but I believe that they do.

CHARLOTTE: Yes, Master.

DAVID: Would you like to be free?

CHARLOTTE: Well, Master. That's a tough question. You know that I love it here with you, Mistress and Reverend John. And you take such good care of us. I honestly can't imagine a situation where I would be happier. But, yes, part of me does wonder what it would be like to be free.

DAVID: I'd like to make you an offer. I'm willing to let you and Benjamin buy your freedom in exchange for some kindness and caring on your part.

CHARLOTTE: What do you mean?

DAVID: I mean, Charlotte, that you are one of the most beautiful women that I've ever seen. Ever since I came back, I've thought about you day and night. Charlotte, if the law permitted I would marry you. I need you.

(He grabs her and kisses her deeply.)

CHARLOTTE: Are you sure the mistress would agree to let us buy our freedom?

DAVID: Don't worry about the mistress. I'm the master of this house.

(The sound of a baby crying. They kiss again. He bends her over his desk, pulls up her skirt and has sex with her very quickly. He should finish after about ten pumps. He pulls out, buttons up, and regains his composure.)

The baby's crying. Go tend to your duties.

CHARLOTTE: Yes, Master.

(She straightens up and exits.)

SCENE 9

David, John, Benjamin, Elizabeth, Charlotte and the Doctor are surrounding Isaiah Junior. The Doctor holds a stethoscope to the baby's heart.

DOCTOR: He's gone to Heaven. I'm sorry.

(Elizabeth starts crying.)

ELIZABETH: No. No. My baby. *(Screaming at Charlotte)* This is all your fault! This is all your fault! You killed him!

(Elizabeth starts hitting Charlotte. Charlotte runs out of the room. John restrains Elizabeth. He puts her in a chair. Then he pulls out a Bible and reads the 23rd Psalm.)

JOHN:
    The Lord is my shepherd, I shall lack nothing.
    He makes me lie down in green pastures,
    He leads me beside quiet waters,
    He restores my soul.
    He guides me in paths of righteousness
    For his name's sake.
    Even though I walk
    Through the valley of the shadow
    Of death,
    I will fear no evil,
    For you are with me;
    Your rod and your staff,
    They comfort me.
    You prepare a table before me
    In the presence of my enemies.
    You anoint my head with oil;
    My cup overflows.
    Surely goodness and love will follow me

All the days of my life,
and I will dwell in the house of
the Lord
forever.

Amen.

ALL: Amen.

SCENE 10

Elizabeth and David are alone. David comforts Elizabeth.

DAVID: Everything's going to be all right, Beth. We cannot stand in the way of God's will.

ELIZABETH: I know. But it upsets me that Isaiah doesn't have an heir to carry on his name. He was such a good man. Our baby was so beautiful.

DAVID: We could have a baby of our very own.

ELIZABETH *(With a smile)*: I'm already pregnant.

DAVID: Really?! Are you sure?

ELIZABETH: Absolutely. I was going to wait and surprise you.

DAVID: This is wonderful. I've always wanted to be a father!
    (He rubs her stomach and starts speaking to the baby) Can you hear me? This is your daddy speaking. Daddy and Mommy are going to take good care of you. I love you, Beth.

ELIZABETH: I love you, too.

(Pause.)

I think we should sell Charlotte?

DAVID: Why?

ELIZABETH: I can't bear to look at her face after what she did to Little Isaiah.

DAVID: She's a good servant, Elizabeth. I don't think that she had anything to do with Isaiah Junior's death. God works in mysterious ways.

ELIZABETH: Charlotte was the one who nursed Isaiah. I know that she neglected him in some way.

DAVID: What about Benjamin?

ELIZABETH: Benjamin can marry one of our other slaves.

DAVID *(Hesitant)*: How— How about we allow Charlotte and Benjamin to buy their freedom.

ELIZABETH *(In disbelief)*: Are you listening to me, David? My baby is dead because of Charlotte and you suggest that we allow her to buy her freedom?! If you ever speak to me about freeing another one of our slaves, I'll see to it that my brother advocates for our divorce. *(Screams)* She killed my baby and I want her sold!

DAVID: All right, Elizabeth. All right. I'm sorry. I'll talk to the trader about selling Charlotte tomorrow.

SCENE 11

Benjamin and Elizabeth are having sex. She is on top. She has an orgasm. She regains her composure and climbs off him. She straightens herself, fixes her hair, etc.

ELIZABETH: I'm going to town for a couple of hours. Take care of the house while I'm gone.

BENJAMIN: Yes, ma'am.

(He straightens himself and climbs out of bed. She exits.
    Benjamin goes to the closet and takes out some of Isaiah's clothes and puts them on. He pretends that he's a slave master.)

(Pointing) Nigger! I'm going to take my supper outside this evening. I want you to stand by my table and swat away the flies.

VOICE OF IMAGINARY SLAVE: Yes, Master.

(Benjamin sits and pretends to eat.)

BENJAMIN: That's not how you swat flies, nigger! You're swatting too fast! Swat in a circular motion like this.

(He demonstrates how to swat flies properly.)

VOICE OF IMAGINARY SLAVE: I'm sorry, Master. Thanks for showing me how to swat flies properly.

BENJAMIN: You're lucky I'm such a good master or I would've had you whupped.

VOICE OF IMAGINARY SLAVE: Thank you, kind Master.

BENJAMIN: This food's too cold. Go fetch me another plate.

(Benjamin gets up. Imaginary Slave exits from Benjamin's mind. A few moments later the Imaginary Slave runs onstage, running in circles, chased by David and John.)

IMAGINARY SLAVE: I didn't steal the meat! I didn't steal the meat!

DAVID: We know you stole it.

JOHN: Give it back.

IMAGINARY SLAVE: I didn't steal the meat! I didn't steal the meat!

BENJAMIN: It's a mortal sin to lie to a white man, nigger! We know that you stole the meat. But I know that that's not all you've stolen. I saw you steal a watermelon from the melon patch yesterday evening.

IMAGINARY SLAVE: I swear that I ain't stolen no watermelon either.

(Benjamin breaks into song. The singing should be operatic.)

BENJAMIN:
Vile Nigger!

(John and David start singing also.)

JOHN AND DAVID:
You're a vile, vile nigger.

BENJAMIN:
Vile nigger!

JOHN AND DAVID:
 You're a vile, vile nigger.

*(They sing the words "vile, vile nigger" in a three-part har-
mony while they tie a noose around the Imaginary Slave's neck
and lynch him. After the Imaginary Slave is dead they sing in
unison:)*

ALL:
 "He that converteth a sinner from the error of his ways
 shall save a soul from death."

*(At this point Benjamin's fantasy ends. He can hear Charlotte
calling him.)*

CHARLOTTE *(Offstage)*: Benjamin. Benjamin? Is you up there?
BENJAMIN: Yes, Charlotte. I'll be right down.

(Benjamin quickly changes out of Isaiah's clothes into his own.)

SCENE 12

Benjamin and Charlotte are eating dinner.

BENJAMIN: You sure do know how to cook up some pig's feet
 and collard greens. I swear you're cookin' is better than my
 mama's.
CHARLOTTE: Thank you, Benjamin.
BENJAMIN: I have to go back out tonight. Master John needs me
 to chop up some firewood and bring it into the house.
CHARLOTTE: I have to tell you something. But I'm hesitant to
 say anything because of all the lies we've been told.
BENJAMIN: What?
CHARLOTTE: Master David told me that he would allow us to
 buy our freedom.
BENJAMIN: Really? When did he tell you that?

CHARLOTTE: This morning.

BENJAMIN: How did this come up?

CHARLOTTE: Master David just brought me into his study and asked me whether we wanted our freedom.

BENJAMIN: What did you have to do for him?

(Pause. She doesn't answer.)

What did you have to do for him?

(Pause. She still doesn't answer. He violently grabs her hair.)

What did you have to do for him, you slut?!

CHARLOTTE: Nothing! I ain't do nothing for him.

BENJAMIN: You lie!

(Benjamin is about to hit her when David walks in.)

DAVID: What's going on here?

(Benjamin releases Charlotte's hair.)

Benjamin, it is a sin to raise your hand against your wife. You must fight your animal instincts and try to be civilized. Now apologize to Charlotte.

BENJAMIN: I'm sorry, Charlotte.

CHARLOTTE: I'm sorry, too.

DAVID: Good. Charlotte, gather you things.

CHARLOTTE: Why, Master David?

DAVID: Don't ask questions, Charlotte. Just gather your things.

BENJAMIN: Where you taking her, Master?

DAVID: Didn't John tell you to chop some firewood? It's freezing in the house.

BENJAMIN: Can't I finish my supper?

DAVID: No, you cannot finish your supper. If you ever question me again I'm going to whip you twice as severely as I whipped you earlier this week. Now chop that wood, nigger!

BENJAMIN: Yes, Master.

(Charlotte and Benjamin just stare at each other for a moment. They are uncertain whether they will ever see each other again.)

Bye, Charlotte.

(He goes over and kisses her.)

CHARLOTTE *(Crying silently)*: Bye, Benjamin. I love you.
DAVID: Stop this nonsense!

(David pushes Benjamin out the door.)

BENJAMIN *(Frantic)*: I love you, too! I love you, Charlotte. I love you.
DAVID: Don't say another word! Just get that wood!

(Benjamin goes.)

CHARLOTTE: Where are you taking me?
DAVID: Never mind that. Gather up your things. Your train leaves soon.
CHARLOTTE: Am I being sold?

(David is overwhelmed with desire.)

DAVID: I need to have you one last time. I'm going to miss this.

(He violently lifts up her skirt and shoves himself into her.)

(Panting) I'm going to miss this! I'm going to miss this! Sweet nigger pussy! I love you. I love you.

(He pulls himself out of her.)

Let's go.

(They start to leave, but then he says:)

Remember, the Lord giveth and the Lord taketh away.

(He kisses her on the lips against his will. They exit.)

SCENE 13

Benjamin is lying despondently in bed. David is sitting on the bed, rubbing Benjamin's arm. Elizabeth is in a chair next to the bed. John brings in a turkey leg and cornbread on a plate. John eats some cornbread.

DAVID: We've let you lie here for two days because of your grief, but now it's time to move on, Benjamin.

ELIZABETH: We know how much you loved Charlotte, but we think that you should take a new wife to console yourself. Are there any of our slave girls that you would like to marry? I've always noticed that you like Frieda.

BENJAMIN: I don't want a new wife. I love Charlotte.

JOHN: God works in mysterious ways, Benjamin. You must toss off your grief and take a new wife.

ELIZABETH: We've brought you a turkey leg and some cornbread to make you feel better.

BENJAMIN: You brung me a turkey leg?

DAVID: Yes. We know it's your favorite.

(Benjamin slowly rises and goes over to the table. He eats ferociously.)

ELIZABETH: Is there any slave girl on another plantation that you like?

BENJAMIN: I don't want another wife. Even though she's been taken away we're still bound by God.

DAVID: Suit yourself, Benjamin, but you must return to work tomorrow.

BENJAMIN: Yes, Master.

ELIZABETH: We're so glad to see that you're feeling better. Remember that we're here to comfort you.

JOHN: We expect to see you at morning mass tomorrow. You can even have a mint julep.

BENJAMIN: Thank you, Master John.

(John pats Benjamin on the back.)

ELIZABETH: Good night, Benjamin.

DAVID: Good night.

BENJAMIN: Good night.

(They exit. Benjamin is left alone.)

SCENE 14

Eight months later. Elizabeth is in labor. John, David and the Doctor are standing around the bed. Elizabeth is screaming.

DOCTOR: Push. Push. You're almost there, Elizabeth.

ELIZABETH: I'm pushing!

DAVID: Just keep it up! You're doing a great job, dear.

DOCTOR: Here it comes!

(Elizabeth gives one final push and scream. We hear the baby crying. The baby is black.)

You have a beautiful baby girl, Elizabeth.

(Doctor hands the baby to David. David and John are horrified that the baby's black but they try to keep their composure.)

ELIZABETH: I want to hold the baby. I want to see her.

DAVID: Not right now, Elizabeth. You should rest.

JOHN: Yes. Yes. You should rest.

ELIZABETH: Just hand her to me for a moment.

DOCTOR: They're right, Elizabeth. You should sleep.

SCENE 15

Later that night. John and David are alone.

DAVID: Are you sure that there's no nigger blood in your family.

JOHN: Absolutely. Don't insult my ancestors!

DAVID: I'm sorry. But that baby is a nigger child. That means that that slut has had relations with some nigger.

JOHN: Elizabeth is a virtuous and righteous woman. There must be some other explanation.

DAVID: Like what?

JOHN: Maybe there's some nigger blood in your family.

(David slaps John.)

DAVID: Don't ever insult my heritage!

JOHN: Maybe she was raped.

DAVID: That slut wasn't raped! She would've had that nigger hung if she had been. She's done the unthinkable.

JOHN: You're right. My fair sister has compromised her chastity. What are we going to do?

DAVID: Kill the child.

JOHN: Can't we—

DAVID: We must kill the child. If we kill it now then people will believe that the child was weak and didn't survive the night. It happens all the time.

JOHN: You're right. We must not let shame be cast upon this family.

DAVID: Will you go get it?

JOHN: Yes.

(John exits, then comes back with the baby in a blanket.)

How should we do it?

(The baby starts crying.)

DAVID: Here. Let me.

(John hands the baby to David. David lays the baby down on a table and strangles it. We hear gasping sounds. Then all is silent.)

Poor, poor, innocent thing. Brought into this world through sin.

JOHN: Let us pray for the innocent nigger child.
Heavenly Father, You have not made us for darkness and death, but for life with You forever. Without You we have nothing to hope for; with You we have nothing to fear. Speak to us now Your words of eternal life. Lift us from anxiety and guilt to the light and peace of Your presence, and set the glory of Your love before us; through Jesus Christ our Lord.

DAVID: Lord Jesus Christ, You comforted Your disciples when You were going to die: now set our troubled hearts at rest and banish our fears. You are the way to the Father: help us to follow You. You are the truth: bring us to know You. You are the life: give us that life, to live with You now and forever.

JOHN: O God, who brought us to birth, and in whose arms we die, in our grief and shock contain and comfort us; embrace us with Your love, give us hope in our confusion and grace to let go into new life; through Jesus Christ. Amen.

DAVID: Amen.

(Pause.)

Let's bury the child in the backyard. We'll bury it by the stream at the edge of the plantation. No one will find it there.

JOHN: Wrap the child in blankets. I'll go get a shovel.

(David starts to wrap the baby. John exits.)

SCENE 16

Benjamin is in his bed sleeping. The ghost of his old master, Isaiah, walks into the room and wakes him. Maybe Benjamin is dreaming. Maybe he isn't. Isaiah's voice should sound majestic.

ISAIAH: Benjamin! Rise from your slumber!

(Benjamin wakes up startled. Scared.)

BENJAMIN: What?! Who's there!?

ISAIAH *(Moving closer to him)*: It's me, Benjamin. Your Master Isaiah.

BENJAMIN: But you's dead, Master. You's must be a ghost.

ISAIAH: We never die, Benjamin. We just take on a different form. Don't be afraid.

BENJAMIN: What do you want with me?

ISAIAH: You are in grave danger. You must leave this place.

BENJAMIN: Why am I in danger?

ISAIAH: I think you know why, Benjamin. Something having to do with a child.

BENJAMIN: Forgive me, Master. I didn't want to do it. I'm sorry.

ISAIAH: All is forgiven. God forgives. But you must leave this place tomorrow.

BENJAMIN: Where should I go?

ISAIAH: Go North. Go to that freedom which I promised you. You'll be safe there.

BENJAMIN: Can I take Charlotte?

ISAIAH: Charlotte's gone, Benjamin. She's gone. You will be reunited with her in Heaven.

BENJAMIN: How can I escape?

ISAIAH: Get thee into a box.

BENJAMIN: What? What do you mean, Master?

ISAIAH: Get thee into a box.

BENJAMIN: What do you mean? What kind of box? Master? Master?

(There is no answer. Isaiah is gone.
  Benjamin gets out of bed and puts his clothes on. He leaves
his room.)

SCENE 17

*Benjamin is in his friend Peter's room. It is the same slave that
played the role of the Imaginary Slave in Benjamin's fantasy.
Peter is sleeping.*

BENJAMIN: Peter! Peter! Wake up!

(Still sleeping, Peter mumbles something.)

Peter! Wake up. It's me Benjamin.
PETER *(Waking up)*: What? Is it time to go out to the field?
BENJAMIN: No, Peter. I'm going to escape tomorrow and I need
  you to help me.
PETER: I don't want to get into no trouble, Benjamin.
BENJAMIN: Don't worry. You won't get into no trouble.
PETER: Why do you need to leave tomorrow?
BENJAMIN: Never mind that. I'll give you half of my money.
PETER: How much money you got?
BENJAMIN: One hundred and eighty-six dollars.
PETER: You got a hundred and eighty-six dollars! Let me see it.

(Benjamin shows him the money.)

How you get one hundred and eighty-six dollars? I never
  seen so much money in my life.
BENJAMIN: I been savin' it for a very long time.
PETER: How much of this you gonna give me to help you?
BENJAMIN: Half?
PETER: How much is that?
BENJAMIN: Ninety-three.
PETER: I want a hundred even.

BENJAMIN: Fine.

PETER: What do you need me to do?

BENJAMIN: I want you to mail me to Philadelphia.

PETER: How can I mail a grown man?

BENJAMIN: I've found a wooden box. It's about four feet by three feet. Once I'm in, I want you to nail the box shut.

PETER: That sounds like a coffin, Benjamin.

BENJAMIN: I know. But with God's help I know that I will succeed.

PETER: Why did you come to me?

BENJAMIN: Because I know that you know how to write. I need you to write "very fragile" on the box, and write "this side up" so that I'm never placed upside down.

PETER: When do you want to do this?

BENJAMIN: At daybreak. I want to be at the post office when it opens. Send the box express. I want you to meet me in my room in three hours. We need to leave before Master is up and about.

SCENE 18

John and David are walking back from burying the baby. They are covered in dirt.

JOHN: Are you sure that it's Benjamin?

DAVID: Who else could it be? He's the only male house nigger.

JOHN: What should we do with him?

DAVID: We should act normal all day tomorrow, so that he doesn't suspect anything. And tomorrow night we should knock him unconscious while he's sleeping, castrate him, then bury him alive.

JOHN: That'll teach the nigger never to touch a white woman.

DAVID: That *will* teach the nigger.

SCENE 19

Peter has the box in the mail office. The Mail Clerk is questioning him about the package.

CLERK: This box is mighty heavy. What you got in this box, boy?
PETER: They're sacks of sugar cane. My master's sending them to his brother in Philadelphia.
CLERK: Sacks of sugar you say. How come it says "fragile" and "this side up"?
PETER: There are also some family heirlooms that my master doesn't want to be broken.
CLERK: All right. How do you want this sent?
PETER: My master wishes it to be sent express. How long that gonna take?
CLERK: About twenty-seven hours. That'll be seven dollars even.

(Peter hands him the money.)

PETER: You have a good day, sir.

(The Mail Clerk doesn't respond. He just goes back to his work. Peter exits.)

SCENE 20

We see various boxes onstage. The box containing Benjamin is in the center. He is upside down. The mail people have not followed the directions on the box which say, "This side up." We hear Benjamin's internal monologue. This should be played over speakers. There's no need to actually have an actor in the box.

BENJAMIN: Oh Lord help me! I've been upside down in this box for an hour and a half it seems to me. I'm feelin' my eyes and head. My eyes are almost swollen out of their sock-

ets, and the veins on my temple seem ready to burst! But
I dare not make a sound. I must not betray my presence.
The only thing that sustains me is the thought of sweet liberty! I won't make no noise. I would rather die in this box
than return to the shackles of slavery. It's victory or death
for me. Victory or death. Please! Please! Lord help me!

*(Two men enter who work on the ship. They're stacking boxes
and moving them around.)*

MAN #1: Let's take a rest. We've been on our feet since mornin'.
MAN #2: Let's sit on this box here.

*(They turn Benjamin's box on its side so that he is no longer
upside down. Then they sit on it.)*

BENJAMIN: Hallelujah! Thank you sweet Lord. Thank you for
delivering me from the clutches of death.
MAN #1: What do you suppose is in this box?
MAN #2: The mail I reckon.
MAN #1: I reckon you're right. It's awfully heavy.
MAN #2: Where's this box goin'?

(Man #1 looks at the box.)

MAN #1: Philadelphia.
MAN #2: Let's get back to work.

(They get up.)

MAN #1: We'll put this with the other boxes bound for there.

(They move the box. They place Benjamin right side up.)

SCENE 21

David enters Elizabeth's room. She is very sick from childbirth. She looks pale and weak.

DAVID: How are you feeling, Beth?
ELIZABETH: I feel very weak.
DAVID: Is there anything that I can get you?
ELIZABETH: A glass of water would help.

(David gets Elizabeth a glass of water. She drinks.)

DAVID: Do you feel better now?
ELIZABETH: Yes.

(He sits in a chair near the bed.)

DAVID: Have you seen Benjamin today?
ELIZABETH: No. I called for him a couple of times but he never came.
DAVID: Neither have I. I've had the whole plantation searched and there's no sign of him.
ELIZABETH *(Alarmed)*: It's almost evening. Why didn't you tell me earlier?
DAVID: I didn't want to alarm you.
ELIZABETH: When was the last time anyone saw him?
DAVID: Last night.
ELIZABETH: That's not like Benjamin. Where do you think he is?
DAVID: I think he escaped.
ELIZABETH: Benjamin loves us. Why would he escape?
DAVID: I think you would know better than I.
ELIZABETH: What's that supposed to mean.
DAVID: Exactly what it sounds like. I think that you would know better than I.
ELIZABETH: I want to see my baby. Can I see my baby now?
DAVID: No. *Your* baby caused this whole mess.

ELIZABETH: David. You're scaring me.

(David gets up and goes over to the bed.)

DAVID: What reason do you have to be scared? You've done nothing wrong.

ELIZABETH: I—I haven't done anything.

(David leans into her and speaks in a sinister tone.)

DAVID: I know what you did. You've dishonored this family.

ELIZABETH: I didn't do anything!

(David slaps her across the face really hard.)

DAVID: You're a damned liar. This is God's punishment for having relations with a nigger, you damned slut!

(He violently puts a pillow over her face and smothers her. Her legs kick. There is a struggle. Eventually she stops moving. He removes the pillow from her face.
David is quiet for a few moments. Then he runs to the door and shouts for John.)

John! John! Where are you?

(David runs out of the room to look for John.)

John! John! Come here.

JOHN *(Offstage)*: What? What's going on.

DAVID *(Offstage)*: Something terrible has happened.

(They enter.)

I came to check on her and she was dead.

JOHN: Oh, my dear sister.

(He goes over to Elizabeth. He holds her hand and kisses her forehead.)

My dear, dear sister.

(John cries.)

God has punished her for her wickedness.
DAVID: I fear he has.
JOHN: Let us pray for her soul.
    Lord, You have been our refuge
    Throughout all generations.
    Before the mountains were born or You brought forth
        the earth
    And the world,
    From everlasting to everlasting
    You are God.
    You turn men back to dust,
    Saying, "Return to dust, O sons of men."
    For a thousand years in Your sight
    Are like a day that has just gone by,
    Or like the new grass of the morning—
    Though in the morning it springs up new,
    By evening it is dry and withered.
    We are consumed by Your anger and terrified by Your
        indignation.
    You have set our iniquities before You,
    Our secret sins in the light of Your presence.
    All our days pass away under Your wrath;
    We finish our years with a moan.
    The length of our days is seventy years—
    Or eighty, if we have the strength;
    Yet their span is but trouble and sorrow,
    For they quickly pass, and we fly away.
    Or Lord please deliver Elizabeth's soul to Heaven and
        pardon her sins.
    In Christ's name.

    Amen.
DAVID: Amen.

(Pause.)

I'm going to free all the slaves on this plantation, John.

JOHN: You should think about this for a couple of days, David. Think about all the money you could get if you sold them.

DAVID: Those slaves are *my* property and I will free them. This is God's will. Now run and tell the overseer to stop all work on this plantation, and let it be known that from this moment all my slaves are free.

(John thinks about arguing with David some more but sees that it's of no use.)

JOHN: I'll tell the overseer.

(John runs out of the room. David opens the window and starts shouting out.)

DAVID: You're free! You're free! Do you hear?

(David runs outside. We can hear him shouting:)

You're free! You're free! You're free!

SCENE 22

Benjamin is alone.

BENJAMIN: God carried me to freedom in a box that was four feet high and three feet wide. Some might call it a coffin, but it was my vessel to freedom.

I reached the post office in Philadelphia at three o'clock in the morning, and remained in the depot until six o'clock, A.M., at which time, a wagon drove up, and a person inquired for a box labeled, "this side up." I was soon gone and carried to the house of my friend, where quite a number of persons were waiting to receive me. They appeared to be afraid to open the box at first, but at length one of them rapped upon it, and with a trembling voice, asked, "Is all right within?" To which I replied, "All right."

The joy of these friends was excessive, and like the ancient Jews, who rebuilt the city of Jerusalem, each one seized hold of some tool, and commenced opening my grave. At length the cover was removed, and I arose, and shook myself from the lethargy which I had fallen; but exhausted, nature proved too much for my frame, and I swooned away.

After my recovery from this fainting fit, the first impulse of my soul, as I looked around, and beheld my friends, and was told that I was safe, was to break out in a song of deliverance, and praise the most high God, whose arm had been so signally manifest in my escape.

Great God, was I a freeman?! Had I indeed succeeded in effecting my escape from the human wolves of slavery? O what ecstatic joy thrilled through every nerve and fiber of my system! My labor was accomplished, my warfare was ended, and I stood erect before my equal fellow men, no longer a crouching slave, forever at the look and nod of a whimsical and tyrannical slave owner.

Long had seemed my journey, and terribly hazardous had been my attempt to gain my birthright; but it all seemed a comparatively light price to pay for the precious jewel of liberty.

(The lights fade to black.)

END OF PLAY

DAWN

PRODUCTION HISTORY

The world premiere of *Dawn* was produced by the Flea Theater (Jim Simpson, Artistic Director; Carol Ostrow, Producing Director) in New York on November 15, 2008. It was directed by Jim Simpson; set design was by Michael Goldsheft, costume design was by Claudia Brown, lighting design was by Jeanette Oi-Suk Yew, sound design was by Brandon Wolcott; the production stage manager was Yvonne Perez. The cast was:

HAMPTON	Gerry Bamman
SUSAN	Irene Walsh
NANCY	Laura Esterman
STEVEN	Drew Hildebrand
LAURA	Kate Benson
CRISSY	Jenny Seastone Stern
ENSEMBLE	Jane Elliott, Alexis Macnab, Bobby Moreno, Jessica Pohly, Sarah Sakaan

CHARACTERS

HAMPTON, a successful businessman, sixty
SUSAN, his wife, forty
NANCY, his ex-wife, sixty
STEVEN, Hampton and Nancy's son, thirty-three
LAURA, Hampton and Nancy's daughter, thirty-six
CRISSY, Laura's daughter, fourteen

SETTING

Florham Park, New Jersey. The present.

SCENE 1

Hampton, wearing an expensive suit, is in his home office, very drunk.

HAMPTON *(Stumbling, heavily slurring his words, wild)*: Let light shine like fire! Through the dawn of these dark times! *(Laughing)* Help us to achieve redemption!

(Pause.)

Teach us the eternal rituals of suffering!

(He stumbles around a bit, trying to take off his suit jacket, but then falls to the floor and passes out.
Susan enters Hampton's office. She wears a negligee, obviously hoping to have sex on this Saturday night. She lies down next to him on the floor and caresses him.)

SUSAN *(Sexy)*: Wake up. Wake up. I've got something that I think you'll like. Wake up, Mr. Sleepyhead.

(When she sees that this isn't working, she undoes his pants and straddles him rubbing back and forth.)

C'mon, big daddy. Don't you want to make mama happy? Mama's all ready for you.

(She tries kissing him, but it's of no use. She gives up. She walks off and comes back with a pillow. She puts it beneath his head. She kisses him on the forehead.)

Good night, honey.

(She exits. He suddenly comes back to life and vomits on the floor, then passes out again. Blackout.)

SCENE 2

Hampton is still passed out on the floor. It is morning. He has urinated on himself during the night. He wakes up. He gets up slowly. His hands are shaking slightly. He takes off his pants and underwear and puts on new ones. He gets a towel and wipes up the piss on the floor. He seems lost. He then goes to his safe, opens it, takes out a bottle of Johnnie Walker Black Label, and takes a couple of shots to ease his hangover and stop the shaking. He hears his wife coming, and quickly hides the booze. She enters.

SUSAN: Good morning, honey.
HAMPTON: Good morning.
SUSAN: Would you like me to make you some breakfast?
HAMPTON: No thanks.
SUSAN: How are you feeling?
HAMPTON: Oh, my stomach hurts a little.
SUSAN: Why do you think that is?
HAMPTON: Maybe it's something I ate.
SUSAN: Maybe you drank a little too much.
HAMPTON: No it's not that.

SUSAN: Honey, you drank a case and a half of beer yesterday.

HAMPTON: What do you want from me? I stopped drinking hard liquor because of you and now you have the nerve to criticize me for having a couple of beers?! It's impossible to get drunk off of beer. Have you ever seen anyone get drunk drinking beer? You said that I could drink as much beer as I wanted as long as I stay away from the hard liquor. I'm holding up my end of the agreement.

SUSAN: I know. It's just that I worry sometimes.

HAMPTON: Okay, honey. I'll drink a little less beer if it'll make you happy.

(She tries to kiss him but he backs away.)

I've got to go shower. I don't want to be late. I've got a bunch of clients to see this morning.

SCENE 3

Hampton has come home in the middle of the afternoon because he knows that his wife will be out. He is carrying a case of Tanqueray gin. He puts the gin down and throws a coat over it to hide it.

HAMPTON: Hello, honey? Susan? Are you home?

(He runs around the house to make sure she's not there.)

Susan?

(After he's satisfied that she's not home, he picks up the case of gin and sets it on a table. He then proceeds to hide a bottle of gin in every imaginable place. He hides gin with the cleaning supplies, in the fireplace, behind books, in the broom closet. Then he empties a gallon of water and fills it with gin, then he takes sixteen-ounce bottles of water and fills them with gin.)

Martini time!

(He downs a sixteen-ounce bottle of the gin.)

This one needs a refill!

(He refills the bottle. He puts the water bottles in the pantry. Susan enters. Hampton puts a piece of gum into his mouth.)

SUSAN: What are you doing home?

HAMPTON: We decided to close the office early because it's Friday.

SUSAN: You remember that we're supposed to have dinner with Jen and Scott tonight. Right?

(He sighs.)

HAMPTON: Oh yes. I can't wait.

SUSAN: You forgot.

HAMPTON: Why do we have to spend time with those people? She talks sooo much and all he talks about are stocks, stocks, stocks. I've never met someone so obsessed with his portfolio.

SUSAN: They're my friends, Hampton. That's why. Please, honey, just try to have a good time.

HAMPTON: I will, honey. I promise.

SCENE 4

Susan and Hampton storm through the door. They are in the middle of a heated argument.

SUSAN: I want a divorce!

HAMPTON: Go ahead! Divorce me, you stupid bitch!

SUSAN: That's the last time you'll embarrass me in front of my friends! I'm sick of it! Do you hear! *(Screaming at the top of her lungs, practically insane)* Sick of it! I'm sick of waking up in a puddle of your piss every night. Our bed is disgusting. I'm sick of nursing you through your hangovers every day. Sick of having a husband who can't have sex because his dick is limp from drinking too much.

HAMPTON: You're sick?! You think you're sick of me?!

SUSAN *(Screaming)*: You haven't been able to get it up for six months.

HAMPTON: I'M SICK OF SUPPORTING YOU! I work hard every day so that you can have your furs and diamonds! So that you can spend all day chatting with your nosy friends at the country club. Sick of having a wife who yells at me every time I have a couple of drinks.

SUSAN: You punched Scott in the middle of dinner!

HAMPTON: He deserved it. He thinks he's better than me!

SUSAN: He just told you that his stocks are doing well.

HAMPTON *(Imitating Scott)*: "Oh, Hampton, you really should switch to my broker. I made a million dollars last month. How much did you make?" Fuck Scott! I wish I had punched him twice.

SUSAN: You'll be lucky if he doesn't sue you!

HAMPTON: Let that faggot sue me! The only reason you married me was so that you can inherit my money when I die. Well guess what? First thing in the morning I'm going to write you out of my will, you ungrateful cunt!

(She gets in his face.)

SUSAN: Who are you going to leave it to? Huh? Your kids won't even speak to you because you've been an absent drunk their whole lives. Your children hate you.

HAMPTON: I'll leave all my money to my ex-wife. She was grateful for everything I did for her, unlike you.

(Susan slaps him.)

And did you ever stop to think that maybe I don't have sex with you because you're unattractive? Because you act like a slob, always belching at the dinner table! Who does that? Now my ex-wife, Nancy, she knew how to take care of herself. She was amazing in bed.

(Susan slaps him again.)

SUSAN: How dare you speak to me like that.
HAMPTON: I'll speak to you any way I want.

(He slaps her across the face and she falls to the ground.)

Let that be a lesson to you.

(He grabs his heart, falls to the floor, and passes out. Susan gets up and goes over to him.)

SUSAN: Are you okay? Hampton? Answer me.

(She checks to see whether his heart is beating. It is not. She calls an ambulance.)

SCENE 5

Hampton is in the hospital. He wakes up. Susan is sitting by his side.

HAMPTON: Where am I?
SUSAN: You're at the hospital, honey.
HAMPTON: What happened?
SUSAN: You don't remember?
HAMPTON: No. I don't remember anything.
SUSAN: You passed out. Your heart stopped beating.
HAMPTON: Am I all right?
SUSAN: Your heart is having trouble working because of all the drinking. Hampton. You need to stop.
HAMPTON: Oh, you're exaggerating. I'm sure it didn't have anything to do with the alcohol.

(Pause.)

C'mon, let's get out of here.

(Hampton starts to get out of his hospital bed when we hear the voice of the Doctor.)

DOCTOR *(Voice-over)*: Hello, Mr. Dempsy, Mrs. Dempsy.

SUSAN: Hello, Doctor.

HAMPTON: Hello.

DOCTOR *(Voice-over)*: How much alcohol do you drink a day?

HAMPTON: I have a couple of drinks every night. That's it.

DOCTOR *(Voice-over)*: Are you being honest, Mr. Dempsy?

SUSAN: He's lying, Doctor. He drinks at least a case of beer a day, and I constantly find liquor hidden around the house, so it's hard to say exactly how much he's drinking, but it's a lot.

(Susan and the Doctor both stare at Hampton for a moment to see if he has a response. He is silent.)

DOCTOR *(Voice-over)*: We want to send you to a detox, Mr. Hampton. Your drinking is putting a strain on your heart and you have cirrhosis of the liver.

HAMPTON *(Worried)*: Cirrhosis? Am I going to die?

DOCTOR *(Voice-over)*: We have medication that can heal your liver if you quit drinking now. But if you don't, you'll be dead within a year.

HAMPTON: What if I don't want to go to detox?

DOCTOR *(Voice-over)*: It's your choice.

SUSAN *(Pleading)*: Hampton. Please. Please go. I need you. I need you to get better.

DOCTOR *(Voice-over)*: It'll only be for three days.

HAMPTON *(Resigned)*: Okay I'll go. I'll go.

SCENE 6

Hampton has just come home from detox. The atmosphere is full of hope. Susan sits on Hampton's lap.

SUSAN: Welcome home, honey!

HAMPTON: It's so good to be home.

SUSAN: How are you feeling?

HAMPTON: Susan, I'm a new man. I feel like I've just walked out of a fog. Like I've awoken from a long, terrible, nightmare.

(Pause.)

I want to apologize to you, Susan.

(They're looking deeply into one another's eyes. Susan is on the verge of tears.)

I know that I've said that I would stop drinking a million times before, but this time is different. This time is for good.

(Pause.)

I want to apologize for all the years of pain that I've caused you. I know that I've been a hard man to live with, and you've been a saint for putting up with me for all these years. But from this day forward I promise to treat you as you deserve to be treated. I'm going to love you like the goddess that you are. Please forgive me, Susan, I promise that I'm going to start being the husband that you deserve.

(She is crying now. Tears of joy.)

SUSAN: I forgive you, Hampton. I'm just glad to have my husband back.

(They kiss.)

C'mon. Let's go upstairs.

(They run upstairs like teenagers. Giddy and giggling.)

SCENE 7

Susan and Hampton are in bed. They have just had sex.

SUSAN: That was wonderful, Hampton. You still know how to please me.

HAMPTON: You were wonderful.

(Pause.)

What do you want to do for your birthday?

SUSAN: We don't have to do anything special.

HAMPTON: How about we take a trip?

SUSAN: Where?

HAMPTON: Wherever you want.

SUSAN: Can we go to Paris?

HAMPTON: We've been to Paris.

SUSAN: So what? I want to go again! I hate going new places 'cause I always feel like I have to see everything. I don't want to spend a week going to museums. This way we can just relax.

HAMPTON: How about Iceland?

SUSAN: Boring.

HAMPTON: Okay, Paris it is.

SUSAN: Yaay.

(They kiss. Pause.)

HAMPTON *(Remembering)*: I still have all those bottles hidden around the house. Will you help me to get rid of them?

SUSAN: Sure, honey.

(They go around the house, Hampton showing Susan the hiding places. They empty the bottles of liquor. While Susan is emptying a bottle, Hampton prepares to empty the gallon jug, but decides to put it back. He can't quite bring himself to get rid of all his liquor even though he wants to.)

Is that it?

(He thinks.)

HAMPTON: There's one more bottle in my safe.
SUSAN: In the safe?
HAMPTON: What can I say?

(They laugh. They go and get the bottle from the safe and pour it out.)

That's all of it.
SUSAN: Are you sure.
HAMPTON: I'm positive. Now we have a clean house.
SUSAN: I love you.
HAMPTON: I love you, too.

SCENE 8

Hampton is lying on the floor with his gallon-sized water bottle next to him. It is only half full. He's been drinking all day. There is a bucket next to him that he's been using to vomit into. He sits up, takes another swig, then lies back down. He vomits into the bucket. Susan enters.

SUSAN: Hampton? Hampton what's wrong?
HAMPTON: I don't feel too good.
SUSAN: Why aren't you at work?
HAMPTON: I couldn't make it. I just couldn't make it.

(She picks up the bottle and smells the gin.)

SUSAN *(Disappointed)*: You've been home drinking all day.
HAMPTON: I'm sick, Susan. I don't feel well.
SUSAN: Drinking a half gallon of gin will do that to you.

(Silence.)

You promised that we emptied out all of your liquor. How do you expect me to trust you? I don't know why I trusted you in the first place.

HAMPTON: You can trust me. I'm sorry, honey. I'm so sorry. I tried. I tried so hard but I couldn't do it. I tried so hard.

SUSAN: You couldn't make it five days?! Five days without fucking drinking. You have no willpower. You're a weak, weak man.

(Pause.)

I'm leaving you, Hampton. I can't live like this anymore.

HAMPTON: I think I'm dying.

(He takes another drink, then vomits.)

SUSAN: You just don't care about anyone? Do you?

HAMPTON: Hold me, Susan. I think I'm dying.

SUSAN: What do you mean you're dying?

HAMPTON: I've been shitting blood all day.

SUSAN *(Suddenly alarmed)*: What do you mean?

HAMPTON: I've been shitting blood. Lots of it. I'm scared.

SUSAN: We've got to get you to the hospital.

HAMPTON: No hospital. Just hold me, Susan. Please.

(She goes over to him and holds him.)

SUSAN: You've got to stop this.

HAMPTON: I know. I love you. I love you so much. Please forgive me.

SUSAN: I love you, too.

SCENE 9

Hampton is in the hospital. Susan is by his side.

SUSAN: There's someone here to see you.
HAMPTON: I don't want to see anyone.
SUSAN: I think seeing some people will help with your depression.
HAMPTON: I think a drink would help with my depression.
SUSAN: If that's your attitude then I hope they lock you up forever.
HAMPTON: How can you say that?
SUSAN: At least you can't hurt yourself here.
HAMPTON: Who is it?

> *(Susan goes out into the hallway and brings back Hampton's thirty-three-year-old son, Steven. They haven't seen or spoken to each other for seven years. Steven is a lawyer dressed in a tailored suit. Hampton stares in amazement, once he recognizes who it is.)*

Steven?
STEVEN: Hi, Dad.
HAMPTON: It's been a long time.
STEVEN: It has been.

> *(Pause.)*

I miss you, Dad.
HAMPTON: I didn't think you were ever going to speak to me again.
STEVEN: That's all in the past.

> *(Pause.)*

I heard that you were sick.
HAMPTON: That appears to be the case.
STEVEN: I can help you, Dad.
HAMPTON *(Chuckles)*: I appreciate that, Son, but I'm beyond help. I don't think that anyone can help me.

STEVEN: I stopped drinking four years ago.

HAMPTON: Why?

STEVEN: Because I'm an alcoholic. I swore that I would never become like you. But I did. It's in our blood.

HAMPTON: Don't blame your problems on me.

STEVEN: I'm not. I know that you have no power over your alcoholism. It's a disease that we both share. I realize now that you treated Mom, Laura, and me the way you did because you were sick.

(Pause.)

And I forgive you, Dad. I forgive you.

(Pause.)

HAMPTON: I apologize, Steven. I apologize for not being there for you. I didn't do it on purpose. I was just so wrapped-up in my own head that I couldn't see anything else. I couldn't see or help those around me. I couldn't be a good father to you and Laura. Are you sure that you can forgive me?

STEVEN: Yes, Dad. It's water under the bridge.

(Pause.)

But I want you to know that there is a solution.

HAMPTON: What is it?

STEVEN: Alcoholics Anonymous.

(Pause.)

HAMPTON: Get out of here! Get out of here! How dare you come in here and start preaching religion to me?! How dare you? *(Yelling)* Susan! Susan! Get him out of here!

(Susan enters. Steven waves her back out.)

STEVEN: Dad. You've got to calm down. It's not religion.

HAMPTON: Don't lie to me! I know all about you AA weirdos and your higher power. I never thought I'd live to see the day that my own son would come to preach religion to me. God does not exist. Only science. If God does exist, then he's a malicious God. Why else would he allow innocent people to get murdered and raped every day? Why does he allow homelessness? Why did he allow the Holocaust? No, Son, you shall not convince me that there is a God.

STEVEN: Are you finished now?

HAMPTON: Yes. I suppose so.

STEVEN: AA saved my life, Dad. And it can save yours, too. You don't have to believe in God, Dad. That's a common misconception that people have about AA.

HAMPTON: Really?

STEVEN: Yes. When I came into the program I felt the same way as you did. You don't have to do anything you don't want to do. The only thing that is a requirement for AA membership is a desire to stop drinking.

(Pause.)

Do you want to stop drinking, Dad?

(Pause.)

HAMPTON: Yes.

STEVEN: Good. Just give it a try. One meeting. If you don't like it, then you don't ever have to go again.

HAMPTON: Okay. One meeting.

SCENE 10

Steven and Hampton have just arrived home from an AA meeting.

STEVEN: So what did you think?

HAMPTON: I think you lied to me.

STEVEN: How?

HAMPTON: All they did was talk about God, God, God. You swore to me that AA wasn't a religious organization.

STEVEN: It's not.

HAMPTON: How can you say that? It even said it on the fucking wall. "Step Two: Came to believe that a Power greater than ourselves could restore us to sanity. Step Three: Made a decision to turn our lives over to the care of God *as we understood* Him."

STEVEN: Exactly! Right there! As we understood him. That's what you have to focus on. AA isn't about Jesus or organized religion. AA just says that you need a higher power. But that power can be anything. It could be AA itself, it could be your car, it could be the fucking doorknob. AA doesn't care what you believe. These steps are just suggestions. The steps are simply what the founders of AA did to get sober. You don't have to follow any of them if you don't want to.

(Pause.)

But I would highly recommend that you do. Those steps saved my life.

HAMPTON: Well, what do you believe?

STEVEN: I believe that God is everywhere. I believe that God permeates everything. God is in the trees. It's the very air that we breath.

HAMPTON: What about the evil in the world?

STEVEN: I don't believe that God dictates human affairs. I don't think that God helps people get parking spaces or makes the subway come on time. I don't think God gets involved with the minutiae of human affairs. I think God is everything that is good. God is about action. If you perform good actions and try to help other people, then you will know and see good. If you perform evil actions, you will know pain and suffering. Choice is what makes humans unique.

HAMPTON: I don't really understand.

STEVEN: You don't have to understand. This program is not about understanding. Just take this leap of faith and follow the program. I promise it'll keep you sober.

HAMPTON: I just don't know.

STEVEN: What do you have to lose? You have to let go of your will. Where has your way of living gotten you?

(Pause.)

It's gotten you cirrhosis of the liver, blood in your shit, and complete alienation from your family. I mean, who are you to say that God doesn't exist? You've tried your way, now try another.

(Something is awakening in Hampton. He is beginning to have a spiritual transformation.)

HAMPTON: You're right Steven.

STEVEN: All I ask, all AA asks is that you have an open mind. And, Dad, you *are* going to know a new freedom and happiness.

HAMPTON: I can do that. I can have an open mind.

STEVEN: All you have to do is get on your knees tonight and pray. Ask for your obsession with alcohol to be lifted. It doesn't matter whether you understand what or who you're praying to. Just do it. I certainly don't know what I pray to, but I know it works. It works.

HAMPTON: I will pray, Son. I will pray. Thank you.

(They hug.)

STEVEN: Now get on your knees and repeat after me.

(They both get on their knees.)

"God, grant me the serenity to accept the things I cannot change . . ."

HAMPTON: "God, grant me the serenity to accept the things I cannot change . . ."

STEVEN: "The courage to change the things I can . . ."
HAMPTON: "The courage to change the things I can . . ."
STEVEN: "And the wisdom to know the difference."
HAMPTON: "And the wisdom to know the difference."

(Lights down.)

SCENE 11

Steven has shown up at his sister Laura's house. Her fourteen-year-old daughter, Crissy, has answered the door.

CRISSY: Hi, Uncle Steven!
STEVEN: Hey, Crissy! Is your mom home?
CRISSY: No. She's at the supermarket. She should be back in like fifteen minutes.
STEVEN: Cool.

(Steven enters the house.)

How's school?
CRISSY: School's fine.
STEVEN: You just started high school didn't you?
CRISSY: No, I'm still in the eighth grade. I got held back a year.
STEVEN: Really? Your mom didn't tell me that.
CRISSY: That's because she's embarrassed. I don't think that it's a big deal. She's being stupid about the whole situation if you ask me.
STEVEN: Your mom just wants you to be successful. That's all. What's a smart girl like you doing failing classes?
CRISSY: I don't know. I just think that school's boring.
STEVEN: What subjects did you fail?
CRISSY: Math and chemistry.
STEVEN: Are there any classes that you like?
CRISSY: I really like painting. I like acting class, too.
STEVEN: I was just like you when I was in high school. I failed trigonometry and chemistry.

CRISSY *(Shocked)*: Really?

STEVEN: Yup. Had to go to summer school twice.

CRISSY: Oh my God! I can't believe that *you* had to go to summer school! But you're so successful.

STEVEN: I'm just letting you know that all teenagers fuck up.

CRISSY: Even Mom?

STEVEN: Even your mother.

CRISSY: What did she do?

STEVEN: I'm not going to get into that.

CRISSY: C'mon tell me.

STEVEN: Well she used to skip class all the time and she dated a few guys that your grandfather hated.

CRISSY: Mom used to skip class! I can't imagine.

STEVEN: But you have to promise not to tell her that I told you.

CRISSY: I promise.

STEVEN: The point is that you still have plenty of time to turn things around. If I did it, then you can do it. You're going to be a great artist one day.

CRISSY: Thanks, Uncle Steven.

(She gives him a hug.)

STEVEN: That's a very nice skirt that you're wearing.

CRISSY: Thanks! I got it at the French Connection.

(Laura enters holding bags of groceries.)

LAURA: Crissy, will you help me with these groceries?

(Laura sees Steven. She is happily surprised.)

Hi, Steven. What are you doing here?

(Crissy grabs a bag and Steven grabs another.)

STEVEN: I just wanted to see my lovely sister.

(He kisses her on the cheek. She chuckles.)

LAURA: Yeah right. What are you really doing here?

STEVEN: I saw Dad.

CRISSY: You saw Grandpa?

LAURA: Go upstairs, honey.

CRISSY: Why?

STEVEN: You need to go study so that you can become a famous artist.

CRISSY: Fine.

(Crissy exits.)

LAURA: How did this come about?

STEVEN: Well Susan called me because Dad was in the hospital.

LAURA: Is he okay?

STEVEN: He has cirrhosis of the liver.

LAURA: That's a surprise. It's remarkable that it didn't happen sooner.

STEVEN: I want you to see him.

LAURA: I don't think so, Steven. I haven't spoken to him in ten years. There's no reason to start now.

STEVEN: He stopped drinking.

LAURA: So what! He's still a cradle-robbing asshole.

STEVEN: This is not about Susan.

(Pause.)

I talked to him and I convinced him to go to AA. I've seen an amazing change in him over the last few weeks. He's undergone a wonderful transformation. He wants to see you so that he can apologize for all the wrong that he's done to you and ask your forgiveness.

LAURA: So he's not going to die?

STEVEN: Not as long as he stays away from alcohol. And I think that it would be really great for Crissy to have a relationship with her grandfather, *especially* now that you and Mark are divorced.

LAURA: Okay I'll see him.

STEVEN: You won't regret this, Laura. Thank you.

SCENE 12

Crissy is alone, sitting in a chair masturbating in front of her webcam with her back to the audience. She wears a bathrobe. She climaxes. She moans loudly. She closes her bathrobe and gets up.

CRISSY: Did you like that?

MAN: You're so hot, Crissy. I've never seen a girl as beautiful as you. I want to fuck you so bad.

CRISSY: You did fuck me. *(Giggles)* In your head.

MAN: I want to fuck you in real life.

CRISSY: I was thinking about that picture of you as I touched my breasts, my thighs and my clit, all for you. I did it all for you.

MAN: When do I get to see you again?

CRISSY: My next session will be Friday night.

MAN: That's two days from now. Why not tomorrow? I want to watch you tomorrow.

CRISSY: I'm busy.

MAN: Sometimes I think about you at work and I get so horny that I have to go into the bathroom and masturbate. I go into a stall at work and I masturbate. I love you, Crissy. I love your young body.

CRISSY *(Matter-of-factly, business-like)*: Oh yeah, I wanted to tell you that I'm raising my fee to one hundred dollars per session.

MAN: What?! Fifty dollars isn't enough?

CRISSY: Not anymore.

MAN: That's highway robbery! I can't afford that.

CRISSY: Well I guess you won't be seeing me anymore.

MAN: Okay, okay. One hundred dollars it is. No price is too high to pay for you.

CRISSY: Thanks. And don't forget to tell your friends about the new price.

MAN: I won't. See you Friday.

CRISSY: See you Friday.

(She turns off her webcam and opens her math book to study.)

SCENE 13

Hampton is alone, praying. He is kneeling.

HAMPTON: God. Spirit of the Universe. Whatever you are. Please. Please take the desire to drink away from me. I can't do this alone. I need your help. And please God. Please help me to clear away the wreckage of my past. Please allow my family to forgive me for all the wrong I've done to them over the years. And please help me to have the willingness to ask for forgiveness and to forgive.

May thy will not mine be done.

Amen.

SCENE 14

Hampton has shown up at Laura's house. Steven is with him. Crissy and Laura answer the door.

HAMPTON: Hi, Laura.
LAURA: Hi, Dad.

(Hampton tries to give Laura a hug but she backs away.)

CRISSY: Hi, Grandpa!

(She throws her arms around Hampton.)

HAMPTON: Hi, Crissy. You've gotten so big. The last time I saw you you were this high!

(He shows her how tall she was with his hands.)

How old are you now?
CRISSY: Fourteen.

HAMPTON: It's amazing how quickly the time flies by.

LAURA: It is amazing. Come in.

(Steven and Hampton enter.)

(To Crissy) Why don't you go do some homework so that Grandpa and I can talk.

CRISSY: Okay.

(Crissy reluctantly leaves.)

STEVEN: I'll leave the two of you alone.

LAURA: Thanks.

(Steven starts to leave but then comes back.)

STEVEN: Is there anything you want me to do?

LAURA: Yeah, you can throw that laundry in the wash if you don't mind.

STEVEN: No problem. *(Shouts upstairs)* Hey, Crissy, do you have anything that needs to be washed?

CRISSY *(Shouting back downstairs)*: Yeah. Hold on.

(Crissy comes back downstairs holding a couple of tank tops, socks, some underwear, and hands them to Steven.)

Thanks, Uncle Steven!

STEVEN: Anytime.

(Steven exits into the laundry room in the basement. The following action takes place simultaneously as the dialogue with Hampton and Laura. Steven starts to separate the laundry. He takes a pair of Crissy's underwear and sniffs them. Then he picks up another pair of her underwear and sniffs and licks them. Then he sits down in a chair and slides one pair of underwear down his pants and masturbates with those while sniffing her other pair of underwear.)

HAMPTON: Thank you for agreeing to see me, Laura. It's been so long.

(Silence.)

I know that I haven't been the best father to you. I know that because of my alcoholism I neglected you, your mother, and your brother for many years, and I'm sorry for that. I wish I could go back in time and change the past but I can't. But with the help of your brother I've stopped drinking. And from this day forward I want to be the father and grandfather that I wasn't able to be for all those years. Can you forgive me?

LAURA: Do you think that because you've stopped drinking you can just waltz in here and be instantly forgiven for all that you've done?

HAMPTON: No. I understand that this won't happen overnight and that this will take time, but I'm asking whether you're willing to start this process with me.

LAURA: Do you know that I've been seeing a psychiatrist for that last ten years to try to get over all the fucking psychological damage that you caused while I was growing up?

HAMPTON: I didn't know that. I'm sorry.

LAURA: What exactly are you sorry for?

HAMPTON *(Hesitant)*: For. For. All the damage that I've caused. For hurting you.

LAURA: Enough with the fucking generalities! Let's get into specifics!

HAMPTON: Okay.

LAURA: Are you sorry for beating Mom in front of Steven and me?

(Silence.)

Are you?

HAMPTON: I didn't think you remembered that. You were so young.

LAURA: Well I do fucking remember! I bet we remember all sorts of things that you'd hoped we'd forgotten. Are you sorry?

HAMPTON *(Starting to cry)*: Yes, Laura. Very sorry.

(Steven should be done masturbating by now. He zips up, finishes putting the clothes in the wash, then comes back upstairs and walks through the living room where Hampton and Laura are.)

LAURA *(Yelling)*: Say you're sorry to Steven. He watched you beat Mom, too.

HAMPTON: I'm sorry, Steven.

STEVEN: Laura? Calm down. What are you doing? Yelling is not going to help.

LAURA: It's helping me!

HAMPTON: It's okay, Steven. Leave us alone. Let us finish.

(Steven exits.)

LAURA: What else are you sorry for?

(Pause.)

I can think of a few things! Do you know what it was like living with you?! I used to walk around in a constant state of fear. We never knew what was going to happen next. That was the worst part. I remember Steven and me huddling in a closet while you were arguing with Mom and destroying everything in the house. We were afraid that you were going to kill her. There was never a moment of peace.

(Yelling) Are you sorry for that!? Are you sorry for ruining my childhood?!

HAMPTON *(Memories are starting to come back to him)*: I'm sorry for coming into your room drunk and breaking all your toys when I was fighting with your mother. I remember you had that Etch A Sketch and I broke it in half. I don't know why I did that. I remember you crying for the rest of the night.

LAURA: You should be sorry!

(Laura is crying now. She is overwhelmed with her dad's admission.)

And? And? What else are you sorry for?

HAMPTON: I'm sorry for not allowing you to go to your junior prom.

(Pause.)

LAURA: No. No. That was my fault. You were right to keep me from going to the prom after you caught me having sex on you and Mom's bed. I must have wanted to get caught.

(She and Hampton are holding each other and crying.)

HAMPTON: It wasn't your fault, dear. If I had been a better father to you then you wouldn't have felt the need to rebel against me. Do you forgive me?

LAURA: Yes, Dad, I forgive you.

(He kisses her on the forehead.)

Do you forgive me for being so rebellious, and for running away all those times?

HAMPTON: I forgive you for everything, Laura. I'm just glad to have you back in my life.

(Steven peeks in, then comes into the room.)

STEVEN: This is much better than the yelling.

(Laura and Hampton chuckle. They motion for Steven to come over and join their hug. He does. Blackout.)

SCENE 15

Hampton has come home from Laura's house. Susan greets him.

SUSAN: Hey, honey. How did it go?

HAMPTON: It was amazing, Susan. It was very difficult, but Laura and I really connected.

SUSAN: That's great, honey.

HAMPTON: And I saw Crissy! She's fourteen now. I can't believe how big she's gotten. Time goes by so quickly.

SUSAN: Maybe we could have Laura, Crissy and Steven over for dinner.

(Pause.)

HAMPTON *(Hesitant)*: I think that's a good idea, but I don't know if everyone's ready for that quite yet.

SUSAN: Why not? I'd really like to get to know your children.

HAMPTON: I know. But I think that they still hold you partly responsible for breaking up me and their mother's marriage.

SUSAN: But that's not true at all! We weren't even dating when you two separated!

HAMPTON: I know. I know. But they refuse to believe it. What can I say?

(Pause. He pulls her close.)

We have to let everything take its natural course. We can't force anything here. I'm lucky that my kids are even talking to me.

(Pause.)

I promise that we'll all have dinner in a couple of months. Okay.

(He kisses her on the forehead.)

SUSAN: Okay. Hey. Do you want to go dancing tonight?
HAMPTON: Sure.

(The stage transforms into a dance hall. We watch Hampton and Susan dance. They're like teenagers in love.)

SCENE 16

Steven has shown up at Laura's house. He knows that Laura is out. Crissy answers the door.

CRISSY: Hi, Uncle Steven!
STEVEN: Hey, Crissy! Is your mom home?
CRISSY: No.
STEVEN: Oh. Where is she?
CRISSY: She's at an appointment with her shrink.
STEVEN: Oh.
CRISSY: You can wait if you want, but she probably won't be back for like an hour.
STEVEN: Yeah. I guess I'll hang out for a while.
CRISSY: Cool!

(They sit down.)

STEVEN: What are you doing home on a Friday afternoon? Shouldn't you be out with your friends or at a sleepover or something?
CRISSY: I don't really have that many friends.
STEVEN: Oh.
CRISSY: It's not a big deal. I'm a loner I guess. I like being alone. All the girls at my school are so superficial.
STEVEN: What about the boys? You're very pretty. You must have to beat them away with a stick.

(He laughs. She doesn't.)

CRISSY: I don't know. The boys my age are so immature. They only want to date the popular girls, cheerleaders and stuff. I think older guys are much cooler.

STEVEN: Do you have a crush on anyone?

CRISSY: There's this band called Gogol Bordello. I have a crush on the lead singer.

STEVEN: How old is he?

CRISSY: Old. He's like thirty-five.

STEVEN: What do you do for fun?

CRISSY: I like to play with my video camera. I was thinking about the conversation that we had the other day and I was thinking that I'd like to be a film director.

STEVEN: That's great! I have some friends in the film industry. Maybe you can intern with them or something.

CRISSY: Awesome! Is there anyone famous that I would know?

STEVEN: Crissy, I'm an entertainment lawyer! I know tons of famous people. But there's something I want to talk to you about before your mother comes home.

CRISSY *(Slightly alarmed)*: What?

(Pause.)

STEVEN: I saw some pictures of you on the internet.

CRISSY *(Extremely alarmed)*: What kinds of pictures?

STEVEN: Well actually they weren't really pictures, they were movies of you—um—of you playing with yourself.

CRISSY *(Horrified)*: Those pictures aren't of me. They can't be of me.

STEVEN: Crissy. There's no need to deny it. I know it's you. I know what you look like.

CRISSY: Oh my God. This is so embarrassing. Are you going to tell my mother? Please don't tell my mother! Please, Uncle Steven, she'll kill me.

STEVEN: I'm not going to tell your mother. But, Crissy, how did this happen?

CRISSY: Oh my God, this is so embarrassing. I didn't mean for this to happen.

STEVEN: What happened?

CRISSY: Well, I was in this chat-room talking with this really awesome older guy.

STEVEN: How old?

CRISSY: He said that he was forty.

STEVEN: Go on.

CRISSY: Anyway, he was really cool and I liked him and we started video-chatting with our webcams, and one day he said that he would give me money if I touched myself while he watched.

(Pause.)

I was hesitant, but a few months ago I read this article in the *New York Times Magazine* about how all these colleges are starting up their own porn magazines and how the students are posing for them, and I thought well those girls aren't *that* much older than me and they're doing it for free, I may as well make some money.

STEVEN: You read the *New York Times*? I didn't start reading the *Times* until I was in college. Anyway. There's a big difference between fourteen and eighteen. And what colleges are these?

CRISSY: Harvard has one called *H-Bomb*, Vassar has one, and Boston College.

STEVEN: I went to Vassar! They didn't have anything like that when I was there.

CRISSY: And a few months ago I was reading in the *Times* about how there was this sixteen year old who had his own porn website and he made like hundreds of thousands of dollars. I thought that it would be no big deal.

STEVEN: But you didn't know that the videos were available for anyone to download?

CRISSY: No. But this became a regular thing with this guy. He would give me money to touch myself, but then one day he asked me if I'd be willing to let some of his friends watch, too, so now all these guys give me money to watch me play with myself.

STEVEN *(With grave earnestness)*: Crissy. You've got to put an end to this. Do you understand?

(Pause.)

CRISSY: I understand. Are you mad at me.

STEVEN: No, Crissy. I'm not mad at you at all. I think what you did is perfectly natural.

CRISSY: Really?

STEVEN: Yes. Humans are sexual beings. We're sexual pretty much from the time we're born. Have you never noticed that kids start touching themselves at four or five years old? They do it because it feels good. And humans are naturally ready to have children at eleven or twelve, but the oppressive society that we live in tells us that it's not right to engage in sexual activity until we're eighteen years old. That's why everyone's crazy! Because of sexual repression! I think children and teenagers should be able to freely express and indulge their sexuality as humans were meant to!

CRISSY: Wow. I agree.

STEVEN: So I don't think that it's wrong that you were exploring your sexuality. I just don't think you're doing it in the proper manner. Under the right circumstances. I think that you need to learn about sex in a comfortable and safe environment, not from some forty-year-old guy on the internet.

CRISSY: Thank you for understanding, Uncle Steven. I've felt so alone. Like no one understands me. But you know exactly how I feel.

(He pulls her close and strokes her hair.)

STEVEN: I do, Crissy. I do understand. And you know, Crissy, you're so beautiful. You're one of the most beautiful girls that I've ever seen.

(He lifts her chin up and kisses her on the mouth.)

You're lips are so soft. I would like to help you explore your sexuality in the proper manner. You should do this with someone who loves you.

(He kisses her again.)

Crissy, are you still a virgin?
CRISSY: Yes.
STEVEN: You're a good girl, Crissy.
CRISSY: Uncle Steven, I don't mean to be weird, but isn't this wrong? I mean we're related.
STEVEN: No, Crissy! That's exactly what I mean by societal repression! We live in this puritanical society that tells us that it's wrong to have sex with family members. Our society tells us that it's disgusting. That it's against God's will. God doesn't care about who you have sex with! Animals have sex with their siblings! Hell the Bible promotes sex with siblings. Think about it. If Adam was the first man and Eve was the first woman and they populated the earth, who do you think their kids were having sex with?! Each other! God doesn't know any sexual boundaries. God wants us to love freely. To love who we're supposed to love, and, Crissy, I haven't been able to take my eyes off of you for the last few years. We're meant to love each other. God wants us to be happy, joyous and free.
CRISSY: I love you, Uncle Steven.

(She kisses him and pulls him on top of her. Her cell phone rings and she answers it.)

Hello? Hi, Mom. Yeah. Actually can you pick me up some tampons from the store? Thanks.

(She hangs up the phone.)

STEVEN: How long until she comes home?

CRISSY: About forty-five minutes. She's going to stop by the grocery store.

(Steven is kissing her neck and putting his hands up her skirt.)

Wait. Do you have condoms?

STEVEN: We're not going to do that today. Today is about your pleasure my beautiful princess.

(He starts kissing her calves and then kisses along her legs until he gets to her inner thigh. She is very aroused.)

CRISSY: I don't think you want to do this right now. I'm on my period.

STEVEN: Your period is beautiful. It's natural. I love the smell. Now just relax.

(He goes back to kissing and licking her thigh and makes his way to her vagina and performs oral sex on her as the lights fade to black.)

SCENE 17

Hampton is alone, praying. He is reading a prayer from the Eleventh Step in the Twelve Steps and Twelve Traditions of Alcoholics Anonymous.

HAMPTON: "Lord, make me a channel of thy peace—that where there is hatred, I may bring love—that where there is wrong, I may bring the spirit of forgiveness—that where there is discord, I may bring harmony—that were there is error, I may bring truth—that were there is doubt, I may bring faith—that where there is despair, I may bring hope— that where there are shadows, I may bring light—that where there is sadness, I may bring joy.

Lord, grant that I may seek rather to comfort than to be comforted—to understand, than to be understood—to love, than to be loved. For it is by self-forgetting that one finds. It is by forgiving that one is forgiven. It is by dying that one awakens to eternal life. Amen."

Thank you, O Eternal Force, for my sobriety. Thank you for not letting me drink yesterday, please help me not to drink today, and help me not to drink tomorrow, and forever one day at a time.

And Lord, thank you for bringing my family back into my life. I'm so grateful to you. It's a joy beyond my wildest dreams. Please let my ex-wife Nancy forgive me and accept my amends as my children have done.

May your will, not mine, be done.

Amen.

SCENE 18

Hampton and his ex-wife Nancy are in a restaurant.

HAMPTON: Thank you for meeting me. I know that you didn't have to.

NANCY: I know that I didn't have to meet you. Why are you telling me that?

HAMPTON: I'm sorry. I'm just nervous I guess.

NANCY: Will you stop beating around the bush and tell me why you brought me here. I'd like to get home in time to watch *Desperate Housewives*.

HAMPTON: Well. The reason that I brought you here. Well. I stopped drinking two months ago.

NANCY: I heard. Would you like a medal?

HAMPTON: C'mon, Nancy. Please don't be like this. Hear me out at least.

NANCY: What? I'm listening. You've barely told me anything except that you've stopped drinking. Do you mind that I'm drinking? I'm really enjoying this martini. You used to *love* martinis. Do you remember the time that you had six martinis and then threw a piano bench out the window? That piano bench missed my head by a quarter inch. You almost killed me!

(Pause.)

Ahh, those were the good old days.

HAMPTON: I'm sorry, Nancy. I came here to apologize to you. Since I've stopped drinking I've been able to see the wreckage of my past. I realize that I was a terrible, terrible husband and father during my drinking years. And I know that I can't change the past, but I want to make right all the wrong that I've done to you. To you, Laura and Steven. I want to make things right.

NANCY: What do you want me to say, Hampton?

HAMPTON: I want you to tell me how I can make things up to you.

NANCY: You can't, Hampton. Can't you see that? You can't. You abandoned me and your children.

HAMPTON: You divorced me! I didn't abandon you!

NANCY: You were never there! And when you were there you were a fucking psychopath drunk! Do you remember the night that you slammed my finger in that big wood door as I was trying to get away from you, and half of my finger came off?! My finger still doesn't work right!

HAMPTON: Why are you dredging all of this stuff up? I came here to apologize.

NANCY: You're unbelievable! You keep saying that you came here to apologize, but you still haven't apologized for anything.

HAMPTON: You know, I see where Laura gets this from! That's exactly what she said to me!

NANCY: Did you ever stop to think that maybe it's you and not us?

(This is a revelation to Hampton.)

HAMPTON: You're right. You're right. I haven't been listening to you.

(He gets down on his knees and pleads with her. This should be very emotional for Hampton, and it should be spoken like vomit.)

I'm sorry for slamming your finger in the door and throwing that piano bench at you, I'm sorry for pissing in our bed every night, and I'm sorry for beating you, and calling you names, and making you have sex when you didn't want to, I'm sorry for not attending to your emotional needs or the kids emotional needs, I'm sorry for never taking Steven to soccer practice, and I'm sorry for putting making money above everything else.

Oh, Nancy, I wish that I could erase my past and start over again. I've wasted my life. I've lived all these years and what do I have to show for it? I just want to make things right before I die.

(She is genuinely moved by this. She is also amused. She is laughing a little.)

NANCY: Oh, Hampton, get up. The whole restaurant is watching.

HAMPTON: I will not get up until you tell me how I can make everything up to you. How can I fix the damage that I've done?

NANCY: You can start by getting up off of the floor.

(He does. Pause.)

I want to ask you something.

HAMPTON: Anything.

NANCY: Were you having an affair with Susan while we were still married? Tell me the truth. This question has been haunting me for years.

(Long silence.)

HAMPTON: No, Nancy. I never cheated on you. I did a lot of terrible things but I was always faithful to you. You were my first love. You've been my only love. I started dating Susan after you left. After I realized that things weren't going to work out between us. Nancy, I have to tell you that I'm still in love with you. When I have sex with Susan I imagine that I'm making love to you. Oh, please take me back, Nancy. We can be one big happy family again! You, me, Steven, Laura and Crissy.

NANCY: Do you even know what you're saying? I'm leaving, Hampton. This is getting weird. We can talk on the phone next week.

(She gets up to leave.)

It was nice seeing you, Hampton.

(He grabs her arm and kisses her on the mouth. They kiss for a few moments. She doesn't stop him. The kiss eventually ends and they stare at each other for a couple of moments.)

Hampton, that was inappropriate. Let go of me.

(She tries to walk away again but he swings her around and kisses her again. This kiss is very passionate.)

Hampton, I don't think that this is a good idea.

HAMPTON: We're old. What do we have to lose?

(They kiss again. Blackout.)

SCENE 19

Hampton and Nancy are in bed. They have just had sex.

HAMPTON: And they say that great sex is only for the young!

(They laugh.)

NANCY: That was wonderful, Hampton. I've been so lonely without you.

HAMPTON: And I've been lonely without you.

NANCY: You know, you're the only man that I've ever been intimate with.

HAMPTON *(Shocked)*: You haven't been with anyone since our divorce?

NANCY: I just wasn't interested in dating. Our breakup really broke my heart.

(Pause.)

I lost my virginity to you when I was nineteen years old.

HAMPTON: I lost my virginity to you, too.

NANCY: Really? You told me that you had had sex with several women!

HAMPTON: I lied. I didn't want you to think that I was a loser. It was the sixties! I must be the only man who didn't take advantage of "Free Love."

(They laugh.)

NANCY: I can't believe that you never told me that before. All those years we were married. Twenty-five years.

HAMPTON: What matters is that we're honest with each other now. I promise to never lie to you again.

(They kiss.)

Are you ready for seconds?

NANCY: I'm ready for anything.

(They start to make love as the lights fade to black.)

SCENE 20

Hampton is at home talking to Susan.

HAMPTON: I want to talk to you about something.

SUSAN: What, honey?

HAMPTON: I want to preface what I'm about to say with the fact that AA says that its members must be rigorously honest if they expect to remain sober.

SUSAN: Okay.

HAMPTON: I want you to know that this is very hard for me.

SUSAN: Just say it, Hampton. What is it?

HAMPTON: I want a divorce.

SUSAN: What? Why? Things have been so great since you stopped drinking. We've grown so much closer!

HAMPTON: Thinks have been great. We have gotten closer. But my sobriety has allowed me to get in touch with my deepest feelings, and I've realized that I'm still in love with Nancy.

SUSAN: You slept with her didn't you!?

HAMPTON: I didn't mean for it to happen. When I got in touch with her my only intention was to apologize, but as soon as I saw her I realized that I'd still been in love with her all these years.

SUSAN: Who cares whether you're still in love with her? That's no reason for a divorce. Plenty of people are married to people that they aren't in love with. What matters is that I've stayed by you all these years. She left you. Don't forget that.

HAMPTON: I'm the one who left her!

SUSAN: Yeah, well, she would have left you.

HAMPTON: Don't worry, Susan, I'm going to take care of you. You can have the house and as much money as you want.

SUSAN: I'm not worried. You should be worried. 'Cause if you walk out that door I will never take you back! Do you hear me? Never. So what's it going to be?

HAMPTON: Be reasonable, Susan! We can talk this out.

SUSAN: There's nothing to talk about. So what's it going to be? Me or her?

(Long pause. They stare at each other.)

HAMPTON: I'm sorry. I'll go pack my things.
SUSAN: I'm sorry, too.

(Hampton exits upstairs to go pack.)

SCENE 21

Crissy and Steven are in bed. She has just lost her virginity to Steven.

STEVEN: That was amazing, Crissy.
CRISSY: Really? I didn't really know what I was supposed to do.
STEVEN: You're a natural. That was the best I've ever had.

(She giggles.)

CRISSY: Thanks.
STEVEN: I didn't hurt you did I.
CRISSY *(Embarrassed)*: I had an orgasm.
STEVEN: Really?
CRISSY: You couldn't tell?
STEVEN: Sometimes it's hard to tell whether someone's experiencing pain or pleasure.
CRISSY: That's true.
STEVEN: I love you, Crissy.
CRISSY: I love you, too, Uncle Steven.

(They kiss.)

What if we want to get married?
STEVEN: What?

CRISSY: What if we ever want to get married?

STEVEN: We'll lie. No one has to know the truth. It's no business but our own.

CRISSY: That's good. Because I want to marry you. When can we get married?

STEVEN: As soon as I save up enough money for us to get away from here.

CRISSY: Where are we going to go?

STEVEN: Wherever you want.

CRISSY: I want to live in Paris. Can we move to Paris?

STEVEN: Paris it is.

CRISSY: Yaay Paris!

(Pause.)

How long have you been attracted to me?

(Pause.)

STEVEN: Since you were about seven. This is a little embarrassing, but I used to get aroused watching you jump rope or doing cartwheels in the backyard. *(Laughs)* You've always been special. When were you first attracted to me?

(Pause.)

CRISSY: I don't know. I know that I used to get—I can't describe it. I just know that I've always wanted to be as close as I could possibly be to you.

(They kiss.)

STEVEN: Did you put an end to the whole video-chatting thing?

CRISSY: Yes.

STEVEN: How did it go?

CRISSY: They're pretty angry. They keep offering me more money and whenever they see that I'm online they start IM-ing and harassing me.

STEVEN: Just block their screen names.

CRISSY: I will. *(Hesitant)* I'm scared. One of the guys threatened me. He said he would kill me if I didn't touch myself anymore.

STEVEN: Do any of these guys know where you live?

CRISSY: No.

STEVEN: Then you have nothing to worry about. Don't worry, Crissy, I'm going to make sure that nothing ever happens to you. I'll protect you no matter what.

CRISSY: Thanks, Uncle Steven.

STEVEN: You're a good girl, Crissy. Thank you for doing that for me. Those guys are total cowards. They're just angry that they can't have you anymore. This will all blow over. You'll see. Now lay back. I want to show you something.

(He puts on some music. He kisses her on the mouth and then starts kissing her neck. At this point Nancy and Hampton ring the front doorbell. No one answers. They have come over to break the good news that they're getting back together. They turn the doorknob and the door opens.)

HAMPTON: That's strange. The front door is open.

NANCY: It's not that strange.

(They walk in.)

I can't wait to see the looks on their faces when we tell them that we're getting married!

HAMPTON: Hello?

NANCY: Hello? Laura?

HAMPTON: Strange.

NANCY: Oh wait. I hear music upstairs.

(Nancy and Hampton walk upstairs to Crissy's room. They walk in on Steven and Crissy in bed together. Everyone freezes.)

I—I—I— What—I—

(Nancy begins to hyperventilate and leaves the room.)

HAMPTON: Steven! Crissy?! Steven? What the fuck are you doing?

(Steven hops out of bed completely naked.)

STEVEN: I can explain, Dad.

HAMPTON: She's your niece, Steven! She's fourteen years old.

(Hampton strangles Steven. He pushes him against the wall.)

You pedophile fuck!

CRISSY: Grandpa, no! You'll kill him!

(Crissy has put on her clothes and jumps out of bed. Hampton lets Steven go. Steven runs out of the room.)

It's my fault, Grandpa. Don't blame Steven.

HAMPTON: It's not your fault, Crissy. You've been abused. He's sexually abused you. Why didn't you tell me?

CRISSY: He didn't abuse me! I love Steven with all my heart and he loves me! We're going to get married some day.

HAMPTON *(Covering his ears and shouting)*: Shut up! Shut up! You don't know what you're saying!

(Crissy grabs his hands and uncovers his ears.)

CRISSY: Grandpa, you have to listen to me. I'm a big girl. I'm an adult. I know what I'm doing. You have to understand that Steven and I don't proscribe to the morals of your society. That's all it is. You think what we're doing is wrong, but animals do it, and Adam and Eve—

HAMPTON: You don't know what you're talking about.

(He grabs Crissy and hugs her tightly.)

Everything's going to be all right.

(He kisses her on the forehead and exits. A few moments later she leaves her room.)

CRISSY: Steven! Steven!

SCENE 22

Crissy is in her room crying. Laura knocks on the door. Crissy doesn't answer. Laura opens the door and walks in.

LAURA: Hi, Crissy. How are you feeling?

(Crissy doesn't respond.)

Look, Crissy. I'm not angry.

CRISSY: You're not?

LAURA: No. I'm just confused. Very, very confused. I just want to get a sense of . . . of . . . I don't know. How did this happen?

CRISSY: I don't know, Mom. I know you think it's weird, but over the last few weeks Uncle Steven and I have grown very close. I've been very lonely. I don't have any friends at school, and Uncle Steven really understands me. He's been the only good thing in my life lately.

(Pause. Laura has a horrified look on her face.)

Why are you looking at me like that?

LAURA: I'm sorry. I'm just listening. Go on.

CRISSY: I guess I've realized that Uncle Steven and I are soul mates. I really love him and he loves me. He makes me happy.

LAURA: Crissy. I think that maybe you're confused about what love is.

CRISSY: Don't talk down to me, Mom. I'm not a little kid. I know what love is.

LAURA: You obviously don't because you can't be in love with your uncle.

(Pause.)

Did he threaten you, Crissy? You can tell me the truth.

CRISSY: No, Mom! You have to listen to me. Steven and I don't prescribe to the morals of your society. What's wrong with two people loving each other? You can't choose who you fall in love with. I've done some research, Mom. In the Greco-Roman period of Ancient Egypt brother-sister, father-daughter, and mother-son relationships were commonly practiced. And the book of Leviticus specifically condones sexual relations between uncles and nieces. Did you know that Judaism considers it to have been an act of great kindness on God's part, to allow Adam and Eve's children to marry each other in order to perpetuate the human race?

LAURA: I didn't know that.

CRISSY: And in Sweden siblings are actually allowed to marry. Uncle Steven and I could go to Sweden and be accepted! And in February 2007 two siblings in Germany sued the government in an effort to have the country's incest laws abolished, so that they could continue their sexual relationship. *And* they had four children. It's true that two of the children have disabilities but those were caused by premature birth and not the fact that they're siblings. And Napoleon abolished France's incest laws two hundred years ago. People have been able to love freely for two hundred years in France! Don't you see, Mom. My love for Uncle Steven isn't unnatural at all.

LAURA: Wow, Crissy. Wow. I don't know. I'm. Uh. I'm going to have to go think that over.

CRISSY: Really, Mom? You'll think about it?

LAURA: Yes. Though it's difficult for me, I'm going to take your view into consideration.

CRISSY: Thank you, Mom! Can I go over to Uncle Steven's house now?

(Pause.)

LAURA: No. Not now. Let me think this over.

(She starts to leave but stops when Crissy starts to speak.)

CRISSY: I've always felt this emptiness inside, Mom. I've felt it my whole life. And Uncle Steven fills that void.

SCENE 23

The next day. Laura, Nancy and Hampton are at Laura's house talking.

HAMPTON: Did you have any idea that this was going on?

LAURA: Of course not.

HAMPTON: I mean you didn't notice anything?

NANCY: Of course she didn't. If she had she would have done something.

HAMPTON: Where's Crissy?

LAURA: Upstairs in her room.

NANCY: How is she?

LAURA: She's pretty upset 'cause I won't let her go to Steven's house. She won't open her door.

HAMPTON: I just don't get it. I just don't get it.

(Laura starts crying.)

NANCY: None of us get it. But we have to figure out what we're going to do.

HAMPTON: What do you want to do?

NANCY: I don't know.

HAMPTON: I don't know either.

LAURA *(Hesitant)*: I think that we should go to the police. I think Steven should be thrown in jail.

HAMPTON: Don't you think that's a bit harsh?

LAURA: He raped Crissy!

(Silence.)

HAMPTON: I don't know. I don't think that I can do that.

LAURA: He raped Crissy! He deserves it.

(Silence.)

NANCY: I agree, Hampton. This is as hard for me as it is for you, but after seeing what we saw yesterday I don't see any other choice. He clearly has a problem, and I think it would be better to get him off of the street.

HAMPTON: I know that you're both upset. But jail is no place for a man like Steven. Think about what they do to pedophiles in prison. They treat them worse than murderers!

LAURA: I don't think that you should have a say in this, Dad. After all, you haven't been around for the last ten years.

NANCY: Look, Hampton, if Steven had murdered someone I would protect him. Hell, if he had raped some stranger walking down the street I would have protected him. But he's done this to our own family. He's done this to our Crissy.

HAMPTON: He's our son.

NANCY: I can't believe your attitude, Hampton.

HAMPTON: He saved my life. I would be dead today if it weren't for Steven.

NANCY: Don't you have any love for our granddaughter? She's confused. She's upstairs hurting right now. Can you even begin to understand what kind of damage he's inflicted upon her?

LAURA: She thinks that she's in love with him! *And* that he loves her! It's sick, Dad! It's twisted. And it's all his fault.

HAMPTON: I don't know.

LAURA: I can't listen to this anymore. Please talk some sense into him, Mom. I'm going to check on Crissy.

(She leaves.)

NANCY: If you're not willing to turn Steven in then I can't marry you. I can't be with a man who would watch our granddaughter get raped and do nothing about it. It's time for you to show your commitment to this family by standing up and being a man. Now are you coming to the police station or not?

CRISSY *(From off, shouting)*: It's my life! Give me back my cell phone!

HAMPTON: Can you give me five minutes alone? Just five minutes?

NANCY: Five minutes.

(She exits. Hampton gets on his knees and prays.)

HAMPTON: God, grant me guidance. I am completely lost. Help me not to take a drink. I've never wanted to take a drink so badly in my life. Please God, Eternal Force, Spirit of the Universe, tell me what I should do about Steven. Yes, he's done wrong, but so have I. So has everyone. Please show me the way. "And God, grant me the serenity to accept the things I cannot change, the courage to change the things I can, and the wisdom to know the difference."

(Nancy and Laura walk back in.)

NANCY: Get up, Hampton. We're going to the police station.

(Hampton stands up.)

HAMPTON: I'm not turning our son in. I'm going to protect him.

NANCY: What about our granddaughter?

(Silence.)

What about our granddaughter, Hampton?

(Silence.)

I guess we won't be spending the rest of our lives together.

HAMPTON: No. I guess not.

NANCY: C'mon, Laura. Let's go. Your father isn't coming.

SCENE 24

Hampton has shown up at Steven's house. Steven answers the door holding a bottle of Grey Goose Vodka. He is extremely drunk.

HAMPTON: Hello, Steven.

STEVEN *(Cheerfully)*: Hi, Dad!

HAMPTON: You're drunk.

STEVEN: I know. It's awesome! You should try it! No, no you shouldn't try it because you're an alcoholic.

HAMPTON: We've got to get out of here right now.

STEVEN: I'm sorry, Dad. I'm so sorry. I don't know why I did it, but I love her. I love her, Dad.

HAMPTON: What's done is done. I'm sorry for hitting you, Steven.

STEVEN: It's okay. Do you forgive me, Dad?

HAMPTON: Yes. I forgive you.

(They hug.)

Now. We've got to go quickly, Steven. Your mother and sister have gone to the police.

STEVEN: They're turning me in?

HAMPTON: Yes. Let's go.

STEVEN: I need to pack. I need to get some stuff.

(He tries to go inside, but Hampton stops him.)

HAMPTON: Don't worry about any of that. There isn't time! I don't want you to go to jail. Jail's no place for a man like you. Let's go.

STEVEN: Okay, Dad.

(They exit.)

SCENE 25

Steven and Hampton have gotten out of Hampton's car. They are in a secluded area in the middle of the woods. Steven still has his bottle.

STEVEN: That took forever. Where are we? I have to go pee.

(He pees.)

HAMPTON: In the Catskills. My dad used to take me camping up here when I was a kid.

STEVEN: Is there a cabin up here or something?

HAMPTON: No. Let's walk down here.

(They walk.)

STEVEN: It's dark.

HAMPTON: That's nature.

(Pause.)

I want to thank you, Steven, for giving me the gift of sobriety.

(He takes a gun out of his pants. Steven can't see it.)

STEVEN: I'm sorry that I'm not sober right now, Dad. I just couldn't deal with the pain. It hurts so much.

HAMPTON: It's okay, Steven. Soon your pain will be over. I love you unconditionally. I will always love you.

STEVEN: I love you, too, Dad.

HAMPTON: Give me a hug.

(They hug. Steven cries on Hampton's shoulder.)

Shh. Everything's going to be all right. Everything's going to be all right, Steven.

(Still hugging, Hampton pulls the gun up to Steven's chest and shoots him in the chest. Steven crumples to the ground. Hampton gets on the ground beside Steven. He isn't dead yet.)

STEVEN: Dad, I'm sorry. I'm—

(Hampton shoots him again. Steven stops moving.)

HAMPTON: I know you are.

(Hampton gets on his knees and stretches out his arms and looks up toward the sky.)

Let light shine like fire
Through the dawn of these dark times
Help us to achieve redemption
Teach us
The eternal rituals
Of suffering.

END OF PLAY

PURITY

Purity was developed by the Soho Repertory Theater Writer/
Director Lab (Daniel Aukin, Artistic Director; Alexandra Con-
ley, Executive Director) in 2005–2006. The world premiere
of *Purity* was produced at Performance Space 122 (Vallejo
Gantner, Artistic Director) in New York on January 6, 2007.
It was directed by Yehuda Duenyas; set design was by Clint
Ramos, costume design was by Jessica Gaffney, lighting design
was by Ben Kato; the production stage manager was Michelle
Chang. The cast was:

VERNON	James Scruggs
DAVE	Daniel Manley
LISA	Alexa Scott-Flaherty
MICHELLE	Kate Benson
CARL	Albert Christmas
ECUADORIAN MAN/GENIE	Spencer Scott Barros
MARIA	Jenny Seastone Stern

CHARACTERS

VERNON, African-American, professor at a prestigious university, forty

DAVE, white, Vernon's best friend and the chairman of the English department, forty

LISA, white, Vernon's wife and a neurosurgeon, late thirties

MICHELLE, white, Dave's wife and a powerful lawyer, early forties

CARL, African-American, a professor in the English department, early thirties

ECUADORIAN MAN

MARIA, Ecuadorian Man's daughter

GENIE

SETTING

New York City. The present.

NOTE

Ecuadorian Man and the Genie can be double-cast. Maria must be played by an actress who is at least eighteen years old.

SCENE 1

Dave is in his office. Vernon enters with bits of vomit on his shirt. Vernon is visibly hung over.

DAVE: Hey. What's up?

VERNON: I have to go teach in a few minutes.

DAVE: What are you teaching?

VERNON: *Wuthering Heights.* It's my favorite book.

DAVE: I know.

(Pause.)

What the fuck is on your shirt? It's disgusting.

VERNON *(Looking at his shirt)*: Oh man. It's vomit. I'm so fuck-ing hung over. I was walking out of the library and I sud-denly I got really nauseous, so I ran and threw up into the first garbage can I saw for like five minutes.

DAVE: That sucks, dude.

VERNON: The worst part is that two of my students saw me vomiting. It's so embarrassing.

DAVE: It'll be okay. Just make up something. Say you ate some bad fish or that you have the flu.

(Pause.)

You really look like shit. Let me get you a fresh shirt.

(Dave goes into his closet and gets Vernon a clean shirt. Vernon changes.)

VERNON: You got something for my hangover?

DAVE: Yeah.

(Dave goes and pours Vernon a glass of Johnnie Walker Black Label. Then he goes to his desk and takes out a mirror with a pile of cocaine on it.)

This stuff is primo, man. It'll blow your mind.

(They both do a line. Vernon drinks his scotch.)

VERNON: Thanks, man. I really needed that.

DAVE: You should never teach sober. That's my rule. I thought you would've learned that by now.

VERNON: Is that right? That's a great motto for the chairman of the English department to live by. You should distribute your motto to all the professors in the department. I'm sure the president would love that.

(They both have a good laugh.)

DAVE: Fuck the president. I should be the president. I don't know why the board gave Michael that job.

VERNON: He's got all that money. That's why.

DAVE: Anyway, I'm thinking about tinkering with the English 211 curriculum a little bit.

VERNON: How?

DAVE: I think we should have students read *Jane Eyre* instead of *Wuthering Heights.*

VERNON: Why?

DAVE: My students aren't connecting to *Wuthering Heights* this semester. I've never had much luck getting the students to connect to this novel. I think they'd find it easier to relate to the themes and plot of *Jane Eyre. Jane Eyre* really speaks to youth.

VERNON: That's the most retarded thing I've ever heard you say. *Wuthering Heights* is the greatest literary achievement of the nineteenth century. Just because you're an incompetent teacher doesn't mean that *Wuthering Heights* should be taken out of the curriculum.

DAVE: Oh. I see the problem now. I'm incompetent.

VERNON: That's right.

(Dave playfully punches Vernon in the chest and they play-fight. It's a play-fight where they're hitting each other pretty hard.)

DAVE: You're the incompetent one! Who threw up in a garbage can in front of his students?

VERNON: Yeah well, you want to fuck Charlotte Brontë.

DAVE: And you want to fuck Emily Brontë. Oh and speaking of fucking, look what I got this week.

(They stop play-fighting. Dave goes and gets some kiddie porn from the drawer of his desk. The pictures are of a ten-year-old girl having sex with a grown man.)

VERNON: Oh my God. This girl is so hot. Jesus Christ. She's so little. Where did you get this from?

DAVE: My buddy went down to Ecuador and took these pictures himself. Their laws are pretty lax.

VERNON: How old do you think she is?

DAVE: Nine or ten.

VERNON: Dude. We *need* to go to Ecuador!

DAVE: That's a great idea. But how could we get away from our wives?

VERNON: We'll tell them that there's an English conference down there. We'll tell them that we want some male-bonding time. It'll be just like when we were teenagers. Sneaking around, smoking pot in your mom's basement.

DAVE: Do you remember the time we were smoking pot in your basement and your dad caught us using his bong?

(They laugh.)

VERNON: He was so pissed.

DAVE: But not about the fact that we were smoking pot. He was pissed about the fact that we were using *his* bong. You're dad's awesome.

(They laugh.)

VERNON: Those were the good old days.
  (Looking at the pictures again) She's so little, dude. It looks like he's splitting her open. Oh God she's so hot.

DAVE: I know, man. I jerked off four times last night. I can't get enough of this little girl.

VERNON: I think I need to jerk off.

DAVE: Go for it. No use torturing yourself.

(Dave gestures for Vernon to go into the bathroom. Vernon does. Dave sits down and does some more coke. Vernon reemerges from the bathroom about a minute and a half later.)

VERNON: Oh my God, Dave. That was amazing. Dude. This little girl. Dude. I came so hard that my cum hit me in the face.

DAVE *(In disbelief)*: No way!

VERNON: I'm totally serious.

DAVE: Really?

VERNON: Yeah.

DAVE: Wow.

VERNON: We need to go to Ecuador, man.

DAVE: Are you really serious?

VERNON: I'm sick of masturbating while thinking about little girls. I need the real thing.

DAVE: Let's do it brother.

(They shake hands.)

VERNON *(Looking at his watch)*: Oh shit! I'm late for class.

SCENE 2

Vernon is at home. His wife, Lisa, walks in.

VERNON: How was your day, honey?

(They kiss.)

LISA: I think I need to stop doing so much coke.

VERNON *(Horrified)*: Don't say things like that. I won't let you slander cocaine's good name in my house!

LISA: I'm serious, Vernon.

VERNON *(Hugging her)*: I'm sorry. What happened?

LISA: Well nothing happened. Well actually, I was performing surgery today and couldn't get my hand to stop shaking. I mean, I'm operating on this guy's brain and my hand wouldn't stop shaking!

VERNON: Did everything turn out all right?

LISA: Yeah. But that's a fluke. The brain's so fragile. One slip on my part and that man would've been paralyzed.

(Pause.)

I think that I maybe need to stop using cocaine at work.

VERNON: How do you know it was the cocaine?

LISA: Vernon. It was the fucking cocaine. Okay?

(Vernon hugs her. He gives her a kiss on the forehead.)

VERNON: I support you no mater what you decide to do.

LISA: Oh, who am I kidding? I'll just try to do a little less. I mean, this is the first time this has happened to me.

VERNON: Now that's the spirit! That's the Lisa I know.

(They kiss.)

LISA: How was your day?

VERNON: Dave told me about this English conference that's going to be held in Ecuador.

LISA: Are you going to go?

VERNON: I'm thinking about it.

LISA: We should go! I've always wanted to go to Ecuador. Some vacation time would really do me some good.

VERNON: Well actually, um, Dave and I were thinking that it would be like a male-bonding kind of thing.

LISA: Oh, I see. You two want to travel around the world drinking and carousing with the local women. You don't want your wives dragging you down, preventing you from having sex with whores!

(She laughs.)

VERNON: That's not it and you know it. It's just that Dave and I don't get to spend a lot of time alone together anymore. I mean usually when we hang out it's the four of us.

LISA: Oh, so you guys don't like spending time with your wives. I'm sorry. I didn't know we were such a burden to you guys. We who support you two poor English professors. Whose money do you think will be paying for that trip to Ecuador?

VERNON: It's not like that. We just want to have some time alone. It'll be like when we were in high school. Don't you ever want to just hang out with your girlfriends?

LISA: I'm just giving you a hard time. I know exactly what you mean. It's good to have some girl time.

VERNON: I love you.

LISA: I love you, too.

VERNON: And don't worry. We're not going to carouse with any women.

LISA: You better not.

VERNON: You're the only woman for me. You're so sexy. I love you more than anything in the world.

(They make out as the lights fade to black.)

SCENE 3

Dave, Vernon and a man from Ecuador are drinking and laughing as the lights come up. Dave and Vernon have flown to Ecuador.

DAVE: I can't believe you shot yourself in the foot!

ECUADORIAN MAN: I was young! I didn't want to get drafted into army! Army in Ecuador not a fun place to be!

VERNON: I think what you did makes perfect sense. I've often thought about what I would do if I got drafted.

DAVE: You're way too old to get drafted now!

(They laugh.)

Would you actually shoot yourself in the foot?

VERNON: If it came to that. I'd probably try to convince them that I was gay first.

(More laughing.)

ECUADORIAN MAN: You Americans don't like homosexual. That's good. We Ecuadorians don't like sinful homosexual either.

DAVE: Yeah.

(Awkward pause.)

VERNON: So. Um. You said you have a daughter?

ECUADORIAN MAN: Yes. I hope she never turn out to be homosexual. She is good girl. She is joy of my life since my wife die.

DAVE: How did your wife die?

ECUADORIAN MAN: Car accident. Four years ago.

VERNON: We're sorry to hear that.

ECUADORIAN MAN: I loved her more than sky and moon.

DAVE: How old is your daughter?

ECUADORIAN MAN: Nine.

VERNON: We were wondering whether we could spend some time with your daughter?

ECUADORIAN MAN: Why you want to spend time with my daughter? She have nothing interesting to say. She just little girl.

DAVE: Not to talk to her exactly. I mean we would. We'd give you money.

(Kind of enraged, the Ecuadorian Man stands up.)

ECUADORIAN MAN: You want to buy my daughter?!

VERNON: Yeah. Kind of.

(Long silence.)

ECUADORIAN MAN: How much you pay me?

DAVE: How much do you want?

ECUADORIAN MAN: One thousand dollars.

DAVE: Deal.

ECUADORIAN MAN: Let's go to my house. We pack her things. Can I come visit her in America? That's where you take her. Right?

VERNON: Oh. You don't understand. We didn't really mean buy. We meant more like rent.

ECUADORIAN MAN: Oh! You want rent daughter. So you no take her?

VERNON: No. We'd like to rent her for a few hours a day if possible.

ECUADORIAN MAN: How long you be here?

DAVE: One week.

ECUADORIAN MAN: How much you give me to rent daughter for week?

VERNON: Two hundred dollars.

ECUADORIAN MAN: Five hundred dollars.

VERNON: Three hundred dollars.

ECUADORIAN MAN: Five hundred dollars.

VERNON: Deal.

DAVE: So when can we pick her up?

ECUADORIAN MAN: You no pick her up. You rent her at my house.

VERNON: We'd rather pick her up.

ECUADORIAN MAN: No! You rent her at my house. Four hours a day. I work field while you rent. No worry. No one will bother you.

DAVE: Okay.

ECUADORIAN MAN: Come to my house one P.M. tomorrow. I live in pink house at end of road. My wife like that color.

SCENE 4

Dave and Vernon at the Ecuadorian Man's house.

ECUADORIAN MAN *(Cheerfully)*: Welcome!

VERNON: Thanks.

DAVE: It's good to see you.

ECUADORIAN MAN: Maria. Come down here. You have guests.

(Maria enters.)

These very nice men have come to spend time with you while I work field. You must do whatever they ask you to. You understand?

MARIA: Yes.

(Ecuadorian Man kisses her on the forehead.)

ECUADORIAN MAN: I love you. I see you in a few hours.

MARIA: I love you, Daddy.

(Ecuadorian Man exits.)

DAVE: Hi, Maria. My name's Dave.

MARIA: Hi, Dave.

VERNON: And my name is Vernon.

MARIA: Hi, Vernon.

DAVE: Where's your room?

(She points.)

MARIA: Do you want to come play with me?

DAVE: Yeah we'll play soon. Can you go wait for us in there? We need to have an adult conversation.

(She nods her head and goes into her room.)

This is awesome! She's so fucking little!

VERNON: We hit the jackpot, dude!

DAVE: What should we do? Should we take turns or double-team her?

VERNON: I think we should take turns. I think double-teaming her might traumatize her right now.

DAVE: You're right.

VERNON: We'll play it by ear. She might be ready to be double-teamed by the end of the week.

DAVE: Who should go first?

VERNON: I think I should go first.

DAVE: Why do you get to go first?

VERNON: I don't know. It's just what I think.

DAVE: Fine. You can go first.

(Vernon starts to go into her room.)

But you can't fuck her in the ass.

VERNON: What? Why not?

DAVE: If you get to fuck her pussy first, then I should get to fuck her ass first. It's only fair!

VERNON: I don't know.

DAVE: Think of it this way. You're taking her pussy virginity and I'm taking her ass virginity.

VERNON: Okay. Deal.

(Pause.)

Do you have something to read?

DAVE: Yeah. But you won't be in there too long.

(They laugh. Vernon exits into Maria's room.)

SCENE 5

Vernon is in Maria's room.

VERNON: Hi, Maria. You're very beautiful. Did you know that?

(He strokes her hair.)

MARIA: My dad tells me that sometimes.

VERNON: I've always wanted a little girl like you.

(He kisses her, then undresses her. He tries to move her to her bed. She is reluctant.)

Don't worry. I'm not going to hurt you.

(She relents and lies on her bed. Vernon takes off his pants.)

You're going to become a woman now.

(He starts trying to get his penis in but it won't fit.)

Relax.

(He finally manages to get his penis inside her. She groans as if she's in pain.)

It's okay. It always hurts the first time someone loves you. You feel so good, Maria.

(He's doing it slowly and sweetly and kissing her face. She pants a little.)

I love you. Divine Maria. You're heaven.

(He ejaculates. He lies with her for a few moments and strokes her hair.)

Now that didn't hurt too much. Did it?
MARIA: No.

(She is crying a little.)

Was that love?
VERNON: Yes. Dave and I love you very much. You're a good girl.

(He puts his pants back on and exits.)

(Offstage) Your turn.
DAVE *(Offstage)*: How was she?
VERNON *(Offstage)*: It's indescribable. She's amazing. So tight. Primo, man. Do you have some KY?
DAVE: Yeah.

(Dave enters the room. He takes off his clothes and gets into bed with Maria.)

Why are you crying. Don't cry. There's nothing to cry about. Now turn over.

(He flips her onto her belly.)

We're going to do something a little different.

(He takes out lubricant and smears it in between her butt cheeks. He then starts to ram his penis into her anus roughly. She screams.)

Yeah. This is going to hurt a little.

(He finally gets it all the way in and starts to pump away furiously without any regard for her. She is crying and screaming uncontrollably.)

This is good for you, you little slut. It'll put hair on your chest. Oh, your little ass pussy feels so good.

(He ejaculates. He puts his clothes back on.)

We'll be back tomorrow. Make sure to look pretty. We're going to be taking pictures.

SCENE 6

Dave has just returned from his trip to Ecuador. He greets his wife, Michelle.

DAVE: Hey, honey!
MICHELLE: Hi!

(They kiss.)

How was your trip?
DAVE: Fantastic! It was warm, the air was clean, and the people in Ecuador are so generous. These people were poor, yet they'd give you the shirt off their back if you needed it.
MICHELLE: I'm glad to hear that you and Vernon had such a great time.

(Pause.)

Did you miss me?

(He takes her in his arms.)

DAVE: I missed you so much. I really missed the way you cradle .me as I fall asleep.

(They kiss.)

MICHELLE: I missed you, too. *(Seductively)* I've got a special surprise for you tonight.

(They make out a bit. Then she stops.)

Not until tonight, mister. How was the conference?
DAVE: Oh you know how it is. A bunch of pseudo-intellectual blowhards droning on and on about Byron, Wordsworth and Shelley. None of these guys knew what they were talking about. I mean, everyone knows that Byron was the greatest romantic poet.

(Pause.)

Anyway, how's work been?
MICHELLE: I'm defending this guy who's a total jerk. Every time I have a meeting with him he makes these creepy sexual advances, like flicking his tongue at me like this.

(She makes the gesture with her tongue. Then she does a line of coke.)

And whenever I tell him to stop, he's like, "I'm sorry but you're just so beautiful." I'll tell you. If he keeps it up I'm going to make sure that he goes to jail for a very long time. See, what these guys don't realize is that I can be saying one thing and inferring another through my gestures. I can say, "My client is completely innocent," and then wink at the judge. Or I can make it clear through the tone in my voice that I don't actually believe anything I'm saying about his innocence.
DAVE: What's he accused of?
MICHELLE: Strangling some chick and then raping her corpse.
DAVE: Oh my God! That's sick!
MICHELLE: Tell me about it.

DAVE: Do you think he did it?

MICHELLE: Oh yeah. He did it. You should have seen the photos from the crime scene. Really gruesome stuff. He carved weird symbols into her skin and cut the webbing between her fingers. I'll tell you. That motherfucker better stop flicking his tongue at me or I'm gonna make sure he goes to jail.

(Pause.)

How was the coke in Ecuador?

DAVE: Oh yeah. It was amazing. Amazing. I brought you a little present.

(He takes a wrapped gift out of his suitcase. She opens it. It is an ounce of cocaine.)

MICHELLE: Thank you, honey! This is so sweet!

(They kiss. Then they greedily do some coke.)

SCENE 7

Dave and Vernon are in Dave's office.

VERNON: How's the hangover?

DAVE: Moderate. On a scale of one to ten mine's a four. How about you?

VERNON: Mine's about a two and a half.

DAVE: Not bad. How much did you drink last night?

VERNON: About a third of a liter of Johnnie Walker. How about you?

DAVE: Half a liter.

(Pause.)

Hey. I got the pictures developed.

VERNON: Where?

DAVE: I took them to the guy who tipped us off about Ecuador.

(Dave takes the pictures out of his desk. They look at the pictures.)

That was some sweet pussy wasn't it?

VERNON *(Sweetly)*: The best. I miss her. I miss the games of hide-and-go-seek that we played.

DAVE: Look at this one. You can't even see my dick because it's so far down her throat. That girl sure knew how to relax those gag muscles.

VERNON *(Sweetly)*: Coming in her mouth was the best feeling I've ever had.

DAVE: I liked coming in her ass. I feel a little bad about making her bleed.

VERNON: I think I'm in love with her, Dave. I can't stop thinking about her.

(Pause.)

DAVE: You're being really weird. It's kind of creeping me out.

VERNON: I'm serious, Dave!

DAVE: I'm serious, too! She was just some good pussy. Nothing more. I mean, what do you think you're going to do? Bring her to America, divorce your wife and make her your child-bride? You're getting love and lust confused.

VERNON: I loved the smell of her black hair. I loved her soft skin.

DAVE: That's lust!

VERNON: I want to adopt her.

DAVE: What? How much coke have you done today?

VERNON: It could work! I'll convince Lisa that we'd be really good people if we adopted a poor Ecuadorian child. Think about it. Think about all the organizations like Save The Children and Feed The Poor Dirty Children In Africa and Latin America. The world is overpopulated, blah blah blah. It could work. And then I'd have her all to myself.

DAVE: What are you going to do when she grows up?

VERNON: I'll do a Woody Allen. Everything worked out fine for him.

DAVE: Listen to me, Vernon. You need to get this girl out of your head. You have a wife who loves and supports you. Let this little girl go.

VERNON: Can I keep the pictures?

DAVE: I'll make you a set after I have someone airbrush our faces out of them so that we can sell them.

VERNON: Okay.

(There is a knock on Dave's door.)

DAVE: Hold on a second!

(He puts away the pictures.)

Come in.

(Carl enters. He is an African-American man dressed in kente cloth and a dashiki.)

Hey, Carl!

CARL: Hey, Dave!

DAVE *(To Vernon)*: I just hired Carl to be one of the new assistant professors in the department.

VERNON *(With no enthusiasm)*: Oh. That's great.

DAVE: And Vernon's a full professor and a good friend.

(They shake hands.)

CARL: Nice to meet you.

VERNON: Nice to meet you, too. What's your scholarly expertise?

CARL: African-American literature.

VERNON: Ah. I see. Very interesting.

CARL: What's yours?

VERNON: Romantic literature.

CARL: That's a good field.

VERNON: What's your favorite book?

CARL: *The Autobiography of Malcolm X.*

VERNON *(Genuinely)*: Does that really count as literature?

CARL: Why wouldn't it be?

VERNON: Well, you know.

(Pause.)

CARL: No. I don't know.

DAVE: I have an idea! Why don't we invite Carl over to have dinner with us and our wives on Saturday night!

VERNON: We could do that.

DAVE: Well, Carl?

CARL: I'd love to.

SCENE 8

Vernon, Lisa, Carl and Michelle are having drinks after dinner at Dave's house. When the lights come up everyone is laughing except Vernon.

LISA: So, where did you grow up?

CARL: Newark, New Jersey.

MICHELLE: Newark's a pretty rough place, isn't it?

CARL: Yeah. It was tough. Mom raised us by herself and we lived in the projects.

LISA: How terrible for you! Where was your father?

CARL: In jail. He died there. My mom had me when she was sixteen years old. My dad was a drug dealer. He got caught with eight ounces of cocaine.

DAVE *(In disbelief)*: They threw him in jail for life! Just for having eight ounces! I've bought— That sounds like racism to me!

MICHELLE: That is racist!

LISA: Totally.

(Vernon sighs loudly. Everyone looks at him for a moment. Pause.)

Honey? Don't you think what happened to Carl's father is racist?

VERNON: I think that people's actions have consequences.

CARL: That's true.

VERNON: I mean if you deal drugs and have children when you're a teenager, what do you think your life is going to be like?

LISA: Vernon, stop!

CARL *(To Lisa)*: It's okay. *(To Vernon)* It's true that actions have consequences, but don't you think there is a sociological problem in the black community that leads to teenage pregnancy and drug addiction?

VERNON: No, I don't think that. I think people in the ghetto are lazy and adverse to doing hard work. Instead of working hard in school and going to college, they decided to deal drugs because it's easy money. They bring it upon themselves.

CARL: How can you say that?

VERNON: How can you say that it's a sociological problem?

CARL: Because I lived it! That's how. Where did you grow up?

VERNON: Short Hills.

CARL: Where did you go to high school?

VERNON: Pingry.

CARL: Oh, I see. You're just a rich boy who never had to worry about anything. You can't understand the problems of the ghetto because you were born with a silver spoon in your mouth!

VERNON: That's not true! Sure we had money. Sure we belonged to a country club. The same one as Dave—

DAVE: Don't bring me into this.

VERNON: But I worked my butt off in school, studying for four hours a night so that I could get into Harvard. I earned it.

CARL: You didn't earn anything. It was all handed to you. How is a child in the ghetto supposed to do well in school when his mother is on crack, his dad is in jail, and he's in an inner-city classroom with forty kids and the teacher can't even control the class? In order to do well in school you need to live in an environment that is conducive to learning. And you need guidance. You had your parents to help you do your homework. You had a spacious room in a comfortable environment. These kids don't have their parents to help them! These kids live in two-room apartments with no electricity and not even enough food to eat!

VERNON: You're exaggerating!

CARL: No, I'm not. I lived it. I was happy if Mama was able to feed us one meal a day!

VERNON: But you made it! You grew up in the ghetto and now you have a PhD. If you can do it, then any of these kids can do it. These kids use their environment as an excuse to justify their behavior. That's all I'm saying.

CARL: I was lucky.

VERNON: No you weren't. You got where you are because of hard work.

CARL: Look, all I'm saying is that there is a cycle of poverty that black people in the ghetto are stuck in. And until white society stops blaming black people for the violence and drugs, and realizes that resources need to be put into reducing class size and offering economic opportunity, then nothing is ever going to change.

LISA: I think you might be the racist, Vernon. I agree with Carl's point of view.

MICHELLE: Me too.

DAVE: Me three.

SCENE 9

Vernon addresses the audience.

VERNON: What the fuck was that? *(Mimicking his wife)* "I think you might be the racist, Vernon." Well so what if I'm a racist! They're all racists, too. They just pretend to care about black people because kente-cloth Carl was there. *(Mimicking them)* "We love Carl. Oh poor Carl had to grow up in the ghetto and he was raised by a single mom. Poor him."

I really hate that nigger! I mean, don't you hate niggers like that? Niggers who walk around wearing kente cloth and a dashiki, celebrating Kwanzaa and lecturing people about the plight of ghetto life. I'm sick of it! Aren't you? We need to lead a revolution against these kente-cloth niggers! I think we should round them up like Hitler rounded up the Jews! He thinks he's so great because he went to Howard University. They call Howard the black Harvard. Well I went to the real Harvard! People go to Nigger Harvard because they're too stupid to get into the real one. We should burn Howard and all the rest of those nigger colleges, too! I hate Carl. Entering my white haven and turning my precious white friends against me. I was so happy. Do you know how hard I worked to surround myself with white people? It's really hard when your whole family is black! But I did it because I didn't want to be around niggers anymore. Do you know how much I love my lily white wife? My white best friend? How I love living every day knowing that that white woman is mine? All mine. It's status for me. When people see me walking down the street with my white best friend and my white wife, they know I'm different. They say to themselves: Ahh. He's not one of those dangerous gun-wielding ghetto Negroes! He's the kind of Negro that I like! The kind of Negro that I'd like to have over for dinner to show that I'm not a racist. The kind of Negro that I just might let my daughter date. A Negro who's not going to go around quoting Malcolm X and exploiting my white guilt like kente-cloth Carl.

SCENE 10

Vernon walks into Dave's office. Dave is working at his computer.

VERNON: What's up?
DAVE: You know. What's up with you?
VERNON: Not much. How's your hangover?

DAVE: I'd say a three out of ten.

VERNON *(Impressed with how mild Dave's hangover is)*: Not bad! How much did you drink?

DAVE: About a third of a liter.

VERNON: Very moderate.

DAVE: How's your hangover?

VERNON: About a six.

DAVE: That kind of sucks.

VERNON: Yeah. I drank half a liter.

DAVE: Half a liter's no good. You need a drink.

(Dave pours Vernon a drink.)

VERNON: Why did you side with Carl the other night?

DAVE: What was I supposed to do?

VERNON: You're my best friend. You could have defended me!

DAVE: Defend you and look like a racist! No way! If I took your side Carl would tell every professor in the department that I'm a fucking racist. I'd lose my job.

VERNON: Do you think I'm a racist for the views I hold?

DAVE: Of course not! I feel the same way! But you can't go around saying things like that in front of black people.

VERNON: I'm black!

DAVE: Barely.

(Dave takes out a mirror with cocaine on it.)

Maybe this will make you shut up and stop your whining.

(Vernon does a line.)

VERNON: Thanks.

DAVE: Check this out! I downloaded all of our pictures of Maria and created a website!

VERNON: You what?

DAVE: Dude. We're going to make so much money.

VERNON: We can't do this. We're going to get caught. The FBI's always arresting people for doing this kind of shit.

DAVE: Don't worry about it. I had my friend hook it up so that no one can trace it back to our computers! How cool is that?

VERNON: You're exploiting her!

DAVE: What?

VERNON: Yeah. You heard me. You're exploiting my little girl!

DAVE: Vernon. You're really starting to worry me. You need to come back to earth. Maria is not your little girl and you exploited her just as much as I did when you fucked her.

VERNON: I didn't exploit her! It was love!

DAVE: It was not love. She just had a really tight pussy. That's what you loved. Nothing more. I've got to go teach. Are you going to be okay?

VERNON: Yeah.

(Dave starts to leave.)

DAVE: Oh yeah. Can you take a look at this book? *(Hands Vernon a book)* It's called *A Heartbreaking Work of Staggering Genius*. It was nominated for the Pulitzer a couple of years ago. I'm thinking about making it required reading for freshman comp.

VERNON: Yeah. I'll take a look at it.

DAVE: Thanks.

(Dave leaves.)

SCENE 11

Fantasy sequence #1.
Vernon is still standing in Dave's office when Maria runs in wearing lingerie.

MARIA: Hi, Daddy!

(Vernon picks her up and kisses her on the lips.)

VERNON: How's Daddy's little girl?

(He puts her onto his lap.)

What did you learn in school today?

MARIA: I learned that George Washington was a good man because he didn't tell any lies. When his father asked whether he had chopped down a cherry tree he told the truth.

VERNON: That's a good lesson, honey. Honesty is always the best policy. Promise me that you'll never tell lies.

MARIA: I promise. I never will! Daddy. There's something hard in your pants.

VERNON: Honey. Would you mind moving your butt back and forth in Daddy's lap? That would make Daddy very happy.

(She starts to grind her butt into his lap.)

MARIA: Like this, Daddy?

VERNON: Yes, Maria. Just like that.

MARIA: Oh, Daddy. You're getting harder. It feels so good.

VERNON: I'm getting harder because I love you. This is how a father shows his daughter love.

MARIA: I'm getting all wet between my legs, Daddy.

VERNON: That's natural, honey. That's what happens when your daddy loves you.

MARIA: Do I feel good, Daddy?

VERNON: Like heaven.

MARIA: Am I making my daddy feel good? All I want is to make my daddy feel good.

(She has an orgasm.)

Oh, Daddy.

VERNON: Oh, Maria. My little angel, Maria.

(Lisa enters wearing lingerie.)

LISA *(Seductive anger)*: What are you two doing?

(They stop.)

Were you starting without me? I told you not to get started
without me. Vernon?

VERNON: Yes, dear.

LISA: Do you love our daughter more than you love me?

VERNON: Of course not, honey. I love you both the same.

(Vernon and Lisa kiss for a few moments then stop.)

LISA: And does Maria love her mommy?

MARIA: Very much.

*(Lisa kisses Maria on the lips. Maria and Vernon start to
make out while Lisa starts to give Vernon a blowjob as the
lights fade to black.)*

SCENE 12

Vernon addresses his freshman English class.

VERNON: I read your papers and I was very disappointed to find
that many of you don't know how to write in proper formal
essay structure. This is something that you should have
mastered in high school. As a matter of fact I'm amazed
that you were able to gain acceptance into a prestigious
institution like this without knowing how to write properly.
I mean, you had to submit an essay to get in.

So listen up, freshman, I'm only going to say this once.
An essay has three parts: the introduction, the body, and
the conclusion. In the first sentence of your introductory
paragraph you must introduce the text you're writing about
and the author. You must underline or italicize the title of
the text. The last sentence of your introductory paragraph
should contain your thesis. Your thesis presents the topic

that you will argue in your paper. The first sentence of each body paragraph is your topic sentence. Your topic sentence states what that particular paragraph is about. Your paper should never stray from your thesis and a body paragraph should never stray from its topic sentence. Focus must be maintained at all times! You must include two quotes from the text in each body paragraph. When you quote you must use parenthetical notation. In the first sentence of your conclusion you must restate your thesis. In the conclusion you must summarize the major points that you made in the essay. The conclusion is also the time to give a personal example from your life or the world.

I don't want to see the word "I" anywhere else in your paper! You don't say, "I think Iago is in love with Desdemona"! You say, "Iago is in love with Desdemona"! The latter is a much stronger statement. The second you say, "I think," your credibility is called into question. If I see the word "I" anywhere but the conclusion you will automatically receive an F. If anyone hands in a paper that's not written in the exact manner that I have prescribed you will automatically fail!

Remember to write all your papers in twelve-point Times New Roman. None of that Courier New business.

You're dismissed.

SCENE 13

Michelle, Carl and Lisa are alone talking in Vernon and Lisa's home.

CARL: And that's how my great-great-grandfather got shot trying to escape from slavery.
MICHELLE: That's horrible, Carl!
LISA: Your poor great-great-grandfather!
MICHELLE: Will you tell us another story about your ancestry?
CARL: I don't know. I feel like I'm boring you.
LISA: Not at all. Nothing could be further from the truth.
MICHELLE: We love hearing your stories!

CARL: Okay. My great-great-grandmother on my mother's side was a great beauty. They say that she was the most beautiful slave on Mr. Higgins' plantation. Everyone was in love with her. Even Mr. Higgins, her owner. Every night, Mr. Higgins would sneak out of bed after his wife had gone to sleep and he would crawl into my great-great-grandmother's shack and rape her.

LISA: How do you know it was rape?

CARL: Well, she didn't have much choice in the matter, now did she?

LISA: I suppose not. Sorry for interrupting.

CARL: Anyway, my great-great-grandmother had a boyfriend on another plantation. She would sneak off at night after Mr. Higgins had returned to his great big house. But Mr. Higgins caught wind of this and became very jealous. One night after he had raped my great-great-grandmother, he told her that she better not go anywhere that night and then he left. She disobeyed him and snuck off to see her boyfriend anyway. When Mr. Higgins found her missing later that night, a blinding rage overtook him. He could not bear the thought of my great-great-grandmother with another man. The next morning after Mr. Higgins ate his breakfast and said his morning prayers (he used to pray for a half hour each morning) he called her out from the field and tied her to the whipping post. He gave her one hundred lashes, all the while shouting, "Nigger Bitch," and, "Nigger Whore," as his wife looked on. They say her blood ran like a river when it was all over.

LISA: Oh my God. Slavery was so terrible for your people. How could he do that in front of his wife, I mean she must have known.

CARL: That's just the way things were then. It was common practice. Do you want to know something else?

MICHELLE: What?

CARL: Mr. Higgins, the man who whipped my great-great-grandmother and raped her every night, is my great-great-grandfather on my mother's side.

MICHELLE: Oh my God! How does that make you feel?

CARL: I don't know. I have very complicated feelings about the matter. I guess in reality I'm part slave owner and part slave. I wish I could destroy my white slave-owning blood. But I can't. I can't. It's just as much a part of me as my blackness.

(He starts to cry. Michelle and Lisa comfort him by showering him with kisses, all the while repeating, "Poor Carl, poor Carl." He stops crying.)

LISA: We should go soon. Vernon's going to be home any minute.

MICHELLE: We can go to my place. Dave won't be home for a couple of hours.

SCENE 14

Carl is having sex with Michelle from behind while Lisa watches and masturbates.

CARL: Oh yeah. C'mon, baby. Say it! *(More forcefully)* Say it!

MICHELLE: Fuck me, ghetto nigger!

CARL: Again!

MICHELLE: Fuck me, you ghetto nigger!

CARL: Good. Good. You're a dirty white bitch. You know that? Say the next thing! Say it!

MICHELLE: Pull my hair, you jungle monkey! Pull my hair!

(Carl pulls her hair.)

Harder!

(He pulls her hair harder.)

CARL: That's right, you stupid white whore. Say the next thing!

MICHELLE: I don't remember.

(Michelle has an orgasm.)

CARL: Try harder. I'm almost there!
MICHELLE: Your dick feels so good.
CARL: No! That's not it!

(Lisa has an orgasm.)

MICHELLE: Oh yeah. Fuck me like a runaway slave!
CARL: Oh yeah!

(He ejaculates.)

LISA: It's not true that all black men have big dicks. Your dick is so much bigger than Vernon's.
CARL: It's your turn, you horny white slut.

(Lisa and Michelle switch places. Carl starts to have sex with Lisa as the lights fade to black.)

SCENE 15

Vernon has just walked into Dave's office.

DAVE: Hey, Vern. What's up?
VERNON: There's something strange going on.
DAVE: What do you mean?
VERNON: I came home the other day and Carl was hanging out with Michelle and Lisa. Isn't that weird?
DAVE: It is a little weird. I think they feel sorry for him. The really seem to be into his ghetto upbringing and plight as a black man.
VERNON: I know. What are we going to do?
DAVE: Do?
VERNON: Yeah. What are we going to do?

DAVE: Why do we have to do anything? I mean, it seems pretty harmless. Besides, I like Carl. It really doesn't bother me that much. Did you get a chance to read *A Heartbreaking Work of Staggering Genius?*

VERNON: Yeah.

DAVE: What did you think?

VERNON: I think it's good. His writing is pretty innovative. Instead of telling a linear story he writes in the way that the human brain actually functions. Making random associations and delving into random pieces of distant memory. It's very sophisticated stuff.

DAVE: I agree. Do you think it's a good book for freshman comp?

VERNON: I think it's a great book for that. The students will think it's interesting. And I was thinking that we could have them write their own memoirs after they've read the book.

DAVE: That's brilliant! They'll read a memoir and write their own!

VERNON: Yeah. Their memoirs will be much more interesting to read than those boring papers written in formal essay structure. It's so fucking boring. Dude. Can't you make a rule that senior professors don't have to teach freshman comp? I really hate it.

DAVE: We all hate it, but there's nothing that I can do. This is the way the president wants it.

VERNON: But senior professors at other universities don't have to teach the lower-level writing classes. They get to teach what they want!

DAVE: I know. I know. But the president feels that freshman should have access to the real professors, not just adjuncts and grad students. He thinks it's a more egalitarian system.

VERNON: That's pure bullshit.

DAVE: I know. Hey. This is for you.

(Dave takes five thousand dollars out of a drawer and hands it to Vernon.)

VERNON: What's this for?

DAVE: It's from our internet site. The pictures of Maria are selling like hotcakes, dude!

VERNON: Really? How much are you selling the pictures for?

DAVE: Thirty-five dollars each and four for one hundred.

VERNON: Jesus Christ. How much is this?

DAVE: Five thousand dollars. I think we should go back and take more pictures!

VERNON: I don't think so, and I don't want this money.

DAVE: Why?

VERNON: You know why.

DAVE: Not this sissy bullshit again.

VERNON: I know you think it's weird, but I refuse to exploit her anymore. I love her.

(He gives the money back to Dave.)

DAVE: I'm not going to fight you on this one. More money for me.

VERNON: Why don't you buy me an ounce of cocaine for my birthday and we'll call it even.

DAVE: Deal.

SCENE 16

Vernon addresses the audience.

VERNON: What the fuck is going on? It's bad enough that Carl exists. But now he's hanging out with my women! My white women! No-siree-bob. I don't like it one bit. There's something fishy about the whole situation. He wants to fuck my women. I know it! He wants to steal my beautiful white goddesses away from me. He doesn't understand white women the way I understand white women. He doesn't know how to cherish and treat them like the beautiful gems that they are. He's probably never even slept with a white woman. He's not good enough to sleep with a white woman. White women don't like ghetto dashiki-wearing niggers like Carl!

Can you believe that he's a professor? Can you believe that some university actually gave him a PhD? For what? Reading Malcolm X? Can you believe that your children might have him as a teacher some day? Do you want your children to be alone in a classroom with him? I certainly don't.

I love Dave's wife. I never meant to sleep with her but it just happens sometimes. You know. The first time it happened we were at a party. Dave and Lisa couldn't make it, and every word we said to one another was filled with sexual tension. I mean, we couldn't control ourselves, so we went into the master bedroom of our friend's apartment, locked the door, and fucked like it was going out of style. And you know what the best thing is? She loves to get fucked in the ass! SHE LOVES IT! My wife won't let me fuck her in the ass. So if you really think about it, it's not really cheating. When I fuck my wife, I fuck her vagina. And when I fuck Michelle, it's usually in her ass. Is anal sex *really* sex? I actually hear that some girls have anal sex to prevent losing their virginity. I wish I had dated a girl like that in high school.

I don't want you to get the impression that I'm fucking my best friend's wife behind his back. I don't fuck her that much and I don't go out of my way to do it. It just happens sometimes. You know?

Carl better stay away from my alabaster queens or else there's going to be trouble.

SCENE 17

Fantasy sequence #2.
Vernon is alone. A magic lamp sits on the floor. Vernon picks up the magic lamp and rubs it. A Genie appears.

GENIE: Hello.
VERNON: Uh, hi.
GENIE: What's your name?

VERNON: Vernon.

GENIE: Vernon, I'm going to grant you three wishes.

VERNON: What should I wish for?

GENIE: You can wish for anything that your heart desires.

VERNON: Anything?

GENIE: Yes anything.

VERNON: My first wish is to be white.

(The Genie applies white makeup to Vernon's face.)

GENIE: Your wish has been granted. What's your second wish?

VERNON: I want to be a Southern plantation owner.

(The stage is transformed into a Southern plantation.)

GENIE: Your wish has been granted. What's your final wish?

VERNON: I want kente-cloth Carl to be my slave.

(Carl enters wearing tattered slave clothing. Lisa enters as a Southern belle. Vernon smokes a cigar.)

CARL: Massa, you wanted to see me?

VERNON: Are you looking directly at me? You put your head down and avert your eyes when you're in the presence of a white man. You understand?

CARL: Yes, Massa. I'm sorry, Massa.

VERNON: Good. Now go fetch me another mint julep, nigger.

CARL: Yes, Massa.

(Carl exits.)

VERNON: How's my beautiful peach today?

LISA: I'm doing just fine. My nigresses have been making me a new quilt! I can't wait for it to be finished. The only problem is that niggers work so slow sometimes.

VERNON: A truer sentence has never been spoken. Take Carl for instance.

(He shouts.)

Nigger! Hurry up with my mint julep! I'm thirsty!

LISA: Now you mustn't get angry, Vernon. Carl can't help it. Being lazy and shiftless is just their nature.

VERNON: I know, but I feel, as an upstanding white people, it is our duty to rid niggers of their animalistic and lazy nature. Now you watch what I do to Carl when he gets back. I'm going to show you how to encourage niggers to stop being so nigger-like.

(Carl enters, running with Vernon's mint julep.)

CARL: I'm sorry it took so long, Massa.

(He hands Vernon the drink.)

VERNON: You spilled some when you ran in. You must learn to be more careful. I paid good money for this liquor and I don't like to see it wasted. Do you like to waste money, boy?

CARL: No, Massa.

VERNON: Good. Now lick up what you spilled.

CARL: But, Massa—

VERNON: Don't talk back, boy!

CARL: But, Massa—

VERNON: Lick it up, nigger!

(Carl licks up what he spilled. Vernon takes a sip of his mint julep.)

How did it taste?

CARL: That's a good drink, Massa.

VERNON: If you think this is good then you have very bad taste. Come here.

(Carl walks over to Vernon. Vernon throws his drink into Carl's face.)

There ain't enough julep in this drink! Now go quickly! Make me another one with more julep!

(Carl runs off. He turns to Lisa.)

Now that's how you teach niggers to act properly.

LISA: You did a good job, honey. I wish I could learn to treat niggers like that, then my life would be so much easier. I bet my niggresses would've already been done with my quilt if I treated them correctly, like you do.

VERNON: You can do it! You just need to be more firm. Your problem is that you sometimes treat niggers like they're human.

LISA: How dare you say that to me?! I certainly do not treat niggers like they're human.

VERNON: Honey, I'm not trying to insult you. I'm just trying to offer some constructive criticism. For instance, sometimes I hear you address niggers by their name. I always address them as "nigger" or "boy" or "girl" in the case of a woman.

LISA: I'd like to do that, but how will they know who you're talking to? I mean, whenever I walk into a room and say "nigger" they all turn around. How will niggers know which nigger I'm talking to if I don't use their name?

VERNON: Hmm. That's an interesting question. You know, I never thought about it like that. I'll have to sleep on it.

(Carl enters walking very slowly and carefully so that he doesn't spill any of the drink.)

You are such a slow nigger. That took even longer than last time.

CARL: Sorry, Massa. I wanted to make it jus' right for you.

(He hands Vernon the drink. Vernon takes a sip.)

How is it, Massa?

(Vernon takes another sip. He rolls the liquor around in his mouth for a while, assessing the quality of the drink.)

VERNON: You've done a good job, boy! This is a fine mint julep!

(Lisa has a coughing fit. Vernon and Carl look at Lisa. Vernon pats her on the back to alleviate the coughing.)

CARL: Do you want me to fetch you some water, ma'am?

(Vernon looks up and sees that Carl is looking at his wife. He stares at Carl in disbelief for a couple of moments.)

VERNON: How dare you look at my wife? How dare you? Your eyes should never gaze upon a white woman's face. Never. I can see it in your eyes. You're lusting after my wife! Do you actually think that a white woman could ever be attracted to a monkey like you? All you niggers are the same. Your most sacred wish is to rape a white woman. That's what you would do all day if we didn't keep you in your places. I'm going to whip that fantasy out of your head, you nappy-headed ashy nigger!

(He roughly strings Carl up to a whipping post.)

This is going to teach you, you filthy rapist!

(He whips Carl seven times. After each lash Carl let's out an excruciating scream.)

I hope you learned something.

SCENE 18

Dave has frantically entered Vernon's office.

DAVE: Dude, you were right. There's something really fucked up about the situation with Carl and our wives.

VERNON: What happened?

DAVE: You don't want to know. I'm so disgusted. I don't even want to say it.

VERNON: What? You have to tell me!

DAVE: I went home this afternoon and they were having a fucking orgy!

VERNON: Please tell me you're kidding.

DAVE: I'm dead serious. He was fucking your wife while my wife watched and masturbated. And she was saying all this weird shit like, "Fuck me, you ghetto nigger."

VERNON: He was fucking my wife?

DAVE: What are you, fucking deaf? Yes, he was fucking your wife.

VERNON: What did you do?

DAVE: Nothing.

VERNON: Did they see you?

DAVE: No. I just walked out. I was in shock.

VERNON: What should we do?

DAVE: I have no clue. The situation is just so crazy. I mean, what do they see in him? He's so ugly! He's got those fucking dreadlocks.

VERNON: Fire him! You have to fire him.

DAVE: I can't fire him, dude. He was just hired.

VERNON: Well, something needs to be done about that motherfucker.

DAVE: Yeah.

VERNON: I'll take care of it.

DAVE: What are you going to do?

VERNON: Don't worry about it. I've got to go.

DAVE: I shut down the website.

VERNON: Why?

DAVE: It was taking up too much of my time. At the rate I was going, I would've had to quit my job and become a professional pornographer.

VERNON *(Confused)*: Okay.

(Lights down.)

SCENE 19

Vernon is tying a noose to a tree branch in Carl's backyard. He then breaks into Carl's house where Carl is sleeping. Vernon creeps up to Carl's bed with a gun. Vernon pulls up a chair and watches Carl sleep for a while with the gun pointed at him.

VERNON: Rise and shine!

(Carl remains sleeping.)

C'mon! Rise and shine, Carl. There's African drumming at the Alvin Ailey Center. Don't you want to see some black people dance and beat drums like monkeys?

(Carl wakes up.)

CARL *(Startled)*: What's going on?
VERNON: I thought we could go see the African drummers at the Alvin Ailey Center.
CARL: Am I dreaming?
VERNON: This is no dream.
CARL: What time is it?
VERNON: Three o'clock in the morning?
CARL *(Notices the gun)*: Why do you have that gun?
VERNON: It's for protection. I hear this neighborhood is pretty violent. Lot's of black people, I hear.
CARL: You're scaring me.
VERNON: When did I start to scare you? You seem pretty fearless to me. Turn over.
CARL: What for?
VERNON: Turn over or I'm going to fucking shoot you.

(He slaps Carl across the face. Carl turns onto his stomach. Vernon straddles him and ties his hands together.)

Good boy.

CARL: Why are you doing this to me?

VERNON: I hear you like white women.

(Silence.)

What? Cat got your tongue.

CARL: Look, Vernon. It's not what you think.

VERNON: Really? Fucking my wife isn't what I think it is? Okay. Then tell me what it is.

CARL: Look, man, she seduced me.

VERNON: Don't you mean "they" seduced you?! Don't forget that you fucked Dave's wife, too. I thought you'd have some respect for the man who gave you a job.

CARL: Okay. They seduced me. They took advantage of me. Hey. The flesh is weak. I didn't know what to do.

VERNON: You're a real coward. You know that? When I first met you I thought you were the upstanding, moral, righteous black guy. I actually kind of admired you. I didn't like you. But I admire people who have morals and values because I have no concept of what that's like. I thought that maybe you were a better person than me. But now I know that you're as guilty as the rest of us. We're all going to have a big party in Hell! Yeah!

CARL: Please, Vernon.

VERNON: Get the fuck up!

(Carl doesn't move.)

I said get the fuck up, you stupid nigger!

(Carl gets up. He is only wearing his underwear.)

CARL: Can I put on some clothes?

VERNON: No. You look great in your underwear, you sexy bitch.

(Vernon grabs Carl's butt and licks his face.)

I see why my women like you so much. Ohh. Ohh. You're so sexy! Makes me feel gay! Makes me want to stick my dick in your ass! Yeeeha!

(Vernon licks Carl's face as he presses the gun into Carl's chest.)

CARL: Where are you taking me?

VERNON: Into your backyard. I've got a big surprise for you. Walk faster, you oversexed nigger! You know, I didn't think a dashiki-wearing kente-cloth nigger like you would've been interested in white she-devils.

(They are at the rope.)

CARL *(Very scared)*: Why are you doing this to me?

VERNON: Do you really want to know?

CARL: Yes.

VERNON: First: put your head through the rope. Then I'll tell you.

(Carl climbs up onto the stepstool.)

Oh, Carl. You smell pretty bad. Don't tell me that you shit yourself.

(Carl jumps off the stepstool and starts to run across the stage. Vernon shoots Carl and he falls.)

That'll teach you to try to escape from me, you stupid nigger.

(Pause.)

I hope that tainting my white doves was worth it for you, because they'll never be the same to me. A dark stain now rests upon them.

(Vernon calmly walks off.)

END OF PLAY

STROM THURMOND IS NOT A RACIST

PRODUCTION HISTORY

The world premiere of *Strom Thurmond Is Not a Racist* was
produced by the Immediate Theater Company (Jose Zayas,
Artistic Director) at the Brick Theater in New York on Febru-
ary 8, 2007. It was directed by Jose Zayas; set design was by
Ryan Elliot Kravetz, costume design was by Mel Haley, light-
ing design was by Jim French, sound design was by Jeremy
Wilson; the production stage manager was Jessica Urtecho.
The cast was:

STROM THURMOND	Hugh Sinclair
CARRIE/ESSIE MAE	Makeda Christodoulos
STROM'S FATHER/TRENT LOTT/	
INTERVIEWER/AIDE	Peter Schuyler

CHARACTERS

STROM THURMOND, a segregationist politician
CARRIE BUTLER, the Thurmond family's black maid
ESSIE MAE WASHINGTON-WILLIAMS, Carrie and Strom's
   illegitimate biracial daughter
STROM'S FATHER
TRENT LOTT, a United States Senator
INTERVIEWER
AIDE

SETTING

South Carolina and Washington, D.C. 1924–2002.

NOTE

All the stage directions that indicate important information about time and location should be projected onto a screen so that the audience is aware of exactly where and when a scene takes place.

The play can be double-cast so that only three actors are needed: one actor to play Strom Thurmond, one actress to play Carrie Butler and Essie Mae Washington-Williams and one actor to play Strom's Father, Trent Lott, Interviewer and Aide.

SCENE 1

Carrie Butler, the Thurmonds' black family maid, fifteen, in her maid's
uniform, is cleaning the Thurmonds' living room. She is vibrant and
sexy. Strom, wearing a suit, twenty-two, enters. It is 1924.

STROM: How are you doing today, Miss Carrie?

CARRIE: I'm doing just fine, Massa Thurmond, and yourself?

STROM: Very, very well. I was wondering whether you would
take pity on a poor country gentleman, and escort him on
a walk in the garden?

CARRIE: But I have work to do, Massa Thurmond.

STROM: Forget about work for the moment. Your problem is
that you work too hard. You need to put aside some time for
yourself to relax. That is the secret to happiness.

CARRIE: No offense, Massa Thurmond, but your family makes
me work seven days a week for sixteen hours a day. When
is there time for me to relax? Us poor folk have got to
work.

STROM: Let's not get too bogged down with details, with the logistics of the manner, but let me just say that you need to learn how to think outside of the box.

CARRIE: What do you mean?

STROM: You just told me that you work seven days a week, for sixteen hours a day, isn't that right?

CARRIE: Yes, that's true.

STROM: That means that you have eight hours a day to yourself, that adds up to fifty-six hours a week, and two hundred and twenty-four hours a month. Don't you see, Miss Carrie, that you could be thinking up wonderful new inventions with that time, and painting beautiful murals of the dawn, singing the night away!

(Carrie looks at him as though he is crazy. She is hesitant, trying to wrap her mind around this point.)

CARRIE: I don't mean to be disrespectful, Massa Thurmond, but your plan doesn't leave me any time to sleep. How am I going to come here and work every day if I don't get no sleep?

STROM *(Shaking his head in disbelief of her ignorance and lazy attitude)*: Carrie, you need to learn to stop letting your mind indulge in such lazy thinking. Now come, let's go into the garden to get a breath of fresh air.

SCENE 2

Carrie and Strom are strolling in the garden.

STROM: Have you ever had the pleasure of strolling in the garden before?

CARRIE: No, sir, the garden is off limits to me.

STROM: I'll speak to my father about that. Everyone should be entitled to some beauty and fresh air.

CARRIE: Thank you, sir.

STROM: Please, Carrie, let's drop the formalities, there's no need for you to call me sir. Master Thurmond is just fine.

CARRIE: Whatever you say, Massa Thurmond.

(She looks around as if she is very worried and nervous about something.)

STROM: Is there something wrong?

CARRIE: Won't your father be angry if he catch us out here?

STROM: He isn't home. Besides, there's nothing wrong with two people enjoying each other's company in the garden.

CARRIE: Yes, sir.

STROM *(Disapproving of her calling him sir, reprimanding)*: Carrie.

CARRIE: Sorry, Massa Thurmond.

STROM: That's much better. Music to my ears.

(Pause.)

I think that you're a very sophisticated young woman, Carrie.

(Pause.)

Do you know what "sophisticated" means?

CARRIE: No.

STROM: Sophisticated means that you're worldly, that you're wise beyond your years. How old are you anyway?

CARRIE: Fifteen.

STROM: Yes indeed, you seem very mature for your age.

CARRIE: Them flowers are so beautiful. I've never been surrounded by so much beauty. What are them purple flowers called?

STROM: Those are called lilacs. Do you like them?

CARRIE: They're the prettiest flowers that I've ever seen in my life. Only weeds grow around my house.

(He picks twelve lilacs and hands them to her.)

STROM: Beautiful flowers for a beautiful girl. May I take your hand?

(She nods her head yes and smells her flowers.)

I've been thinking, Miss Carrie. I've been thinking that a girl as smart and sophisticated as you deserves more than to be a maid. Don't get me wrong, I think that the work you do is very noble, but my conscience tells me that you deserve an education, and since I am a teacher, I feel obligated to help you. It is God's will, and we cannot stand in the way of God's will.

CARRIE: Thank you, Massa Thurmond. You are truly a noble man. I believe that God will bless you for your good deeds. No one has ever been this nice to me before.

(Strom takes her cheek in his hand.)

STROM: You are so beautiful. Just like an angel.

(He kisses her for a long time, then pulls away abruptly, realizing the error of his ways.)

I'm so sorry for my indiscretion, Miss Carrie. That was unbecoming of a Southern gentleman. Please forgive me.

(She nods her head yes and smiles broadly. She obviously enjoyed the kiss very much.)

Well, you should get back to your work before I am led further into temptation.

SCENE 3

Strom is kneeling beside his bed. He says a short prayer.

STROM: Our Lord, who art in Heaven, please hear my prayer. Dear Lord, please forgive this poor wretched soul, I was led into temptation today. Please give me the strength not to be led into temptation ever again. Lord, also give me the strength to make the world a better place. I see such terrible storms brewing in the world today, please give me the strength to always stand up for what I know to be right and good and to always do your bidding. And please, please, Lord; always protect the glorious state of South Carolina. It is truly God's land. In Christ's name, amen.

SCENE 4

Carrie is cleaning the living room.

STROM: Carrie, stop your cleaning for a moment, it's time for your first lesson.

CARRIE: But your father will be furious if I don't finish my work.

STROM: Miss Carrie, you must learn to trust me. My father will be out for the rest of the evening. We've got the whole house to ourselves. Now sit down.

(She does.)

Carrie, do you know how to read?

CARRIE: I know the alphabet, sir.

STROM: I did not ask you whether you knew the alphabet, Miss Carrie. I asked whether you knew how to read.

(Pause.)

There's nothing to be ashamed of.

CARRIE: I didn't get no schooling beyond the first grade. I had to leave school to help my father around the house after my mama died. So no, sir, I don't know how to read too well.

STROM: Well, we're going to change that! Now read this poem by William Wordsworth.

(She tries to read but struggles. She tries to sound out the words. This should go on for an uncomfortably long amount of time.)

CARRIE: I wa- wa- wan- d- d- der- ed- l- l- lon- e- l- l- l- y-a-
a- ass—

(He grabs the book from her.)

STROM: That was good work, Miss Carrie.
CARRIE: Thank you.
STROM: Now listen.

I wandered lonely as a cloud
That floats on high o'er vales and hills,
When all at once I saw a crowd,
A host of golden daffodils;
Beside the lake, beneath the trees,
Fluttering and dancing in the breeze.

Continuous as the stars that shine
And twinkle on the milky way,
They stretched in never-ending line
Along the margin of a bay:
Ten thousand saw I at a glance,
Tossing their heads in sprightly dance.

(He stops reading and stares at her.)

CARRIE: That's beautiful, Master Thurmond.
STROM: You are the most beautiful girl that I've ever seen, Miss
Carrie.

(He kisses her and they have sex.)

SCENE 5

*Strom and his father are sitting on the couch smoking cigars. It is
six months later.*

STROM'S FATHER: Do you enjoy teaching?
STROM: I like it well enough.

STROM'S FATHER: I mean, are you passionate about it? Do you want it to be your career?

STROM: It's hard to say. I really haven't thought about it that much.

(Pause.)

Why do you ask?

STROM'S FATHER: Don't get me wrong, teaching is a fine and noble profession, and it's fine for you as a young man, but I eventually want you to aspire to something higher.

STROM: Like what?

STROM'S FATHER: Like law or politics. You have such a great intellect; I'd hate to see it wasted.

(Carrie walks into the room to clean. She is six months pregnant.)

Your grandfather—

(He notices Carrie. They get distracted from their conversation.)

It's a shame.

(He shakes his head disapprovingly as he looks at Carrie.)

STROM: What is?

STROM'S FATHER: It's a shame how these nigresses go around having children out of wedlock. They pop out babies at the same rate that dogs and rabbits do. It's not their fault though. Niggers are like animals.

(Strom is uncomfortable because Carrie is in the room and can hear everything.)

STROM: Dad!

STROM'S FATHER: Don't try to protect her. She needs to hear this. It'll be good for her.

(He goes right back to his point as if he hadn't been inter-
rupted. Carrie just keeps cleaning and tries to ignore what he's
saying as best she can.)

Niggers have no virtue or self-control, unlike white people.
That's why they need us to set an example for them and be
their guides.

STROM *(Challenging tone of voice)*: That's enough, Dad.

(Strom's Father slaps Strom hard across the face.)

STROM'S FATHER: What's gotten into you, boy?! This is my house.
Remember that. Don't every interrupt me again.

(Pause.)

Where was I? Oh yes! The Emancipation Proclamation was
the worst thing that ever happened to these niggers; someone should have shot Lincoln sooner, so he wouldn't have
ever had the chance to sign that sinful God-hating docu-
ment. Isn't that right, Carrie?

(She runs out of the room.)

I wonder what's gotten into her.

(He laughs in a sinister manner.)

SCENE 6

An orange grove behind the Thurmond Mansion. Carrie is alone
crying. Strom comes to find her. He stares at her for a moment
before he starts to speak. The moonlight shines brightly.

STROM: Please don't cry, Carrie. I hate to see you cry.
CARRIE: What are you doing out here?
STROM: I came to find you.

(He tries to put his arm around her but she moves away from him.)

I'm so sorry about the things my father said in front of you. I know it must have hurt.

CARRIE *(Not knowing how to say what she wants to say)*: Strom?

STROM: Yes, Carrie?

CARRIE: Do you think the way your daddy does? Do you think black people are like animals?

STROM *(In disbelief)*: How can you even ask me that?

CARRIE: You didn't try to stop him!

STROM: I tried!

(Pause.)

What could I do, Carrie? What could I do?

CARRIE *(Realizing that there's no reason for her to be upset because this is the society that they live in)*: Nothing. I don't know why I'm angry. It's just the way our world is.

(He puts his arms around her and looks into her eyes.)

STROM: I love you, Carrie. I have never felt love the way I feel with you. You make my soul feel free. Like a shooting star lighting up the midnight sky!

(They kiss.)

CARRIE: Strom, I love you so much. I just wish things could be different. I wish that we could live in a world where we didn't have to hide our love for each other. A world where we could walk down the street hand in hand and not be thrown in prison.

(Pause.)

I want to raise a family with you, Strom!

STROM: And I with you.

(He kisses her belly.)

Nothing would make me happier.

CARRIE: Do you think we ever really could, Strom? Do you think things could ever really change?

STROM: I hope so, Carrie. I hope our dreams aren't in vain.

(Pause.)

CARRIE: I've made a decision.

STROM: What?

CARRIE: When our child is born I'm going to send it up North to live with my sister. She'll take good care of our baby.

STROM: I wish we could keep it here. I want to see our baby grow. Can't we send the baby somewhere closer?

CARRIE: This is for the best, Strom. We can't have a mulatto child running around here. People would talk. I want to see you succeed, Strom! This baby would ruin your career. I want to see you become the great man that you're destined to be.

STROM *(Sadly)*: We'll send the baby up North.

(Pause.)

I want to make a promise to you, Carrie.

CARRIE: What's that?

STROM: I promise to support you and our child for the rest of our lives. No matter what happens.

SCENE 7

Strom's Father is in the living room reading alone when Strom enters, very excited.

STROM: Dad! What was it like to work for Governor Tillman?

STROM'S FATHER: Working for Ben Tillman was the best time of my life, Son. We were inseparable. Why do you ask?

STROM: I've been reading this book by Tillman and it's the most amazing philosophy that I've ever read. The most profound part of this book is when he describes the Anglo-Saxon race as being "The Flower of Humanity" because white people are responsible for civilization as we know it.

STROM'S FATHER: That's absolutely true. He was a genius.

STROM: His words really spoke to me, Dad. It made me realize that I have a higher purpose in life because God selected me to be one of the chosen few.

STROM'S FATHER: It makes me so proud that you appreciate Ben Tillman. Many of those Yankee nigger lovers had the nerve to call him a racist for speaking the truth.

STROM: That's the problem with Yankees. They refuse to face reality! Instead they keep on lying to themselves by preaching that niggers and whites are equal when clearly niggers are inferior to white people. It's insulting to the white race.

STROM'S FATHER: I wish you could have really met Governor Tillman. He was the first to hold you when you were a tiny baby. Said he thought you'd make a great governor some day. You two would have really gotten along.

STROM *(Very seriously)*: If white people are the flower of humanity, and niggers are the equivalent of barbarian beasts, then where do mulatto people fit in?

STROM'S FATHER: That's an excellent question, Strom. I've often pondered this myself. Mulatto intelligence varies based on the proportion of white blood in their veins. You see, mulattoes are more intelligent than pure-blooded niggers and maybe even more intelligent than the lower types of whites, but on the whole they are a frustrated and futureless class of people.

STROM: What about Booker T. Washington? Everyone seems to believe that he's a brilliant man. Theodore Roosevelt even invited him to dine at the White House.

STROM'S FATHER *(Clearly angered about Roosevelt inviting Booker T. Washington to the White House)*: Roosevelt set the South back forty years by entertaining that nigger! We had to lynch a thousand niggers before they learned their place in the South again! Niggers got uppity after they saw the President of the United States shaking hands with one of their kind.

STROM: What do you mean they got uppity?

STROM'S FATHER *(Ranting, enraged)*: When the niggers saw Booker T. Washington shaking Roosevelt's hand they started to feel equal to whites. This was a dire mistake. You see, niggers are a barbarian and savage race. The only thing those animals are good for is picking cotton, plowing fields and plundering the innocence of our chaste white sisters. Any progress the colored race has shown itself capable of achieving has come from slavery.

When Niggers were brought over from Africa they were pure barbarians. Noble white men civilized and Christianized those savage beasts. Slavery was the best thing that ever happened to those niggers, and they knew it! Niggers didn't go running North at the first shot of the Civil War. Most stuck by their masters! Even fought alongside them!

But these uppity niggers got infected with the virus of equality after they saw Roosevelt shake that nigger's hand. They wanted the State House, and then they wanted the White House. Damn uppity niggers started thinking they were good enough to marry white women! And when those niggers realized that they couldn't marry white women they reverted back to their savage natures. The poor African became a fiend! A wild beast seeking to devour, rape and murder white women! And that is why niggers have to be lynched sometimes! We must prevent them from reverting to their primal jungle instincts.

We must defend White, Southern, Female Purity at all costs! Lynching is chivalrous! Don't ever let anyone tell you differently.

STROM: I won't, Dad. I promise. I promise to lead the Anglo-Saxon race to greater glory! I think Ben Tillman was right. I'm going to run for Governor of South Carolina some day.

(They hug.)

SCENE 8

*1948. Twenty-three years after the previous scene. The setting is the
South Carolina Governor's Mansion. Strom Thurmond, now forty-
five, is the governor. He is speaking to an Aide. He is about to break
away from the Democratic Party so that he can run for president with
the newly formed Dixiecrat Party. Harry Truman is president.*

STROM: The Truman administration is engaging in completely
unconstitutional acts. I love my country! And as a retired
major general I believe that the army should overthrow the
Truman Administration.

AIDE: I agree with your position, sir, but you can't say that publicly.

STROM: Why not? I have always advocated that the military should challenge the civilian authority if the civilian
authority engages in unconstitutional acts. What's wrong
with saying that in my speeches?

AIDE: Again, Mr. Governor, I completely agree with your position, but not everyone sees President Truman's actions as
being unconstitutional. If you say you want the government
to be overthrown then people will think that you're a fanatic.

STROM: Anyone who doesn't see Truman's actions as unconstitutional is a nigger lover and a communist. They're the
fanatics. South Carolina is an autonomous state. The federal government can't just come and tell us that we have to
let niggers into our schools, movie theaters, churches, restaurants and homes. Desegregation is against God's will!
And mark my words, our country will be a sea of blood if
Truman tries to force his socialist values on us. We've had
a shaky armistice with the North since the Civil War, but
if he does this it's all over. The Soviet Union is run from
Moscow. If we let the United States be run by a bunch of
nigger lovers in Washington, then we're going to turn into
a goddamned communist state.

(The Aide looks at his watch.)

AIDE: Uh. I think your daughter is here. She said she'd be here at three o'clock.

STROM: Send her in. We'll finish this discussion later.

AIDE: Yes, Governor.

(Essie Mae enters. She is the biracial child that Strom fathered with Carrie Butler. She is twenty-one and in college. She goes to South Carolina State University. She is well dressed.)

ESSIE: Hello, Daddy.

(Strom gets up and gives her a hug.)

STROM: How's my sugarplum doing?

(He kisses her on the forehead.)

ESSIE: Just Fine.

STROM: And to what do I owe this visit from my lovely daughter?

ESSIE: Three things. Number one, to see my handsome father.

STROM: You warm my heart.

ESSIE: Two, for some shopping money. There is this lovely dress—

STROM: I bought you a whole new wardrobe just six months ago! I swear, you women go through clothes the way pigs go through garbage.

ESSIE: Please, Daddy.

STROM: I'm sorry, Essie, but you're going to have to wait at least another six months before I buy you new clothes. I'm not made of money. You need to learn the value of the dollar.

ESSIE: Come on, Daddy! These clothes are practically rags now! And my sorority sisters will make fun of me if I'm not dressed in the latest fashions.

(Strom is resigned. He knows there's no use in fighting her.)

STROM: Fine, Essie. Whatever you like. You know that I always give in to your sweet melodic voice.

(She is very excited.)

ESSIE: Thanks, Daddy. And third—
STROM: Let me guess. It's tuition time again. I've go it right here.

(He opens a drawer in his desk and takes out a thick wad of cash and gives it to her.)

This is for your tuition.

(He goes into his wallet and takes out some more bills.)

And this is for your new clothes.
ESSIE: Thanks, Daddy.

(She kisses him on the cheek.)

STROM: Tell me about school. You're keeping your grades up I hope.
ESSIE: Straight A's. And my sorority sisters have chosen me to plan our spring ball in April. I'm so excited, it's such a great honor. I hope I do a good job.
STROM: You're going to do just fine. I'm sure you'll knock 'em dead. What's the name of your sorority again?
ESSIE: Delta Sigma Theta.
STROM: Why can't I remember that?
ESSIE: 'Cause it's a Negro sorority—
STROM: Please forgive me. And you're attending church every Sunday I hope.
ESSIE: Of course, Daddy.
STROM: Always remember that God is what keeps us strong. If you have Jesus in your heart you will never go wrong. Tell me. Do your classmates drink alcoholic beverages?
ESSIE: Some of them do, but I don't, because you always say that . . .
STROM AND ESSIE *(In unison)*: Alcohol is the devil's water.
STROM: That's my girl. One day we're going to bring prohibition back, and end all the sin in the world. Don't you worry.

ESSIE: I can't wait.

STROM: I hate to cut our time together short, but I have a radio interview to attend.

ESSIE: Bye, Daddy.

(They hug and kiss.)

STROM: And don't—

ESSIE: I know, you don't want me listening to your interviews and I don't.

STROM: You're a good girl. Bye, sugar.

(They kiss. She leaves.)

SCENE 9

September 1948. Strom is in an interview. He is the presidential nominee for the segregationist Dixiecrat Party.

INTERVIEWER: Governor Thurmond, why did you and your fellow Dixiecrats feel it necessary to break away from the Democratic Party to run your own nominee for president?

STROM: The Democratic Party has abandoned its time-honored and traditional principles of states' rights, home rule and local self-government. In place of these principles the Democratic Party has adopted a program of misnamed civil rights, calling for a police state in this country, in which the federal government will use its army to force the Negro into the schools, movie theaters, and the homes of white Southerners. States' Rights Americans resist this shameful betrayal of our national character. States' Rights Americans stand beside God and the Constitution of the United States with drawn sword.

INTERVIEWER: Some of your critics call you a racist. They say that your only motivation to run for president is to keep segregation intact to further oppress black people. How do you respond to this?

STROM: I am outraged that anyone would call me a racist! I am not a racist! I am a soldier of the Almighty. It is a Northern communist misconception that blacks are oppressed in the South. Northerners are so ignorant that they don't understand that "separate but equal" means that blacks receive the same treatment as whites in the South— As a matter of fact the Negro is treated like royalty in South Carolina— the greatest state in the union—which I am proud to be governor of.

INTERVIEWER: What about the frequent lynchings that occur in South Carolina? Records indicate that last year over two hundred lynchings took place in your state.

STROM: I have no comment about that. I haven't seen these statistics. I believe that your statistics have been fabricated by the Northern press. I have personally seen to it that Negroes are treated with the utmost respect under my governorship.

INTERVIEWER: If blacks are treated equally in your state, then why go through the trouble of having segregation in the first place?

STROM: I'm glad you asked me that question.

(Pause.)

We have segregation because God doesn't want blacks and whites to mix. It's a sin. Maybe you should get more acquainted with the Bible. Then maybe you'd stop asking me such silly questions.

INTERVIEWER: Why should you be elected the next President of the United States?

STROM: Because I'm the only candidate running that will prevent the United States of America from getting itself into the type of mess that Europe got itself into during World War II.

INTERVIEWER: I don't exactly understand what you mean by that. Can you elaborate?

STROM: Hitler offered the people of Germany a shortcut to human progress. He gained power in Germany by advocating human rights for minority groups, just as the Democrats and Republicans are advocating human rights for the Negro. The Negroes already got human rights. That's what emancipation did. Under Hitler's plan, the constitutional rights of the people were destroyed. We oppose these disciples of political expediency, who, today emulate Hitler and who offer the ill-fated European experiment as a shortcut to human progress, which ended in tears, blood, disillusionment and tragedy. Mark my words: if the federal government engages in the unconstitutional action of forcing the Negro into the Southern home, then God will see to it that the United States ends up just like Germany did during World War II.

INTERVIEWER: There have been rumors swirling around which state that you support a Negro child from Orangeburg. The rumors also suggest that this Negro child is your illegitimate daughter. Are these rumors true?

STROM: That is the most ridiculous assertion that I've ever heard. Let me say this clearly: I do not have an illegitimate Negro child. I am a respectable Southern gentleman. I would never and have never engaged in the vile, disgusting and sinful act of having relations with a Negro woman. This rumor was created by my Northern enemies to inflict character assassination on my good name.

INTERVIEWER: Thank you for coming on my show. It's been a pleasure.

(They shake hands.)

STROM: Thank you.

SCENE 10

Strom is visiting Essie Mae at South Carolina University. He has just arrived. He is carrying a box.

STROM: How's Daddy's little girl?

(He gives her a hug.)

ESSIE: Fine.

STROM: How was your sorority ball? Did you knock 'em dead with your planning?

ESSIE *(Sad)*: It went well.

STROM: I brought you a present.

(He gives her a present. She opens it. It is a new radio.)

ESSIE *(Not excited at all)*: Thanks, Dad.

STROM: Don't you like it? These just came out. It's the newest radio technology. I don't even have one yet!

ESSIE: I like it just fine.

(Strom takes her under his arm.)

STROM: Why's my little magpie so gloomy? I hate to see you sad.

ESSIE *(About to cry)*: I heard your radio interview.

STROM *(Holding her closer)*: Now, honey, there's a reason that I tell you not to listen to my speeches and interviews.

ESSIE: I know, but I wanted to hear what you had to say. My dad's the Governor of South Carolina and might be the next President of the United States and I can't tell anyone. *(Softly)* It makes me sad sometimes.

(Pause.)

Did you mean all the things that you said in the interview about race and stuff?

STROM: Honey, that's just politics. It's political talk. That's what I have to do at work. It doesn't mean anything.

ESSIE: Really?

STROM: Yes, darling. You're my daughter. You mean more to me than anything else in the world.

ESSIE: Then why do you deny that I'm your daughter?

(She cries.)

STROM: I told you, honey, it's just my job. My opposition would slaughter me if they knew the truth.

(Pause. He's beginning to realize something.)

How does it make you feel that I deny you publicly?

ESSIE: It makes me feel— It makes me feel like you don't really love me.

STROM: But you know I do!

ESSIE: You become a different person when you stand in front of cheering crowds giving campaign speeches. You're unrecognizable to me. You act and speak completely different from the man I know. The man I know is loving and wonderful to me, the man onstage speaks venomously of my kind. It makes me wonder which is the real you or if there's a real you.

STROM *(Pleading)*: This is the real me, Essie. How could you doubt that after all the love I've shown you? The man that walks out in front of the crowds is just a politician. He's just doing what he needs to do to make a living. The way I am with you is the real Strom.

ESSIE: I know. It's just hard to hear the way you talk about me and black people in public.

STROM: I am an honorable man, Essie. If you want me to reveal to the world that you're my daughter, then I will. I didn't realize how much this was affecting you. I would never, ever consciously do anything to cause my beautiful Essie pain. Do you want me to tell the world?

(Long pause.)

ESSIE: No. I want you to succeed. I want my daddy to be the next President of the United States. I believe in you. It's more important to me to have a good relationship with you than a bad one or none at all. I'm glad you came into my life after Mama died.

(They cry while holding each other.)

STROM: That's my girl. I love you, Essie. You're a wonderful daughter, but please, please don't listen to my speeches and interviews anymore. It's all rubbish. You don't need to hear those kinds of things. Okay?

ESSIE: Yes.

(He pulls her chin up and wipes the tears from her eyes and then looks directly into them.)

STROM: You promise?

ESSIE: I promise.

(They hug.)

SCENE 11

Strom is in his family home with his father. They are smoking cigars in the living room.

STROM'S FATHER: I just want to tell you that you're doing a great job. You've made your old man proud.

STROM: Thanks, Dad.

STROM'S FATHER: It was twenty-three years ago that I sat you down in this room and told you that I wanted you to pursue politics. A lot of children no longer honor the commandment "Honor thy mother and father." But you did. That sets you apart from the rest. You're a good son and a true Southern gentleman.

STROM: That means a lot to me.

STROM'S FATHER *(Hesitant)*: Strom?

STROM: Yes, Dad?

STROM'S FATHER *(Very bluntly)*: Is there any truth to these rumors that you fathered a nigger child?

STROM *(Furious)*: How dare you ask a God-fearing man a question like that?

STROM'S FATHER: I'm sorry, Strom. It's just—I hate the way the Northern press has been slandering our good name.

STROM: I know. I'm sorry I snapped. It hurts me, too.

STROM'S FATHER: Calling us nigger lovers! As if anyone that bears the good Thurmond name would have relations with one of those nigger monkeys. I'd rather be torn apart by a pack of rabid dogs, rather than touch one of those black-skinned beasts.

(Pause. Strom is on the verge of breaking down.)

STROM: Dad?

STROM'S FATHER: Yes, Son?

STROM *(Quietly)*: Please forgive me.

STROM'S FATHER: For what?

STROM: I lied.

STROM'S FATHER: What are you trying to tell me?

STROM: Remember our maid Carrie?

STROM'S FATHER: Are you trying to tell me that—

STROM: She was my first. She was my first experience with a woman.

(Very, very long pause. Then Strom's Father puts his hand on Strom's shoulder, consolingly.)

STROM'S FATHER: I've suspected that for a long time. I always wondered why Carrie had that baby shipped to Pennsylvania rather than raising the child herself here. We would've helped her.

STROM: I made her do that. I didn't want to bring shame upon our family by having a mulatto child running around our household. *(On the verge of tears)* Everyone knows about it now. Can you ever forgive me?

(Pause.)

STROM'S FATHER: There's no shame in what you did, Strom.

STROM: How can you say that? Of course there is.

STROM'S FATHER: My first experience was also with a negress.

STROM *(Shocked)*: Really?

STROM'S FATHER: She was a slave girl that my family held onto after Lincoln freed the Negroes.

STROM: Some people still had slaves after Emancipation?

STROM'S FATHER: Oh yes. Some families kept their Negroes by threat of violence, and some Negroes stayed voluntarily, 'cause they had nowhere else to go. The girl I had my first experience with was only a baby when Lincoln signed the Emancipation Proclamation, and both of her parents had been sold to other plantations, so my parents decided to keep her.

STROM: Did you have a child with her?

(Pause.)

STROM'S FATHER: Yes. Two children.

STROM: What happened to them? Where are they now?

STROM'S FATHER: I don't know. It's a right of passage for most Southern gentleman. We learn about women from the promiscuous negress. They tantalize us. There's something irresistible about them. We demonize them by day and crawl into their beds at night.

STROM: But we never let the truth be known. It's our open secret.

STROM'S FATHER: So you take care of this girl?

STROM: Yes, sir, I do. I started taking care of her after her mother died. She was sixteen.

STROM'S FATHER: You're a better man than I. You did the right thing.

SCENE 12

August 29, 1963. Strom Thurmond, now sixty, is in the United States Senate. He is talking to an Aide. It is the day after the March on Washington. Strom is heatedly ranting to the Aide.

AIDE: You've got to calm down, sir. The whole office can hear you.

STROM: Good! I hope the whole senate can hear me! I wish the White House would wake up and listen to what I have to say!

AIDE: Sir—

STROM: Instead of preventing these niggers from holding their march, Kennedy shuts down the Capitol and provides security for them! Extra security! That's the pinnacle of nigger-loving.

AIDE: Kennedy is a terrible man.

STROM: If I had been elected president, you can bet that none of this nonsense would be going on.

AIDE: The world would be a much better place, sir.

STROM: If I were president those niggers wouldn't have been invited to the Capitol! That's liberal craziness! They would've been greeted with attack dogs and rubber bullets.

AIDE: That would've been the right thing to do, sir.

STROM: But nothing made me more furious than the head nigger's "I have a dream" speech. That really got by blood boiling.

AIDE: It was reprehensible.

STROM: What does that nigger think? That he's the only one who's got a dream? I've also got a dream, too. I have a dream that I go back a hundred years and shoot Lincoln the day before he signed the nigger-lover Proclamation! I have a dream that I go back in time and shoot Truman before he integrated the military and started letting those monkeys serve along good white soldiers! I have a dream that I go back in time and blow up the courthouse where Brown versus Board of Education was fought, so that our white daughters wouldn't have to be raped by those black-stained animals in the classroom every day.

(Calms down. Sad) I have a dream that maybe one day, white people won't have to endure this injustice, and will be able to live in peace.

SCENE 13

Spring 1964. Civil rights legislation ending racial discrimination has just been passed. Strom is visiting his daughter, Essie Mae, now thirty-seven. They are hugging. Strom is sad.

STROM: How's my magpie?

ESSIE: I'm doing just fine.

STROM: How is teaching?

ESSIE: It's just wonderful. I'm teaching a class that's almost equally split. Half black and half white. Isn't it amazing?

STROM *(Darkly)*: Yes, it is amazing. *(Trying to change the subject)* I used to be a teacher, you know.

ESSIE: Yes, I know. That's how you met Mama.

(She goes right back to what she was talking about before.)

Who would've thought that race relations would have come so far in such a short amount of time?

STROM *(Even darker)*: Yes. Who would have thought.

ESSIE *(Noticing his condition)*: What's wrong, Daddy?

STROM: I have this horrible feeling, Essie.

ESSIE *(Very alarmed)*: About what?

STROM: I see the images of the Book of Revelations all around us. I feel that the world is coming to an end.

(Essie puts her arms around her father to console him.)

ESSIE: There's nothing to worry about, Daddy. The world is getting better every day.

STROM: The only positive thing that's happened recently was Kennedy getting shot.

ESSIE: Don't talk that way in my house!

STROM: I'm your father! I'll talk any way I want. You don't give me orders. You understand?

ESSIE *(Resentful)*: Yes, Dad.

STROM *(Trying to make her see the light)*: Don't you see that Johnson signing the Civil Rights Act means that the end of the world is coming upon us?

ESSIE: No. I don't see that.

STROM: Essie. The Bible clearly states that the mixing of races is not permitted.

ESSIE: You mixed yourself up with Mama.

STROM: The Bible clearly states that the mixing of the races is not permitted. The beginning of the end was the Emancipation Proclamation. It's no coincidence that Kennedy's shameful, disgusting legislation was signed almost exactly one hundred years to the day after Lincoln signed Emancipation. God is punishing us for letting things get so out of control.

ESSIE: I don't think the Civil Rights Act is shameful at all. I think it is good for the country. I think that it is a blessing from God.

STROM *(Snaps)*: That is the most ignorant thing that I've ever heard in my life. Revelations states that—

ESSIE *(About to cry, softly)*: Why are you talking to me this way?

STROM *(Calming down)*: In what way?

ESSIE: About how you think the Civil Rights Act is shameful and means the end of the world. It hurts me, Dad. You're talking the way you do onstage. You've never spoken this way to me before.

STROM *(Realizing his error)*: I'm sorry, Essie. I'm just so upset about what's happening in this country. I've fought so hard for so long, and now I've been defeated. Everything is crumbling around me.

ESSIE: You have fought hard.

(Pause.)

But, Dad, I'M BLACK! Don't you understand that when you talk about your hate of desegregation, that you're saying that you love to oppress me? I'M BLACK, DAD! Don't you understand?

STROM: Don't ever refer to yourself as being black. Have some dignity!

ESSIE *(Completely bewildered)*: What on earth do you mean?

STROM: Am I black?

ESSIE: No.

STROM: Then neither are you. REMEMBER THAT!

ESSIE: But, Dad, I AM BLACK, THAT'S THE WAY THE WORLD SEES ME!

STROM: It doesn't matter how the world sees you! You're Strom Thurmond's daughter. It doesn't matter how you look on the outside, 'cause on the inside you've got the Thurmond soul. You're white on the inside. Your soul is pure white, like snow. I can see it, and God blesses you for it. Do you understand?

(She doesn't really understand, but since he really seems to believe it, she doesn't fight it.)

ESSIE: Yes, Father.

STROM *(Lovingly)*: Do you really understand?

(She shakes her head yes.)

Good. Then say it. Tell me what you understand.

ESSIE *(Wants to cry but holds it)*: My—my soul is pure white.

STROM: That's my girl.

(He gives her a big hug.)

Well, I've got to get back to Washington. I'm glad we had this talk.

ESSIE: Me, too.

(They hug again. He leaves. Essie sits down and cries alone. The lights fade to black.)

SCENE 14

December 2002. Trent Lott is giving a speech at Strom's one-hundredth birthday party. He is the Republican senator from Mississippi, and the Republican leader in the senate. Strom Thurmond is in a wheelchair looking a bit dazed and mentally empty. There are other Republican senators present.

TRENT LOTT: I feel privileged to be here celebrating Strom Thurmond's hundredth birthday with him. Strom Thurmond is the greatest politician of the twentieth century. There's only one person that I admire more than Strom Thurmond, and that's Jefferson Davis, the great President of the Confederacy!

(Wild cheering from the Republican senators.)

Strom Thurmond once said that all the laws of Washington and all the bayonets of the army cannot force the Negro into our homes, our schools, our swimming pools and our churches!

(More wild cheering.)

And Strom Thurmond's 1948 Dixiecrat campaign platform read: "We stand for the segregation of the races and the racial integrity of each race."

(More cheering. To Strom:)

I hope I'm not embarrassing you by going on for so long about your wonderful achievements. But I can't help it, for you are truly a great man.

(Strong applause.)

Now I want to say this about my state: when Strom Thurmond ran for president, the people of Mississippi voted for him. We're proud of it. And if the rest of the country had followed our lead, then we wouldn't have had all these problems over all these years either.

(Wild cheering.
The cheering dies out and is replaced by the sound of funeral bells as everyone exits.
Eventually Essie Mae, now seventy-five, enters.)

ESSIE: Strom Thurmond was a good man. He did and said many inflammatory things that I disagreed with, but he was my father, and in my heart of hearts I know he was good.

Let he who is without sin cast the first stone. All of God's creatures have faults. Our duty to God is to try to change our sinful ways. He did that. He tried. I know he did.

As time went on, my father became more and more accepting. In 1983 he voted to make the Reverend Martin Luther King's birthday a holiday. Hallelujah! That's a far cry from the fiery rhetoric that he used to describe Dr. King in the 1960s. I'd like to think that I had something to do with that.

Yes indeed, blacks have come a long way, but people like Senator Trent Lott make me question whether black folks have really come as far as we think we have. It seems to me that Trent Lott wants to turn back the hands of time, and do away with all the good work that has been done.

Dr. Martin Luther King was a great man, and so was my father. I just wish that they could have seen eye to eye while they were still alive. They had much more in common than they could've ever imagined. Death puts to rest the differences that humans have with one another while they are alive. In the end we're all the same. Death sees to that. Death unites us all.

(She turns to the coffin.)

I'm going to miss you, Daddy.

END OF PLAY

THOMAS BRADSHAW's plays include *Carlyle* and *Mary* (Goodman Theatre); *Intimacy* and *Burning* (New Group); *Job* and *Dawn* (Flea Theater); *Fulfillment* (Flea Theater, American Theater Company); *The Bereaved* (Crowded Fire Theater, Partial Comfort Productions and Theater Bielefeld in Germany); *Southern Promises*, *Purity* and *Prophet* (PS122); *Strom Thurmond Is Not a Racist* and *Cleansed* (The Brick). He was the recipient of a 2009 Guggenheim Fellowship, the 2010 Prince Prize and a 2012 award from the Foundation for Contemporary Arts. He has been featured as one of *Time Out New York*'s "10 Playwrights to Watch," in the *New Yorker*'s "Best Performances of 2008," was named "Best Provocative Playwright" by the *Village Voice* and as one of Chicago's most important people in film and TV by *Newcity Film*.

He has received commissions from Soho Theatre (London), the Goodman Theatre, Soho Rep. (New York), the Old Vic (London), Manhattan Theatre Club, the Flea Theater, Theater Bielefeld (Germany), the Whitney Museum, Partial Comfort Productions, Marin Theatre Company and the Foundry Theatre. He has received fellowships from the Lark Play Development Center, Soho Rep. (Strelsin Fellow) and New York Theater Workshop, where he is also a Usual Suspect.

He received his MFA from Mac Wellman's playwriting program at Brooklyn College and he is an associate professor at Northwestern University.